WILD JOURNEY TO THE LIGHT

BY
ALLISON BEE LEVY

I dedicate this book to all of my readers, the lost souls, and those who are struggling. May you find healing and comfort on your journey to living your truth.

Warning: This book contains sensitive content, sexual topics, explicit language, and drug references that may trigger those struggling with addiction or suffering from sexual trauma. Some names have been changed to protect their identities. My intent is not to make anyone feel uncomfortable; it is only to share my truth. I do NOT recommend that you attempt my ways of researching in the dark to find your light. Everyone has their own journey; follow your heart to find yours.

TABLE OF CONTENTS

CHAPTER ONE

WHEN MY INNOCENCE
WAS RIPPED AWAY

The summer before my first year of high school at Robert E. Lee set me up for a rude awakening. With blinders on, I only saw what I wanted to see. I was innocent. I was young, alive, pure, free, and becoming a woman. Curiosity got the best of this kitty, and let's just say, I found a play toy. To be frank, I spent one night with this boy. It was one wild night that would haunt me for years. We sure had fun in the moment though! It was my first sexual experiment. I was thirteen and didn't know any better. For some reason, I thought butt sex wasn't actually sex, and tried it this way first. I quickly learned that it wasn't pleasurable enough to endure dry, forced, abrasive entry into my body, and unsurprisingly, I didn't want to finish. I was doing my best to keep my virginity, or so I thought. He popped my cherry with his aggressive fingering, so either way, that untouched innocence was ripped away. Although that was the only night we spent together, it was enough to cause his girlfriend to break up with him. Little did I know, since I was still in middle school at the time, that

I got between the most popular couple in high school. To make matters worse, his ex-girlfriend's sister was a senior when I became a freshman, and initiation into high school was right around the corner. One night with that boy would mess with my world for years.

Initiation at Robert E. Lee High School was something that everyone looked forward to. If you were cool enough, you would be initiated, and if you weren't, you were kind of forgotten about. It is a tradition that has been going on now for over 50 years. It was a big deal; I mean, the movie Dazed and Confused made this tradition even stronger because everyone thought it was based on our high school. Our high school's name was even on the buses used in the film, even though it was actually about another school. That being said, it was the "cool" thing to do. Growing up during puberty, with social pressures mounting, who wouldn't want to be a part of that?

Little did I know, there was a line of girls that were out to get me. I figured I would be okay because my sister's friend ended up picking me as her freshman fishy. She would take care of me and make sure that nothing happened, or so I thought. As I left the house in the tacky freshman shirt and mismatched shoes that my sponsor made me wear for my first day of high school, I walked away from an innocent and easy life.

After school, all the freshman girls were taken to the parking lot to lay on the hot pavement and burn our bodies. After that, we were taken to a field in the back of a bunch of pickup trucks. The trucks were swerving and skidding out, and doing donuts in the field once we arrived. All the girls in the back were trying their best to hold on and not fly out. Scared for our lives and confused with what was going to happen to us, we all stopped smiling. Once we arrived at the field, they called my name to come stand up front to begin the initiation. That's where it took a nosedive. At that moment, all eyes were on me. I was in front of the entire school minus the freshman boys. The Queen B, as I will call her, slammed eggs on my head as an intro to start the chaos. She didn't crack them on me; she was hitting me with them. The Queen B is the older sister of that summer boy's girlfriend, and boy was she mad! She had a posse of girls after me! The meaner they were to me, the happier she was, along with her sister who was watching all of this. I soon learned that this wasn't a fun game or any way to enter into high school. This became a game of who could haze and belittle me down to nothing first. It was war. I was their prey; they wanted to attack, torture, humiliate, and tear my soul out, which they accomplished successfully over the course of the next five hours. People were drinking, which only led to things getting completely out of hand and the girls becoming more vicious.

I had a pig foot in one hand, a dead fish in another, along with cat food and vinegar in my eyes. It was hours of sloppy hitting and painful sauces all over us. The Queen B got a full ketchup bottle and put it right up to my ear, filling my whole ear canal until I couldn't hear. It helped me later on because I had her whistling repeatedly in my ear to sing the senior song, which I could not have cared less to memorize. After 15 minutes of continuous yelling, she got bored and asked a popular freshman to step forward and show me up by singing the whole song, perfectly. There was a point where I was singled out and taken in front of all the boys who attended the high school. The Queen B put me on my knees and said "Alright boys! Allison Levy is the biggest fucking slut at Robert E. Lee!" and continued to beat me on the head with about ten more eggs, all because I was pretty and I made a mistake with that fuck boy. There were two or three other pretty girls who were singled out because the older girls' boyfriends thought we were cute. All four of us were completely hated, and we suffered the worst of the hazing. My sister's friend who was supposed to take care of me was nowhere to be found. Her job was to trick me into coming here by telling me that I would be safe, and then once I arrived, I was to be released to the girl who wanted to humiliate me.

The part that sticks with me the most is that my older sister was a senior when I was a freshman. I wish so badly that she would have taken me home and protected me, but she was key to helping out the whole in a positive way. She was doing her best to pass around paper towels to everyone to help wipe the vinegar out of our eyes. It makes sense that she assumed the role of medic, as she is now a nurse. She was trying to pick up the pieces of this out of control mess that the graduating class of 2000 made. There were a few other girls trying to help, but they would get called out by the popular ones and so most were terrified to rebell. This included my sister. She came up to me a few times asking if I was okay and I wish so badly I had been real and said "No, take me home." Instead, I was trying to play like I was tough and could handle the abuse I was going through. I was also in shock as to what all was happening around me and to me, and eventually, I became numb and shut myself down.

To make it even more humiliating, I, alongside the three other targeted "pretty girls," had to pick up all the trash in the field at the end. Let's just say that was one of the worst experiences of my life; one that changed my perspective on the world from that point on. I was singled out, verbally, mentally, and physically abused, and labeled on my first day of high school as the "biggest fucking slut." Life couldn't get much worse for a fourteen-year-old. I couldn't talk, didn't eat, and barely got out of bed for ten days. I was in shock, still numb, and had PTSD from the abuse I went through. I was ashamed and felt like hiding away. I never had experienced suicidal thoughts before then, yet that's all I could think of. Luckily, my mom let me stay at home the following week because I didn't want to get out of bed. I couldn't bear more of the torture that I would have experienced if I had gone back to school right away. I wasn't ready for it yet, and my mama could feel that.

*Side Note: No wonder children these days are going around shooting up schools. Much of this has to do with being hazed, degraded, mistreated, scared, and abused in our school systems. We have to stop this epidemic of righteousness and entitlement. Being someone who suffered this trauma firsthand, I understand how badly it can affect adolescence. Most kids at that age don't know how to process or get past these deeply cut wounds, and they continue to affect them into adulthood. HAZING IS NOT OKAY TO DO TO ANYONE, EVER!

Being the strong mama bear that she was, my mother wasn't going to simply stand by and let this fly without causing a scene! She went on the news to make it known what had happened. Yes, my mother did this in her best attempt for the greater good. Tyler, Texas, is a small town, and my family's reputation was at stake. My mom is a strong, creative, and loving person, but if you attack her babies, you've got another thing coming! I've never seen such sadness in her eyes. She became something else. She was ready to ROAR, and she wasn't going to be silent like me. She went to the school board and filed a complaint, along with going on the news to make sure this didn't happen to any other child. She was trying to stop this tradition, or have it regulated at the very least. She filed a police report, and it got even worse. Every student had to be pulled out of the classroom to write a police report because of the underage drinking that took place. Not only was I hazed throughout this process, but I was hated by most of the school for ratting everyone out. I was the tattletale that couldn't handle my emotions, and my mom was the snitch for stopping the fun and the tradition. It was us against them. Most of the other students' parents didn't want to get involved because, for most of them, it was a harmless tradition. It wasn't their child that got the worst of it, *so why speak up?* Plus, so many of the girls who got hazed didn't speak up. Countless things went wrong that day amidst the chaos. *Yet, how did they all think this is normal?*

Societal pressure, social status, fakeness--is it worth the pain? It's all so worth it to fit in and be popular and liked, right? I found out as I got older that initiation was never the same after me. At least, it was never an extreme event like ours was. It was tamer, sweet, and smaller.

Long story short, the news story and investigation went nowhere, and neither the school board or the police filed any charges. They turned a blind eye and looked at my family differently from that day on. My mom wallowed in a funk for the next two years. She wrote a short story about my silent cry and saved so many newspaper articles of research on the dangers of hazing. People started to reach out to her and speak up about their stories; some former Robert E. Lee students even came forward. It was a giant eggshell smashed on our reality, and things were never the same after that. One thing's for sure: our family's bond grew closer from the pain.

My depression and withdrawal from reality got even worse as the school year progressed. It didn't stop with the initiation. The "popular mean girls" tortured me at my home as well. The street in front of our house was shoe polished with vandalism. It had the word, "slut" with arrows pointing towards our house. We were toilet papered nearly every weekend, with bananas hanging in condoms off our porch. I was so badly degraded that I could barely look at my own face. It was as if I had stepped into a giant ant pile, and the ants just kept biting and slowly eating me alive. If it weren't for the love of my family, I probably would have killed myself.

This was the point where drugs became my saving grace, and my best friend. I started to fade and felt better when I was numb. The world became black. No one meant anything to me; I trusted no one. I vaguely remember most of my high school life because I was so intoxicated; I just wanted to numb the pain and all of the hate and ridicule. I started to abuse alcohol, Xanax, painkillers, Adderall, and anything that helped me feel nothing. I didn't want to face the humiliation and the pain that I had created for myself. I had to relive this every day I went to school. There was always someone who picked on me. I began to develop an eating disorder and barely ever ate, mainly due to my drug use, but also from wanting to fade away. I was evaporating, and completely checking out. I didn't care about myself, my body, what people were saying to me or about me behind my back. I just wanted to get all this over with and didn't know how to make anything better.

I remember my mom tried so hard to get me out of my depression. She was desperate and knew I needed to take my aggression and anger out on something. She bought me a punching bag and put Queen B's picture on it. She encouraged me to write. My favorite thing that worked for me was art. My mom put a canvas and paint in front of me and told me to paint how I felt. I remember painting my first piece. It was all red and fiery, filled with hate. Fierce with purpose. I cried after I released it, and still have it to this day. That was probably the best gift my mother ever gave me. Painting was a great release for me. *I'm not talking to anyone but the canvas, yet the canvas understands me in my raw state.* Those methods started to break me out of this protective shell I was putting myself in. Being creative and having that release were such valuable tools. I didn't have to speak to anyone; it was just me and my heart.

As the struggle with my peers continued, I found that instead of trying to fight what people were calling me (the biggest slut), I might as well have fun with it. I began to have many nights of not remembering what happened to me. Most of it resulted from my own choices, but not all of it. By my own doing, I found myself in precarious situations and vulnerable positions that severely impacted my weakening mental state. I would be drunk and on Xanax, knowing that I could easily get anyone I wanted. I could get them just by looking at them, and they'd wonder if the rumors were true. Unfortunately, some of these situations were to the detriment of my personal growth, and they continue to haunt me to this day. This was when I started to get the wrong idea of what love is, and how it works. I was too young to have this kind of power. I must say, I fucked up my teenage brain by giving away my body before I was ready. This was when I got my signals and wires mixed up on how a healthy relationship should look. I had a couple of boyfriends throughout high school, but these relationships were filled with drama and multiple breakups.

CHAPTER TWO

MY SECRET

A year went by. I was a sophomore in high school, continuing on this destructive path and not giving a shit about myself, when I wound up in a predicament. I was asked to go to a party with this cute football player I had been after. Of course I said yes and put on my best black dress! It was at our classmate's house, but he and his sister weren't there. They were out of town, but for some reason their dad decided to throw the high school a party. Most of the high school's in-crowd was there, so it was weird, but not questionably weird at the time. This man who was throwing the party worked with children in the healthcare industry, so he had a nice house, good surround sound music, and a pool. It was the perfect party house.

As soon as I arrived, the owner of the house offered me a glass of wine. I followed him inside, happily sat at his little bar in the kitchen, and accepted his offer. I noticed the array of fish that he had in aquariums placed throughout the kitchen. I had never seen anything like it. Mesmerized by my surroundings, I drank my first glass of wine fairly quickly due to my nerves, and also because it was delicious. He noticed my glass became empty, so he offered me a second round while we were inside. I was about three sips in on my second glass when all of a sudden, I began to lose control of my body. I could sense all of my limbs becoming weak, and I couldn't hold myself up in the bar chair any longer. I started to slide off the chair when the dad came and caught me before I fell to the ground. I became confused and weak, unsure of what was happening. My body felt as if it wasn't mine anymore, and I had lost all control of my motor functions. I soon realized that he had purposefully drugged me with something that paralyzed my body, but not my mind.

After he caught me from falling off the chair, he held me up by holding his arms under my armpits from behind. He then proceeded to drag me down the hallway into the garage. I was aware of everything that was happening, but I couldn't move my body. I was confused and asked what he was doing, but I couldn't make sense of what was happening. Within 30 minutes of walking into the party, I became a limp, helpless, and defenseless girl who was being taken somewhere hidden away from the party. He brought me into the garage where he hoisted me up into his RV. He only took me to the entryway of the RV, where he proceeded to take my clothes off. He began to touch my vagina in a creepy, soft, and curious way that made me squirm inside. He licked me all over my body. I can remember his gross pointy tongue rubbing up against my clitoris in the worst way that still triggers me to this day. If I could have moved, I would have slapped his face away. I wanted the touching and kissing to stop, and I remember asking him why he doesn't just have sex with me and get it over with. I was so confused about everything that was happening. I was sure he was going to have sex with me, but something inside of him said that touching and kissing were his limit. Probably because he was married and that would have crossed the line. Who knows, but I'm so glad he didn't go all the way with me. All I wanted was for this to be over with and for him to stop fondling and touching me down there.

I couldn't move, but I could feel and remember it all. I tried to run away and yell, but I was disassociating myself with my body because I couldn't do anything else. It was like one of those nightmares that you wish you could forget, but it gets burned in your brain so you think about it every time you lay down in bed. *Why couldn't he have drugged me with something that erased my memory, too?* Was this my Karma? *"This is what I get for being the biggest slut at my high school,"* or so I thought. My classmate's dad raped me. *Was this all planned? How cruel can these kids, and their parents, be? Did the cute football player get paid to do this and set this up? Tell me I'm dreaming. Why would an adult do this to a 15-year-old?* I had all of these thoughts swarming in my brain while I was being raped. This event will haunt me for the rest of my life. After this, I became completely traumatized with any man touching or kissing me down there.

It must have been at least 30 minutes to an hour of this, but it felt like forever. I got to a point where I had mentally checked out. Afterward, I sat on his RV floor still unable to move or speak. I was dead weight; he realized he needed to do something to get rid of me and make this mistake disappear. The dad asked the cute football player who invited me there to get me out of the house without anyone seeing. He opened the garage, and the football player slung me over his shoulder like a ragdoll and walked me down the driveway with his friend. They ended up taking me to his friend's lake house to hide me there for the night until I sobered up. No way they could've brought me home and laid me on the front porch in that condition. I couldn't even function at all for the rest of the night. The next morning, I woke up next to the football player overlooking the lake, wishing it was he who had touched me the night before. I tried to hug him, hoping that last night was a nightmare and it hadn't actually happened. His reaction confirmed that it did. He brushed me off and gave me the most piercing look of disgust as in *don't touch me*. He scrambled to get my stuff together for me as if he couldn't have gotten rid of me fast enough. Never heard from that boy again.

I felt so much shame and pain in my soul the next day, and it stuck with me for years to come, shit, even to this day. There was a lot of shame around getting raped by my classmate's dad before I was even old enough to drive. I carried a lot of shame for thinking that the popular kids wanted to be my friends, or that I was putting myself in situations to be taken advantage of so easily. I felt ashamed for being so naïve, unaware that what had happened was even possible. If you've ever been drugged and molested, you can understand that foggy morning after waking up from it all, feeling as if the weight of the world is crashing down upon you. Your mental state and perception of reality are torn, leaving a gaping hole filled with questions that will never be answered.

As the years continued, I buried this secret with me. For ten years, I hid this away. Part of me had no idea what to do or say, how to react, or how to tell my story. Following my traumatic entrance into high school, I didn't want to be scrutinized anymore. I was done with the unforgiving spotlight. No one knew, except for the boys that took me home. The rape caused me to deal with relationships in a fucked up way. For the longest time, I couldn't have a hand go down my pants without thinking it was the man who raped me. I slapped a person's face away if they tried to kiss me down there. I had an automatic reaction and pushed so many people away from me, unable to let anyone in. To this day, I believe it has strongly affected my orgasms. I always have a fear flashback of that night if someone touches me in a similar way, or if they kiss me the wrong way, and when that happens, it totally ruins the mood. Even 17 years later, it is still with me. Most of the time, I can't fully orgasm and I feel like it has to do with my rape and my trauma from this fuck-head creep. I have a hard time trusting people and letting them in on that level. If I do, they have to touch me completely differently, and if they do touch me in the same way, it's game over and I'm done trying. I become tense and basically have a panic attack. I feel bad for any guy I try to date, because how would he know how someone in the past touched me? I can explain it all with time, but most guys don't get it. I've only met about two or three that I could open up with sexually.

I felt so misunderstood and I didn't exactly know how I could tell people this story. I had PTSD from this for so many years, especially from keeping it inside and not sharing it. I felt so ashamed, as if I had brought it upon myself, just like the nickname I had in high school. I am to blame partially for not caring about my body and what I put in it, but not like this. Nobody deserves to be raped. This event hit the core of my soul, and the pain is real here. This is happening to so many women and so many of them, like myself, have a hard time reliving it. Being able to talk about it is painful. Being at peace with it is even harder. Finding a healthy outlet for our pain is not often the case, which causes it to leak poison into any meaningful relationship, therefore destroying it before it has a chance to thrive. It's hard to come to terms with this trauma, especially when you bury it and forget it ever happened. But this happened to me, and I have to keep my head up somehow. I finally was able to speak to my parents about it ten years later, after I had so many years of fucked up relationships, and more numbing. I was going through therapy eight years later to try to figure out why I was so sexually fucked up and unable to let love in. It all stemmed back to my first traumatic rape. I still haven't been able to confront the man who did this to me. He knows who he is, and eventually, this story will leak out. The sad part about all of this is that I know I'm not the only one he did this to. As I began to share my story with some of my classmates, the same rumoring stories were told back to me. It haunts me to this day that I didn't speak out then. I could've prevented so many other girls from experiencing this. It's a lot harder than you think to speak up about this kind of thing. Writing this chapter in my book is my way of speaking up. I hope the man who did this reads this and feels shame for what he did to me, and to the other women he victimized. I'd love some justice for his actions, but this is my path. This is how I have chosen to feel justified. I've broken my silence.

*Side Note: Please, if you are experiencing something similar, reach out and ask for help. It may not be easy. It will most likely be scary as fuck! But you'll start the healing process. You're not alone and it is NOT YOUR FAULT!!! As stated by one of my teachers, Jenn Wooten, "Shame corrodes the very part of us that believes we are capable of change." Shame keeps us silent. Repressed. Broken. It strips our pride away and keeps us stuck in this cycle of thinking that this is who I am. Jenn Wooten has also said, "Get to know your shame. Make friends with it. It's a hard-wired facet to be human, but don't let it stifle your growth, your voice, or your longing for progress."

Having this experience at such a young age, along with the label of being the "biggest fucking slut," I created an unhealthy mindset of what love is and how to treat my body. I misinterpreted how to show and receive love for so many years of my life. I could fuck around with anyone, but when it came to a committed relationship, I didn't do it in a healthy way. It was always heated and filled with drama, drugs, and fighting. Not understanding or dealing with the pain, shame, or guilt that had been weighing on my shoulders from being hazed and raped, I continued down a dark path.

I was young and realized I had a whole side of my sexuality to explore since my innocence was already ripped from me. I realized I had this shell of a body that made it easy to get what I wanted. I used it to my advantage and took it for granted. It was a game to me, to go after my prey and have the night end the way I had planned it to. This game messed with my mind and my reality of what love should be. I never played this game sober. I was only able to open up when I drank or got high. I would lose control, and when I did, I wouldn't fucking care. When I didn't care, I would get to this place where I blacked out. It's as if my brain blacked it out to save me from remembering my horrible decisions. Sometimes I'd be thankful, other times not so much. When I don't remember, it blocks out the pain, shame, and humiliation. Yet, why was I continuing to do this? These guys didn't respect me because I wasn't respecting myself. Trust me, I have years of guilt that I'm just now processing at 34. Now when I try to meditate, all the black-out moments come back to life. As I get older, I start to think back to all the shit I need to let go of--and trust me, it comes back to bite you in the ass later on.

I went through phases in high school where I would get into long-term relationships to keep me in control. Sometimes I needed a wingman to help take care of me or to spoil me with blunts, food, and parties. Most of these relationships were codependent and unhealthy. I was confused with what love was because once I would try to commit, I would lose sexual interest. I felt accepted when someone liked me, but it was all for the wrong reasons. I wanted to be loved by someone, not fucked. Sex was feelingless and emotionless to me, so how was I supposed to intertwine that with someone I have feelings for? Honestly, it has always been a challenge for me to truly accept a healthy love, or to even find one in the first place.

During high school, the world can be a cruel and vicious place. The sick-minded prey on the weak, waiting for the attack. They enjoy your suffering as if it's a feast for their twisted egos. Your pain is their gain, no matter the cost. Most of them don't even realize that they are partaking in the thrill of watching others suffer. Everyone copes differently with the sadness, pain, anger, and hatred boiling inside of them. I handled it by drowning out the outcome with self-induced confusion, numbing the pain with drugs and alcohol. I hid it well. I was eating Xanax daily and basically blacking out my high school life. I don't really remember most of my classmates. I walked with my head down, wishing they wouldn't see me or judge me, and avoided getting close to anyone. The less they knew about me, the less they could hurt me. I had a small group of friends in the grades above me, so I stuck with them and that's about it.

My parents tried to reach me any way they could and even sought therapy. I don't remember much from that time, but my mom told me I grew more and more distant after each therapy session. Being 14 and 15 and having those horrific stories, no one here knew how to handle them. I didn't know how to handle it, let alone speak about it. I wasn't ready to deal with everything just yet. So even in therapy, I kept my secrets close and pretty much faked my way through, telling the therapist what she wanted to hear. I was a sneaky little one. My poor mother and father did their best to love me unconditionally and accept me, no matter where I was in my life. I am so grateful that I had nurturing parents who always did their best to show their love and support for me. I'm sad I gave them such a painful time.

Most of high school was a blur, but my junior and senior years were better because the older girls who hated me were gone. There were only a small handful of people that I can remember from my circle of hippy friends. We were the trouble-makers that liked to party, take mushrooms, go camping, and get wild! We took any prescription drug we could get our hands on. Surprisingly, it was all too easy. We were all somewhat self-sabotaging, reckless, and didn't give a fuck anymore. I wanted to drown out the pain. I would get stress and tension migraines on the regular, causing me to vomit and be in incredible pain. It was most certainly my body reacting to stress, resulting in more suffering. *What's a girl supposed to do other than cover it up with more drugs, right?* I found myself with a prescription for Vicodin in hand, which only put a patch on the hole in my heart. Thanks, Doc.

CHAPTER THREE

MY MOVE TO AUSTIN (2004)

Cheers to being young, wild, and free! *Watch out world; I'm coming for ya!* I hit the ground running as soon as I was old enough to leave the nest. I was over the moon when I first got out of that small East Texas town and moved to Austin when I turned 18. I felt relieved in Austin because they didn't know my past. This was my fresh start in the world. Austin welcomed me with open arms. The freedom to see live music provided me with an outrageous nightlife. I found myself lost with others who were lost, and we would get wild with adventures and stories. Not all who wander are lost, or maybe they are and don't realize it or care that they are lost. There are also those who are happy being lost and don't care about which way the wind blows. That was me. I felt like being lost was my path. I needed to be worry-free, and to do that, I needed to be open to the possibilities of life. I had no limitations on what I could do and felt like I won the world!

I remember the third night I was in Austin, I met this one dude at a party wearing red Elvis glasses. I was on the hunt, looking for a pipe or papers to smoke the goods. I figured if anyone had one, it was this guy. I confidently walked up and asked him if he did, and he fumbled around stuttering his words, "Uh, uh, I know there's a bong around here somewhere!" And then anxiously scurried off to find the bong. From that moment on, it was smiles for days! I instantly knew this guy needed to be a part of my life. He was nearly ten years older, but at that time, age didn't matter. I loved his view on life and his wisdom, and I wanted to hear more of it. This relationship went super fast, though; I straight U-hauled that shit. I moved in after knowing him for only three weeks because my living situation with my best friend got rocky. I had the sense that this man was going to teach me things that I hadn't learned living in a small town. He was well-traveled and had plenty of stories of his adventures. I felt safe in his arms; I felt at home. He felt the same, too. He wanted to take care of me and pamper me, and to be honest, I didn't mind it at all. I was scared of falling on my face, and I had a guy that was willing to help take care of me at the beginning of my new journey. He had this parental wisdom to guide me and teach me the ways, but in a best friend kind of way. I was in awe that someone could love and care for me the way he did. He worked hard to be able to provide for us, and his love truly showed. I was honestly a lost puppy that didn't mind being lost and learning new things from him. I was learning my instincts, my limits, and gaining knowledge about the spiritual side of life. He was a computer programmer with a creative side, and he also did lighting for concerts. I was always getting into free shows and living the Austin night scene dream. I went backstage and had my private area to dance in where no one bothered me. It was a wonderful environment to grow and get lost in.

My first wild adventure with him was to see Phish in Vermont for their supposed last show. Tickets sold out within 30 minutes, but we had ours! My dad warned me not to go and had been trying to stop me from going to one of these shows my whole life. I knew it would be crazy, filled with drugs and zombie people walking around, but I wanted to experience a live show for myself. I was a rebel and went even though my dad was pissed at me for it. I knew he'd get over it. It was a wild ride up to Vermont, and it gave us a chance to bond and work as a team.

During that trip, I fell in love with this man. I ended up spending the next seven and a half years with him. He took me on adventures that I would have never experienced on my own. He had a safe and comfortable home, I was fed, he supplied the party and the shows, and I became dependent. I seamlessly went from relying on my parents to depending on this man. I never took the time to figure out who I could've been if I was on my own. My identity became entwined with his.

As I tangled myself in the party scene in Austin, I became what they call a "Penny Lane." (If you have ever seen "Almost Famous" you'd understand my reference) My boyfriend did lighting for live concerts, and therefore, I got VIP everything when we went out. I got used to being backstage and the protective barricade that surrounded the front of the house to make sure we all had space. I went to many festivals and owned it! I never got hassled when I was backstage because I learned the "I belong here, I know what the fuck I'm doing" walk. I met many famous artists, but it never fazed me. I mixed in perfectly with this scene because I never got starstruck. I never really knew who was who, because I didn't care that much or get super fan-crazy about any artist. I was a natural and played the part well. I don't know how I did it, but I was able to have long nights of raging at epic parties. Looking back, I feel like being young had a lot to do with how long I could hang for. I had many wild nights filled with drugs and vague memories of flashes and glitches. That was just the beginning. This little Penny Lane had a lot to learn. Drugs and alcohol are also depressants, so when taken by someone who is depressed, it becomes more of that vicious cycle of always trying to catch up to normalcy.

I wouldn't necessarily say I was depressed, but life was like a rollercoaster. I found out my boyfriend had bipolar disorder and that was why it was also such a bumpy relationship. His stress and the chemical imbalance in his brain pushed him to a point of snapping. Literally, he was living on the edge of his breaking point daily, and I was the first person he'd take it out on. This got even worse over time. I always felt bad for him when he would lash out and call me names. I knew it wasn't always him doing this because sometimes he wouldn't even remember what he had just said when he was done yelling at me. I was trying to love him unconditionally, and I wasn't ready to give up. I learned to deal with it instead, which led me to become a victim of his gaslighting and verbal/mental abuse.

Since my world was filled with disillusions, I tried to grasp onto reality with the help of those around me who loved me. I was too codependent to understand how to stand on my own two feet and succeed at it. At least, that's what my confidence level thought. Over time, my self-worth began to decline. I became confused about how to be stable on my own or in a healthy relationship. I learned how to become uncomfortably comfortable in a drama-fueled relationship. I have a big heart, and normally have the tendency to put other people's wishes before my own. I became so wrapped up in trying to keep him happy that I forgot who I was, what I enjoyed doing, and what makes me, *me*. Living life this way only creates an imbalance of energy. You can become resentful, drained of energy, and confused about what you're living for. I clung onto this relationship because I didn't know any better, like it was the only thing that could keep me from fully drowning. I had a mindset that I wouldn't be able to successfully make it on my own, simply because I had honestly never done it. We all fear what we don't know, *right*? I had some things going for me, though. I had a roof over my head, food in my stomach, a person who said he loved me, but showed me differently with his actions. Yet, I had this overly loving personality that just spiritually bypassed (overlooked) all the horrible things he would say to me.

I started fighting with depression and pent up anger again, so when I became intoxicated, I would go back to not caring about my body or my values. I would only care about being the life of the party because I was good at it. Really good. That was how I got most of my attention. Unfortunately, this created a false sense of reality for me. This also didn't make my boyfriend too happy, and he would regularly end the night with a fight about "*what a slut*" I was. Dealing with my pain by taking drugs and drinking alcohol might not have been the best outlet, but I survived to tell about it, somehow. There were too many mornings I woke up in a blur, with a hole in the wall and me in the guest bedroom. I would blame it on the crazy Alli-sin coming out. (Alli-sin is my shadow side persona that lives inside of me and only comes out when I get too intoxicated.) Once I get to a certain level of fucked up, I absorb something or someone else's energy.

When you get fucked up, you open up your crown chakras, becoming vulnerable to the unknown. They call alcohol a "spirit" for a reason. Not having control of your body is also the same as not having power over your spirit and your force field. When my guard was down, something else took over my body. I don't always remember, but it wasn't the sweet Allison everyone knew. Sometimes it was fun, but other times it was a nightmare. I can't remember how many times I have said I am sorry because I did something outrageous, yet had no idea what had happened. Looking back, I can see how this nature had control over me, my lifestyle, and my decision-making process. I had created a cycle for myself to become more depressed. I was giving him reasons to lash out at me because I was young and didn't know how to gain control. I wasn't even legally allowed to be drinking at this age. Things would only get worse the more I tried to play it off like it was nothing. I didn't see that I had a problem with holding my liquor. I felt like I was just young and had my moments. I didn't realize what I was doing, because a depressed addict only cares about numbing the pain and humiliation of the past and the present. Most people in this position don't realize they are the victim of a serious illness, and the cycle continues until some epic event shakes you from its grasp, or an intervention takes place. It was as if I had two personalities. Allison and Alli-sin. (You know it's bad when you name your drunk self.)

Being the stubborn little twat that I was, I never could take the easy route. I continued to drink and take drugs as if nothing was wrong. I continued to stay in this toxic relationship and eventually became addicted to creating fights and drama to keep the connection alive. Being in this situation inevitably led me to continue this vicious cycle. What lessons could be learned by playing it safe and having a calm and simple life in your late teens and early 20's? My mentality was, I had gotten used to having a hard life and thinking that this is what I deserved. I had grown thick skin and learned how to cope and adjust to my environment. I thought I had control over my life and didn't see how it could be the worst thing to have a little fun and put up with someone who wasn't perfect all the time. I thought this was normal. Couples fight and people mess up. I didn't think I had a problem or was doing anything wrong. Maybe I was young, maybe I was weak, maybe I was manipulated, or maybe I didn't want to get categorized as an alcoholic or drug addict in an abusive relationship. In my mind, there was no issue. I was young, in love, and partying like everyone else around me.

CHAPTER FOUR

THE ENERGY SUCKING GHOST

I had something rattle my soul to the point where I questioned reality. One night, after a long weekend of taking Molly, my boyfriend and I were at home fighting once more. We fought so badly all night long until I was too exhausted to argue anymore. I couldn't even be next to him because he had made me so mad. It was so bad that I was trying to sleep in the other room on the floor. As I was lying on my back on the floor crying, when something even more terrifying than fighting with my boyfriend happened. It started with a sound. A *whomp whomp whomp* sound that was moving closer to me. If you've ever taken a whip it, or fainted, or were on the verge of passing out, it was that tunnel vision sound of no control. It happened within seconds, moving closer to me until it surrounded me. Not only was there a sound warning that it was coming closer, but when it reached me, it paralyzed me. I call it "it" because it wasn't human. It was an evil, unseen force. It scared the shit out of me, knowing that it had the power to freeze my body, take my breath away, and suck out the little bit of energy I had left. It must have pinned me down and raped me of my light and energy for nearly ten minutes. Too scared to move, too stubborn to run to my boyfriend for comfort, I laid on that floor, shaking. I tried to fall asleep, thinking I'd be less vulnerable lying on my stomach. I was wrong. Just before I drifted off, I heard it racing towards me through the walls, and then it jumped on me again. It pinned me down and sucked me dry a second time. After this, there was no way I could be alone. I sucked up my pride and ran back into our bed, terrified, shaking, and dumbfounded. The room was still cold and stale with the lingering energy of this *thing* that invaded my space.

Spirits, like humans, prey on the weak. They feed off the fuel of all the unnecessary energy wasted in toxic relationships or compromising situations, like when you drink. The evil, or dark, spirits are drawn in like vultures to that kind of angry and explosive energy. This was the perfect home for them to feast. On top of that, my drinking and drug problem made me a perfectly ripe and naïve target. When we are not in control of our bodies, our spirits play a game of *catch me if you can* with devils. It makes us vulnerable, especially if we are sensitive and empathic beings. If you find yourself in a severely weakened state, you can easily become some spirit's meal. He will use your energy to strengthen himself and thrive for longer amounts of time. This happened on two other nights in this home when we had fought. After this, we decided to start looking for other places to live. That place grew so toxic that it became haunted by this dark, heavy energy that practically started our fights for us. It was the fuel behind all of it. None of it made sense, but I knew what I was feeling, and it wasn't good. We had to get out of this house.

I didn't quite understand the full extent of what was going on until many years later. Being empathic and not understanding the power that comes with it, while being sensitive to the other side and not knowing how to deal with it, along with eating Xanax and drinking too much to hide all of it away, was a recipe for disaster. I was a walking doorway for disembodied souls to feast on. I also strongly believe that these souls would take over when I was blackout drunk, making holes in the walls as an outlet for their rage. Yeah. It's heavy to type this, but it's true. I thought I could ignore it. I thought it would go away once I numbed the discomfort and weirdness that happened every day. I learned how to sit with the happenings and swept it all under the rug, pretending it didn't exist. At the time, I didn't think I was possessed. I didn't think I had a problem. I didn't think I was clairvoyant or empathic. I questioned it but was scared of it. I didn't have anyone to talk to who would understand, nor was I open to sharing this weirdness with others. I kept it to myself and my pill bottle. It was affecting my boyfriend, too. He was perpetually grumpy and ready to fight, depressed, and taking plenty of Xanax and Adderall to get up in the mornings and go down at night. He wasn't the same anymore. He became so intense that I wasn't even comfortable sitting next to him.

To make matters more confusing, two years into that relationship, I wanted out. I tried to walk away before it sucked me dry. I told him this news after a night of crazy partying. He was super unstable, desperate, and willing to do anything to stop me from leaving. He got a shotgun, put it up to his head, and told me he would kill himself if I left. I was shocked and terrified! I didn't know what else to do except to call his mother. I was stuck with someone's life in my hands, and I didn't know how to handle someone dying because of me. So, of course, I stayed and tried to calm him down, called his mother, and went with it. His mother alerted his father, and he called the police. The police were dispatched to the house, and we were quickly surrounded by six cops trying to take over the situation. They retrieved the gun and took him to the psychiatric ward in Austin. Boom. That quick. If you threaten suicide with a deadly weapon, this is the standard procedure.

Following this mess, leaving him wasn't an option. It got worse before it got better. His cry for help worked on me, hitting me where I was most vulnerable; when I see someone in pain, I can't abandon them, even if it is to my own detriment. I had the weight of the world on my shoulders, and I felt guilty and responsible for him being in this torturous place. Little did he know that while he was in the psych ward, I felt just as trapped as he did in there. No way could I leave him now. I don't know what I would've done if he pulled the trigger. My grandma had to witness my grandpa shooting himself in the head while he was drunk one night. I already felt like I was reliving my grandma Buzzy's life, and there was no way in hell I wanted to go through that kind of pain of losing someone like this.

The doctors wouldn't let him out until he showed better behavior. They put him on some hardcore anti-depressants that made him zombie-like, which wasn't helping the situation. I don't know why I didn't run away while he was locked up, when I had the chance to move all my things out. He stayed at the ward for over a week, heavily drugged and under close observation. I remember spraying my perfume on the pillow I brought to him, per his request, to help comfort him. I felt his pain in my veins like it was mine. Plus, he had done so much taking care of me when I first moved out of my parents' house. I felt as if I owed him this much to help him in his recovery. I tried to visit him every day that week, but it was hard to be there. My soul hurt with so much confusion and sadness. It was like the ghost in that house made us both crazy. Whatever this *thing* was, it had won. I wanted to do the right thing, but I didn't know what that was.

The doctors diagnosed him with depression and bipolar disorder, making sense of the wild mood swings and super highs along with super lows, especially when combined with mind altering drugs such as Molly, ecstasy, acid, Xanax, or Adderall--all of which were our drugs of choice at the time. He was released after about a week with a new prescription that made him different. I tried to be kind and gentle but also needed to leave for a while. Between the hauntings and the unexpected flip-switch of my boyfriend's moods, my confused soul just wanted to breathe. It all became too much for me. I had to move out. I got my own apartment down the street and hid out there for a few months while he stayed in the haunted house alone. I got the cutest place, too! It was all mine, and I finally felt safe enough and financially secure enough to breathe. I could sleep well at night, knowing that I could make it on my own if I needed to. It was the confidence I needed at that time in my life.

I could do whatever I wanted and needed to do for my happiness, and I ended up building and creating a cute place filled with love and my own spark. This was exactly what I needed to have at this time; I needed my own space to come back to. I was still kind of talking to my boyfriend during this time, but I needed space to get away from his craziness. He wasn't the same after this, and part of me was scared of what he would do if I left completely. He was a mastermind of manipulation and made me feel guilty for everything I would do. It was still too soon after his suicidal threats to coldly walk away and block him. That wasn't my style at the time because my heart was too big and naïve to know. I was out, but not freed from him. I was still under his spell of entrapment. He was a pro at making me doubt my ability to make it on my own, and in the next breath, he'd reassure me that he'd be there when I inevitably failed and needed to come running back home. He knew he could play this card with me. I wanted to keep making it on my own and I was in a six-month lease, so I was going to use all of this time to make a decision.

The few months living on my own were nice, but tight. The struggle was real to live on your own as a young person in Austin! I became lonely, depressed, and poor from spending all my resources just trying to make it. He was right; maybe I couldn't do it on my own. My self-doubt bellowed in my belly. I was still unhappy being separated from this man. My confidence and sense of self-worth were dwindling.

He continued to suck me in with his sob stories of missing me, crying out to me as he battled depression and suicidal thoughts. His life wasn't worth living if I wasn't in it. His energy was dragging me down and I could feel his pain. I was still being sucked dry of energy, but this time, from a human. I guess we were each other's crutch. I believe they call these kinds of relationships "trauma-based."

I ended up giving up on living separately and moved back in with him within the year, and felt oddly connected to the sadness. I wasn't anyone when I was on my own. I was something with him. That made the biggest difference in my mind at the time. I was linked with his well-being and happiness. Sure, that made me feel worthy, but also responsible for his emotions. I didn't want anything to happen to him, so I stayed with him out of guilt and fear for what he might do to himself. There were many nights when he threatened to kill himself because I was considering leaving him. He knew that he could manipulate me that way because I was wrapped in his gaslighting mind games. Manipulation on that level distorted reality, and I struggled to walk away. I was usually the one who tried to make it work, even if it was unhealthy and killing me slowly. (To reiterate: My grandfather also shot himself in the head while he was drunk long before I was born. It was possible family trauma passed down from my grandmother Buzzy's experience, or my mother's experience.) Nonetheless, I was determined to change the outcome. This burden, this trap, this cry for attention is the main part of why I couldn't leave for so long. I was trapped in the idea that if I left, he would kill himself. I didn't want anyone to die because of me. I didn't want that burden to be on my shoulders. I couldn't live with that, so I chose to stay and fight the fights, cry the tears, all the while, I found myself becoming more brittle as time went on.

*Side Note: 1) You are not responsible for how anyone else is handling their emotions. You cannot make them happy, and you cannot make them sad; that is their doing. You can contribute to their outcome, but in the end, how they choose to show up is on them. 2) No matter how much you drink, or how much Molly or drugs you take, it will never fix your problems. This will only make things worse.

CHAPTER FIVE

EACH LOVE IS A LESSON

In my mind, if you loved me, you were there for me. If you didn't, then Boy, bye. He was one of the few that never walked away, so I didn't either. It wasn't a healthy relationship, but we were on that journey together. Every relationship is a learning experience where you love and learn from that love. You're both in each other's lives for a reason, and I was fascinated to find out what these lessons were. Maybe they are there to be a stepping-stone, or to be your support, or to keep you sane, or to drive you insane!

I've got to say that even though that relationship was wild as hell, I learned some valuable lessons along the way. It wasn't all a shit show. I grew into the person I am today because of the genuine, kind soul that he had hidden underneath the depression and bipolar disorder. Some days were good and some were hard; that was just life, or so I thought. I had to roll with the punches with this guy and learn to adapt. In the end, I am forever grateful for the lessons I learned in this relationship and how this man shaped me into the woman that I am now.

I learned about synchronicities, action-reaction, free will and destiny, and the power of now. My mind was slowly being expanded, filled with curiosity, and the desire to learn more. As I started down this path, I slowly learned to follow what the world was trying to tell me. I found that hearts were my synchronicity. I saw them everywhere and felt guided in the right direction when I found them. I began to see them in rocks, gum that was stuck on the ground, clouds, water droplets, basically in everything. If I was lost but saw a heart pot-hole, I'd feel like this was my path and be at peace with being lost. I started trusting the universe and my inner voice.

I was young. I was naïve. I was weak. Yes, but I was a lost soul clinging on to this information and knowledge, and I felt like he truly loved me. I was looking for guidance, lost in the awe and security of an older man, hoping that he'd show me the ways of life.

When he talked about those extra ten years of life experience, it made me curious as to what it would be like if I explored more and found these epiphanies on my own, instead of relying on him to teach me. He talked about traveling, he spoke of life's awakening moments, and I was living vicariously through him. We were so far apart age-wise that when we would talk about settling down, it was unsettling to me. He didn't realize it, but he was making me dream of taking off traveling to all the could've, should've places! *I mean, I'm young, what am I waiting for?* I wanted this, but he wanted to settle down in Austin for a while, and traveling like this was already a thing of the past for him.

I wanted so badly to be loved and taken care of, nurtured, and respected. Is it possible to have all of those comforts at the same time? I got so used to the mental and verbal abuse that I tricked myself into believing this was my life and this is just how relationships were. I had a roof over my head, clothes on my back, and food in my belly. I was in survival mode, bypassing what was happening to me on a soul level.

I tried my best to please him, but he was one grumpy little fucker. I remember trying to go to strip clubs to "spice" up our relationship and try to appease him. His biggest fear was that I was going to cheat on him, so this was my way of exploring others without going behind his back. It made sense at the time. I had wandering eyes, and he was right; I probably would've cheated on him if our relationship continued the way it was going. Setting boundaries only to walk on the edge of them is never a good idea, especially not when the relationship is already rocky. We had our fair share of fun on Molly, finding a stripper, and playing with the idea, but it never felt right or ended well when the post-rollie blues set in. Then the insecurities turned into my biggest nightmare. I was 22 at this point and had already spent four years with this man. For me, it was harder to change what I was used to, than to start fresh with the unfamiliar. I got used to being uncomfortable after a while. I did know that I needed a change, but I had no idea what that would even look like.

One day, a lady came up to me at the coffee shop I was working at. She was a gentle, soft-spoken, kind-hearted regular named Betty. Underneath her voice, she said "Your angels really want to speak to you." I took a step back and was somewhat shocked, but not surprised. I had been asking for guidance and direction in my life in the quietness of my own head, but had never actually expressed it out loud. Curious, I asked her what she meant. She replied, "I do a healing technique called Akashic Record Readings, where I am the middleman between you and your angels. I would love to give you a reading." This message came at the perfect time in my life, as do most of these kinds of occurrences. So, get this! We all have our own team of angels and spirit guides to help us on our journey. It's like our own personal army. Each angel or spirit guide for you has their own specific task or role in helping you on your path. For instance, there is one to help you with compassion and in relationships, one to help you learn your lessons, one to help in your career, one to help you with family, etc. We have about five to eight depending on the person and what is needed in their life. We all have the ability to speak with our angels and spirit guides, but it takes discipline and practice.

I was intrigued by this medium who could unlock the keys to my future happiness. I felt the guides wanting to communicate with me, but I couldn't quite hear them over all the drugs and alcohol I was consuming. She was very specific about being clear-headed before my session, and advised that I shouldn't do anything to alter my reality. The messages would be louder and more transparent this way. It made sense that I wasn't able to hear them. I was numbing, I was ignoring, and I was abusing. I was not listening, feeling, or comprehending my path. She convinced me to come over for a paint party and then we could do the reading after. We waited a day or two for me to get clear from medications and alcohol, and then I was ready for my reading. It was so hard to go out on my own because of my boyfriend's trust issues and possessiveness, so it was a big deal for me to leave at night for a long period of time. If I ever did go out, it was always a battle, especially when it was time for me to come home. He seemed understanding at the time, so I thought I'd be good for a while.

I arrived at Betty's house and she greeted me with the warmest hug. I had known this woman as a regular over the past year, and she felt like a motherly figure to me. She had a way of checking in on me and asking how I was doing. Do you ever get that feeling like there are people here on this planet who are walking angels? I'm referring to those people who go out of their way to help you on your path, the ones who see something special in you, or appear out of nowhere to save your life. Well, Betty was my first encounter. This woman had the presence of a walking angel, and soon she would be telling me my records and communicating with my team of angels. It was like a board meeting!

She painted me this beautiful piece that I still have hanging over my desk as I write this. She painted me a picture of a bright yellow star in the middle of the canvas. (I'm guessing this was in the middle of the galaxy) It is abstract, but she explained to me, "This painting is a resemblance of you. You are this big, bright light that's shining inside." Little did I know that this would be my mission on this earth to find this bright light within and write a book about my journey finding it. This painting has been my inspiration; I've kept it safe for ten years now! I look at it and am reminded that we are all spiritual light beings in the midst of our human experience.

After the painting was completed, we both sat down in the living room facing each other. She brought over a piece of paper and a pencil, and recommended that I take down notes because a lot of information would be coming in, and it's best to write these tips down! How an Akashic Record Reading works is you have to have specific questions that require more than a yes/no answer. Your guides will respond, but they won't respond in regards to love with an answer to stay or leave. They will hint around it, though. We began the reading with an opening prayer asking for our guides to help give us a clear passage to the other side. It was quite magical to see how comfortable Betty was and how confident she was in her first message. She told me, "Your Grandma Buzzy is your teacher guide! She helps you learn all your lessons in this lifetime." I always felt her presence around me even though I never met her. I wear her ring religiously and never take it off. It was perfect that this is her role, and this was the first thing she said. She said that Buzzy had been trying to talk to me for a while now. I found it super comforting to know she's always there. She continued to tell me that I have seven guides helping me on my journey. A few were relatives, two were unidentified, one is like royalty, and one is like a warrior. We tried to ask names but the only clear one was my grandmother. My first question was mainly regarding what direction I needed to go. I was at a crossroads and knew I needed and wanted something more than what I was doing, but I had no clue where to start. The response was that I needed to go to school to become an event planner. *What?* I never thought about it, but it would be perfect! They went even deeper there and directed me into a specific field: planning yoga and healing events. I didn't do much yoga at the time, but okay. *Sounds nice.* They also informed me to have faith and to follow my heart. Walk the path less traveled. Break out of the normal. I drew a picture of an angel with a rose. I asked about what to do with the man that I was seeing to see what they would reply with, and they told me I knew what I needed to do; I needed to follow my heart. They told me I would travel to do these yoga and healing retreats and that I was here to help people.

At the time, I didn't fully understand the extent of my conversation with my angels. I did get a lot of joy being able to follow their advice. I took what I learned from this reading and enrolled in school to become an event planner. Austin Community College, here I come for an Associates Degree in Hospitality, specializing in Meeting and Event Planning! I was ready to go in that direction, and I felt like such a cute little student. I didn't realize how easy event planning came to me. I think the only book I read at the time was Hospitality Law, just because I didn't want to mess with breaking the law when it came to planning events. I was able to get all A's and B's solely by showing up, without really studying or reading. I was a natural. It felt right. I could go into different fields, working with hotels, festivals, private events, etc. The doors were opening and this was giving me a new focus and a purpose. My favorite type of event to work was working hospitality at festivals. We had to do a lot of volunteer work for school, which turned into some pretty good gigs for my future. I found that I loved the rush that festivals had, with the walkie talkies and golf carts. It's like working in the ER versus a nursing home. It was long and hard hours, with lots of responsibility. I was able to get VIP everywhere I went, and I knew exactly what to do before it was even asked of me. I felt so natural working the events; everything flowed like I was a composer. At the time, I was taking Adderall. This drug made event planning easy. My brain was running at full speed and that helped while working 20 hour days in rough conditions. I also found it helped with not eating, so I didn't have to use a Porta Potty as much.

All this being said, I was starting to love my new path and was finally able to feel something go right in my life. It was my choice on this one, with some guidance, to go to school for something that I was good at. Unfortunately, event planning jobs are kind of hard to get on a full-time basis, so I had to keep my main job managing a coffee shop. I am so grateful to Betty for opening this door and this new path for me. I now have event planning experience under my belt with a whole new perspective on my passions. This reading changed my life! If you ever get a chance to experience an Akashic Record Reading, I strongly recommend doing it. Come with an open mind, not under the influence, and with a pen and paper. Game changer! This is a perfect healing session for those who are lost and need some direction and advice from their guides.

After this reading was done, I became more curious and ended up stumbling upon a psychic's website. All I did was plug in my birthday, and I got an immediate response that told me I had a dangerous decision to make that would determine my fate. I was in a transition period of my life and if I took the wrong course, it could be detrimental to my future. The catch was that I had to buy the full reading for $100, which I didn't have. I waited two days, and grew more and more concerned about what that reading might say, when they messaged me back saying that this is urgent, that it can't wait, so they offered me a lower cost which I still couldn't afford. I waited another day, then she gave me an 80 percent off offer that I couldn't resist. I wish I still had this ten-page reading about my life and my journey. I know that in the Akashic Record Reading, my guides couldn't tell me if I should or shouldn't leave my boyfriend, but this lady was quite clear that I needed to leave and get away from the toxic weights that were drowning me, and my growth. It was exactly what I needed to do, to a T. I wasn't sure about risking my home life on what this reading was telling me, but it definitely shook me up and made me question things even more than I already was. Sometimes these readings help, but sometimes ignorance is bliss.

To nobody's surprise, the stubborn version of myself kept trying to make things work with this boy. I wasn't ready to give up when I had so many signs and messages to leave. I continued to hold on in an unhealthy way. I should've trusted the guides and the warnings, but I was also unsure if these readings were real and if I should make such a drastic lifestyle change based on a psychic reading. I had these messages tucked away in the back of my brain as a side note that got swept under the rug. My guy had a sneaky way of buying my love back by taking me on a great vacation, or blowing my mind with VIP passes to a festival, and I would get brainwashed into believing everything was okay again. With this information in mind, tucked away because I didn't want to believe it was true, I continued on the path with this guy, falling deeper into his mess.

After about six years of being with him, it was getting pretty real. People started to ask the question, *"When are you going to get married?"* The social pressure of what you do if you're with someone for that long starts to set into the relationship, causing a whole new dynamic to emerge. It was either we get married or break up; *which direction are we going to go?* I felt like I could marry this man, but I had my doubts because of everything he'd put me through. I wasn't sure if I could be happy, yet I've never been with someone, loving them unconditionally, for this long. Sure, there were some red flags; the biggest was his lack of trust and his fear that I was going to cheat on him, though I never did. His insecurities were too much of a burden. I thought most of it stemmed from his low self-esteem, so I felt like sealing the deal with this man and showing him I was "*his*" could make him feel better about my intentions. I was happy to take a stable marriage with the security that would come along with it, over breaking up and becoming homeless. So, we had some big talks, big decisions, and big moves to make. All of my other classmates were settling down and starting their families. Maybe I could do it. I just wasn't sure if I was ready yet.

CHAPTER SIX

MAKING MOVES

I was only doing what I thought was right to build a stronger relationship with this man. I could see a future with a family, and moving on with the next phase of my life like everyone else my age was doing. I saw his potential. I was blinded by the gaslighting, bribes, and manipulation throughout the years and ended up not knowing how to live any other way. I was putting up with the degrading, demanding, repulsive behavior because I honestly wanted to make him happy. When I could make him happy, it was great! Being a Taurus, I took this as a challenge because I'm a lover at heart and don't always understand how to walk away. It seems that I have to learn my lessons the hard way, on my own time. I am one of those that will stick with it until my breaking point, when most people would've already taken off.

I waited around for when he was happy and sat miserably uncomfortable when he wasn't. All I wanted was someone to love me, and that was all that mattered, not *how* he loved me. Even if that meant sacrificing my own happiness forever. It was my fate to have this rollercoaster of a relationship. It was what I deserved, or so I thought. I also met this man as soon as I moved out of my parents' house at 18, and I never explored any other option. The talk was on the table with this one about making it work for life. I kept thinking about how I felt about the words *for the rest of my life*. Those words are so powerful once you are committed, or "trapped in a marriage," as some may say. *Could I do it?* I had mixed feelings, but I was also getting swept up in the idea of marriage and how this *should* be the next step with this guy.

*Side Note: Don't beat yourself up for what you don't already know. It takes a lifetime to understand these lessons. It takes diving into the dark to understand the uncomfortable reach for sanity. Know that repeating the same patterns over and over again while expecting different results is commonly referred to as the definition of insanity. You only know what you know based on how you were raised and your experiences. Learning and growing include getting out of your comfort zone and trying something new.

On my 23rd birthday, we spent the night at a concert followed by the strip club after the clubs closed. It wasn't that fun of a night because the Molly we ate hurt my stomach and I wasn't really feeling like myself. Afterwards, we went back to the house, and I passed out on the couch. I was super wasted, coming off my Molly high, and couldn't even make it to bed. As I was passed out on the couch, he set up his lighting right in front of me. He had the spotlight shining at me and shook me to wake me up. I woke up to him on one knee. Still in a haze of confusion, I kind of knew what was happening but felt as if I was dreaming. He whipped out my ideal Simon G. engagement ring that I had been drooling over, and all I could see were the sparkles shimmering. He knew what he was doing; the spotlight was perfectly positioned to make this ring pop!

Still buzzed and fuzzy-headed, I fell on him, screaming "Yes, yes, yes!" Little did I know at the time, I was about to make one of my biggest mistakes. I knew after six years it was either we get married or break up, but to be honest, part of me wanted to marry him to help him with his insecurities and jealousy. I wanted to show him I was his, and he didn't need to worry about anything. I thought marriage might work as the last option to fix our relationship before giving up on us. I was willing to try anything to make it work. Part of me also wanted stability and not having to worry about finding *the one,* so I settled for what I knew.

To top it all off, I partially wanted to get married so I could plan my first wedding. I know it sounds egotistical, or like I was getting married for the wrong reasons, but I didn't want to plan someone else's wedding for my first! I saw it as a challenge and an opportunity for growth.

For the girls and guys out there thinking about marriage: Don't get married for any of these three reasons: 1) you don't know if you should get married or break up 2) you are trying to help with insecurities 3) you are doing it so you can plan a big party. (Trust me, you will regret it and it will come back to bite you in the ass.) Guys, here's a little hint for you: Don't ever ask your future wife to marry you after a long night of drinking.

There was no turning back in my mind at this point. I had already said yes. He bought me my dream ring. I took all this as the natural path of a young adult and was welcoming the new venture into my new reality. This experience would end up shaping me so much and teaching me my biggest relationship lessons to this day.

I was more than excited to be planning this event, though! I had so many wonderful ideas and put my heart into making it a special surprise for our families. I tried to ignore any silly fights and brush them under the rug because I didn't want anything messing with my bride-to-be vibe. In the back of my head, I still had the whispers of what my psychic reading had told me about getting into a devastating situation that could hinder my growth. I ignored the warnings and chose to push through, hoping that it wasn't true. I always had a feeling about it being wrong, but our relationship was now taking steps into the unknown, and it was as if things were escalating so fast that there was no way to put brakes on the momentum. It was possible that our relationship could get better with this change we were willing to endure together. When entering into marriage, one would think it'd get easier knowing you have a partner that has your back. With marriage, there is the growth and acceptance of one another that should happen. I had faith that it was all going in a positive direction. Although, if I'm being honest, I was also a hopeless romantic. There were so many red flags along the way, I could have made a bouquet out of them, leading up to the time before the engagement. I wanted so badly for this to work out and to go on living my fairytale of happily ever after, so I turned a blind eye and kept marching forward with the plans.

I enjoyed planning the wedding, which is why I ignored the awful state of our relationship. Planning the wedding was the easiest part. I was given a small budget and I made something so beautiful out of it. I did a lot of it on my own because I wanted it to be a surprise for my family and friends, but that didn't fly too well with the people funding the event. I got backlash and tons of questions from my family and my soon-to-be husband telling me I was the *"worst event planner"* because I *"wasn't communicating."* I was spending their money while trying to keep everything a surprise, which, in the end, caused a lot of tension as to where their money was going. I was pouring all of my love into this event. This was my coming out party as an event planner and I really wanted to impress those I loved. I wanted to blow everyone's mind with what I could create, but there was some doubt as to what I was capable of since it was my first event. This hurt, but when you're working with thousands of dollars, people want to know where it's all going.

Nonetheless, planning all of this gave me a focus and a drive. It showed me how much I loved event planning and made me feel like I was finally in the right place. All of this joy was crushed with money pressures, communication issues, and the stress of trying to keep it quiet while still sharing only what they needed to know. My partner and I started fighting more once the planning began, which made everything harder because I found myself questioning why I was even planning a wedding with him in the first place. My fiancé didn't want anything to do with the planning, and I still had a shit storm to come home to every night. *Yay! For the rest of my life! I don't know what the fuck I got myself into, but it's nearly too late to get out now. I've invested so much of my time and energy into making this wedding special. Maybe it's the stress and pressure of this "unknown" factor that's making us fight,* or so I thought. We're all so scared and have fear-based thoughts about the things we don't know about, the things that haven't happened, or the pain or fear of failure. I convinced myself that this was normal and stuck it out.

Fast forward to the wedding day--April 30th, 2011. I picked that date because it was my Grandma Buzzy's birthday, and I wanted her to be there in spirit. Funny enough, she is my teacher guide, and boy was she there! This was the biggest lesson my teacher guide could've given me. I remember getting my hair and make-up done and driving out to the venue on the lake. I had to pull over on the side of the road to throw up because of my nerves. I knew I was doing the wrong thing, yet I couldn't be that runaway bride. I just couldn't. Everyone was waiting for me out at the property. We had already spent so much money on this wedding. I couldn't leave my fiancé hanging like that. I didn't even know what I would do if I did run. I'd be homeless. After my throw up session on the side of the road, I continued out to the property where I would inevitably sell my soul. Once I made it out there, I got on the drinking train and began to numb the nerves. I had so many piña coladas that I was automatically singing the "If you like piña coladas and getting caught in the rain" song. I saw my soon-to-be husband before the ceremony, and he had a bag of Molly for the party afterwards. Of course I couldn't resist and begged him for some beforehand. I felt like I couldn't go through with the wedding unless I had something to take the edge off. So, yes, I got married while rolling balls on Molly. In case you were wondering, it did help with the process, but I don't recommend it. Apparently, I was the comedian for the night! I was so buzzed coming down the stairs with my dad, that I forgot my bouquet of flowers. I had stayed up late the night before making all of my floral arrangements. I realized I had forgotten it once I started walking down the aisle, but it was too late.

Later on, my parents told me they felt the most distance from me in my life on my wedding day. My mom felt like she had no connection with her daughter that she was giving away. It could have been the result of all of the secret event planning, or maybe it was because I was ashamed and knew I was doing the wrong thing by marrying him. I was trying to fake it until I made it, or maybe because I was too fucked up to be present. Any way you shake it, my parents could tell that I wasn't being true to myself.

After the ceremony, it was dinnertime, and I couldn't even eat the expensive meal in front of me. Once dinner was over and the dance party started, I stepped aside to throw up in a trash can. It was humiliating and telling of the fact that I was doing the wrong thing. My nerves were too much. The first night as a married couple was not super exciting, either. It was kind of a blur, and the sex wasn't POW! It was, meh. Nothing to report home with.

The next morning we had to leave early to catch our flight out to Turks and Caicos. We were at the airport, hungover off Molly and champagne, when my husband started munching down on some Xanax. He suffered from super bad anxiety when flying, or so he says, and therefore spent that whole day in a fog. It's so hard to travel hungover and with someone who isn't even in the right state of mind. The combination of post-rollie blues and Xanax overload was a recipe for disaster on our honeymoon. On the second day, secluded on a private beach in North Caicos, I was dressed in lingerie trying to please my new husband and cheer him up. His response to this was, "What the fuck did I do marrying you? This is such a mistake!" My mouth dropped. After all that I had endured, on top of pushing through and keeping these doubts and fears to myself, I got slapped in the face with this. These words of his would end up haunting me for the rest of our relationship.

Xanax and Molly were this guy's biggest downfalls. He would say the meanest things to me in the fog of this drug combination. For me, once it is spoken, it is extremely hard to get it out of my head. This was my first week of being married, and I hated it. *What an accomplishment; we have officially made the biggest mistake of our lives.* We both realized we fucked up once it was too late to get out. That was the worst week in paradise, stranded on an island with my husband. Well here we go; welcome to marriage!

When we got back to the States, I was a mess. I became trapped in a world that wasn't right for my heart, mind, or soul. I became super depressed and resumed a heavy addiction to Xanax. It was the only way I could tolerate the anxiety I got from my husband.

*Side Note: If you have to take anxiety medicine to be with your spouse, maybe that's a sign to reconsider the relationship. I don't recommend slowly killing yourself and numbing away your life, like I did. Consider leaving the issue and walking away from the things that cause anxiety; then, maybe you won't have to take medicine.

The pattern of his gaslighting tactics would only get worse now that we were married. In his mind, I had now become his property. The fights intensified, and the intake of my anxiety medicine did as well. I would freeze most of the time with this blank stare at the wall, numbed to my environment. He yelled demeaning things in my face, sometimes even so close he was spitting his words on me, but it was as if I had "checked out." I thought the more still and quiet I was, the lesser the attack would be. The fights did seem to fizzle out more quickly when I choked on my words, shoved my feelings down my throat, and didn't try to stand up for myself.

Once we got married, everything changed. I wasn't Allison anymore; I was now referred to as *my wife*. "My wife needs to have dinner ready and the house cleaned when I get home. My wife needs to not go out at night." I honestly hate that word now because he used it in every sentence when he talked to me, and only me. It was weird and unsettling how he was using this word in a way that assumed I would suddenly change because of my new title. He knew me and my ways before we married, but now I must shape up, change, and do everything in my power to be a *good wife*.

I was someone without an identity and without my own choice. I became weak and brittle. I became used to being in pain like when I was in high school. I knew what it was like to be in pain. I had no idea what a healthy life was. It was almost as if I had accepted that this was what life was like. I didn't blame him for the way he treated me either, because I strongly believed that *you only know what you know*. I only knew how to live in the pain and drama at this point in my life. He only knew how to treat women from what his parents and past relationships were like. He was already engaged before, but his ex-fiancée left during the engagement process, which is why I felt that I couldn't do it to him, too. His parents were divorced and spiteful towards one another, and they would have screaming matches in front of the kids and his mom would leave and disappear before they officially split. We learn from our parents and our past and, without a doubt, bring this into our future relationships. We often recreate our connection from a trauma-driven place, even though you might genuinely care for someone, and not realize it's toxic. My parents are still together and in love, and I guess this gave me hope. I was searching and wanting this for myself, but the person I attached myself to was someone who would never give me this security. We did not learn to love one another in a healthy way.

"Someone can love you desperately with their feelings and still not know how to love you correctly with their actions."
–Unknown Author

One day, lost in the blur, trying to make sense and salvage a freshly commenced marriage, I cried out to my mother for help. My dear, strong, warrior of a mother that I love so much. She gave me the best advice that I will never forget. She said, "Honey, you need to get out before you're too weak to get yourself out." She, too, had been in an abusive first marriage. She knew the signs. It was as if I was reliving her past. (Technically, trauma is passed down for up to seven generations through our DNA. Encoded, whether we would like it to be or not. *Don't be so hard on yourself. It's not your fault.*) Her words will always stick with me, no matter what situation I am in. I try to remember her words, especially when I find myself losing my strength, my will, and my soul to someone who is abusing me or misusing their power to overrule me.

As I deteriorated in a dark cloud of depression and seclusion. I was a zombie, eating Xanax to get through the day and deal with my husband. I was gaining so much weight and didn't even have the energy or the strength to exercise. I was turning into a zombie in this dark place where I felt lost and hopeless, like I ruined my life, and there was no going back. The pressure of this new reality and this being *for the rest of my life* was eating me alive. I had no friends that wanted to talk to me anymore because I was a Debbie Downer to be around. The friends I did have were his friends, and I didn't feel close enough to any of them to talk with them and seek council while I navigated my thoughts. I was alone this time. I had my husband to talk to, but that wasn't pleasant, so I kept our conversations to a bare minimum. Instead, I chose to keep my mouth shut for the first six months of our marriage, eating my medicine, and getting on with my so-called happy life.

To release my sadness, I started creating more as a form of escape. I made large, abstract paintings that took up the whole garage. He continued to bother me when I painted, so I came up with another outlet: writing. Around the same time, this book came to exist. I needed to express and release these emotions that I couldn't hide whenever they came up. I carried the weight of knowing I needed to leave but was too afraid to go through with it. I couldn't go out because he didn't trust me, and I didn't want to be home and bothered by him, so I made excuses to go grocery shopping. It was one of the only things I could do on my own. I found myself in the grocery store parking lot with a journal, which soon became my new indulgence: writing before therapy shopping. Journaling my anxiety and confusion allowed me to see things from a new perspective. This would become my pep talks to myself, to regain my confidence and self-worth. It was the only time I had to myself. I found myself desperate enough to enjoy my secret writing sessions. If I were to have written back at the house, my husband would've gone through all of my secrets about how I dreaded being his wife, and it would've ended badly. I kept my book hidden in my car and only wrote before I went grocery shopping. I soaked up every minute of this duty as a stay-at-home wife and would "forget" things so I could return sooner.

I started by journaling to myself, almost like I was writing personal pep talks to get through my daily struggles. I tried to cheer myself up and show myself that there was hope. I went back and forth with different personalities, depending on my mood and what I was channeling at the time. In my handwritten book, I have identified three different personalities or identities. There are the journal entries that explain what is going on at that time in my life, there is a higher self that I channel that gives uplifting and valuable insight, and then there is the dark side, which is me writing while super intoxicated, swimming in my circle of mistakes.

(In this book, I'll weave in my reality at the time it was happening through my journal entries. If you see a date above and fonts *italicized,* that's from the original handwritten book. Everything else in between is my interpretation and perspective in the present moment.)

CHAPTER SEVEN

THE HANDWRITTEN BOOK BEGINS

August 31st, 2011

My life has led me to this moment. I accept responsibility for all of my actions and the words I have spoken to others and myself on my way here. It's not so much a burden I am feeling right now, as much as I feel like this is my moment. I can choose to be sad, I can choose to be strong, I can choose to do nothing, or I can take action. I'm tired of feeling sad. I'm tired of feeling scared or fearful of others' reactions. That's not any way to live.

As someone who is open-minded, I feel like we all have these patterns and mistakes that we keep reliving from a previous life, until we have fully learned the lesson. The cycle will continue until you are ready to break it. It takes putting in a conscious and mindful effort to combat these challenges the right way during this lifetime.

I want to live like every day is my last. I am crying out for the love, support, guidance, intuition, and strength to do what's right for my own True Self's happiness. I am the only one in charge of my happiness. It's time I stand up for myself. I deserve that. No one else will do that for me. It's time I learn how. At 7 PM, August 31ˢᵗ, 2011, I vow to myself that I will be strong and do what is best for myself from this point on. I will not let fear run my life. I will not sit here and do nothing. I will not let my frustrations get in my way. I am putting all the extra time and energy I have into finding my True Inner Self. That happy Allison that everyone loves so much is still inside me, waiting to burst and release without setbacks, limitations, or my fears getting in my way. I will stay cool, calm, and collected. I welcome only positive people who can make a positive impact in my life. On my journey to self-discovery, I open my arms to the magic the world has in store for me. Maybe I will join the Peace Corps or do something to give back to our community and the environment. I want to travel, live, and feel passion in my life! I want to find my inner voice and let it be heard! The time for change is now! I FEAR no more!!!

September 7th, 2011

A note to myself: Hello!!! Wake up! Are you paying attention? You should be! I have a feeling this is going to be the most important three to four months of your life! Pay close attention to the signs and synchronicities that lie ahead. Trust and listen to them. Stay strong when you feel the weakest. Keep your head up, Darling. Surround yourself with the people who love and care about you, and take pleasure in receiving. It can be difficult right now, but nurture yourself. Love yourself. When times get tough, that is when you will grow the most. Stay strong, be your own individual, and don't let fear run your life. Your awakening will awaken the people you love the most around you. Your example of pain and suffering is an aid to help you connect with the divine. Your road leads here. As you feel that pain in your stomach, remember not to be fearful. Replay all the good times in your life and tell yourself "I love you first!" You are the only one who can make yourself feel a certain way.

Try to stay on a positive path and keep the ones you care about near. For a collaborative strength creates more energy than a solo one. You can look deep within yourself and hear your inner voice on your own, but do not feel like you must go about this journey alone. There are what I call "Walking Angels" who will always be with you! They can take shape or form of whatever is happening to help you get a message. Once you learn to listen to these angels, your inner voice, and life's synchronicities, you'll have a different perspective and appreciation. You will need loving hands to lift your spirit when times get tough. This is the beginning of a whole new you! -Allison

September 8th, 2011

Today is a big day! It's time to shine! I have what it takes to charge through any doubts or reservations. It is time to open the gates of Eden and be reminded of the powerful nature of the laws of attraction. It is said, if you want something, create it, do it, live it! No need to waste any more time! It will only come if you have the courage to make an effort to make it come true. The Divine is urging me to take the next step. I can feel my angels, and I can almost hear them saying how proud they are that I can acknowledge their presence! They love this because what I need right now is to know that I'm never alone, which is quite comforting.

September 9th, 2011

Today comes with its own set of challenges. Everything happens for a reason, and knowing that makes it easier to accept that challenge. Below is a list of things that I wish I had in my soulmate. I would want him to be strong, courageous, and personally happy to the point where he could take care of his own mental and physical needs. I would want him to show me what it takes to be a good example for our offspring. I want someone who stays calm in heated situations. I want someone who treats me like a queen, cares about my feelings, and would never speak to me in a demeaning way. I want someone who will do everything in his power to keep my heart fluttering and alive with passion and spontaneity. I know my knight in shining armor is out there in this world. I also know it's not the man I chose to marry. Are these the traits of my husband? Definitely not. I vowed to do everything in my power to love and cherish this man for life, but I honestly don't think I can. It shouldn't be this way. What did I do? I fucked up, and now all I have is a daydream of what life "should" be like. At least my daydream isn't hurting my heart: it's giving me hope.

September 16th, 2011

My days go by, and I wonder if this is real happiness. I'm trying to stand my ground, make my decisions, go about my somewhat enjoyable life, but at the end of the day, it doesn't add up. Is it worth the effort? It was to me, but all of that is fading because it isn't worth the effort for my husband. He isn't even trying to make things work. He stays in his grumpy depression and never has a good way to relate or communicate with me anymore. It feels like he gave up once we got married and became this angry mess. Most everything I do pisses him off. The more I detach and branch off by trying to make my own decisions, the more he gets upset. The more I relax and try to be myself, the more I hear him nag and complain about my faults. I want someone to love me for all of who I am, good and bad. Isn't that what we vowed to do on our wedding day? I need acceptance and forgiveness, along with more happy moments than negative ones. I miss seeing him smile. I can imagine all the blissful memories and most of them only happened because of drugs. We got back together because of a drug. We got married on that drug. It seems that drugs are one of the only things that can connect us and allow us to have a good time together. How messed up is that? Does this mean that our relationship isn't even real? Or is our relationship a delusional dream? More like a nightmare. It's interesting how I feel a connection, a spark, a memory of a past life with my husband, but only when we are holding each other and not saying a damn word. It seems to be the only time we get along these days is when we are silent or high. It's sad to admit this. It's as if I'm always walking on eggshells and they are all over the floor, impossible to miss. What have we done? I got myself into this mess; I need to find a way out. I have to get out. I know it. This isn't what I want for the rest of my life. I can't put myself through this torture and mundane hell. It will break my heart and his if I were to leave now, but it's as if the walls are caving in on me. It will be uncomfortable, but I have to let go of this weight that is dragging me down. My divine wants to shine. My light in my so-called home of a heart seems to get dimmer and dimmer as the days go by. The only way out is to leave, and I'm finally coming to terms with this. I don't want to change anything about who I am and what makes me uniquely me; not for anyone, not even my husband, nor should I have to. I also don't think it's my place to try to change him. He is the way he is because he chooses to be. We all have a choice as to how we want to show up. I am the only person who is in charge of changing myself and building my own life. I'm the only person that is going to stand up for myself and how I want to be treated. No one else can do that for me. I have control and I have a choice. I can pack my bags and leave tomorrow if I want to. My online reading told me a giant shift would happen on September 17th, which is tomorrow. I asked my angels for the courage and the strength to help me make the right decision at the right moment. It won't be fun or easy, but this is something that I know has to be done. It may not be tomorrow, but I'm listening to my wisdom, intuition, and guidance to show me the way. I'm too young to be this miserable. I should be living a happy life, focusing on school and my career. I deserve to smile and come home to a safe haven. I'll change jobs, change numbers, or change everything in order to get a fresh start! Little reminder: make sure that whomever you let inside your divine circle respects you, trusts you, gets along with you, and loves you for who you are. Honestly, I can't say that any of those requirements applied to my husband. There's a greener pasture of abundance out there in the world, waiting for me to discover it! All I can do is trust that my decision is what's right for my heart, and find peace in that.

September 17th, 2011(a.m.)

Traps to Avoid: *1) Don't do nothing! This creates a stagnant and stale environment where resentment and constant arguing over the same things will happen. (I've been chasing my own tail, repeating the same mistakes.) 2) Don't focus on failures and the unseen future. We are living in today, not yesterday, so learn and grow from all of the past failures for the future. Don't let your mistakes stunt your growth. 3) Avoid being fearful. Fear keeps me locked in a cage of being comfortably uncomfortable because it is all I know. Most of us fear the unknown more than anything. Let this fear go. Instead of being fearful, turn this energy into excitement. 4) Avoid making drastic, life-changing decisions when angry, sad, drunk, or experiencing any other radical emotion. Try to make a game plan first and wait it out to see how you feel in the morning when the dust settles. 5) Don't always follow what is socially acceptable for others to find your happiness. I am unique, and only I can be the one to build my own happiness. It doesn't matter what other people think in the end. It only matters how I think and feel. 6) Let go of old beliefs and ideas to move forward on your journey. Examine what my actions are. How am I behaving and why am I doing these things? This speaks volumes on the current state of being and the vibration that is being put out into the world. Notice the beauty in the growth. This growth was made possible by the darker times and there has to be some acknowledgement of that. 7) Staying positive and patient throughout all of this will bring grace and understanding.*

September 17th, 2011 (p.m.)

Talk about bad timing. We just got married five months ago. Is it too soon to call it off and run away? Is it fair? Is it normal? I know the first year is supposed to be the hardest, but I didn't realize it was going to be this hard. Once we got married, I wasn't me anymore. I became his "wife," and therefore had to act a certain way all of a sudden. His wife wasn't allowed to do much other than please him, which pisses me off. I lost my identity as an individual and I honestly didn't even recognize myself anymore. My husband's words on our honeymoon, "What the fuck did I do marrying you? I made the biggest mistake," keeps haunting me every time I look at him, making things worse.

I know I need to do what will make me happy in the long run, but it scares the shit out of me to end it. The timing has to be right for me to end it in a healthy way. But, I mean, will there ever be a right time? The biggest thing holding me back is my stability, security, and survival needs. I feel like I would be uprooting everything I have in hopes that my new choice will be able to provide this. I feel like I'm too weak, like an unwatered plant, slowly withering away in this marriage. I have to be patient and figure out a plan before I take this leap into the unknown. I somehow need to muster up the strength and courage to take charge of my life. I deserve to be happy. I want to make sure I land on my feet and not my face once I make the jump.

September 26th, 2011

Wow! I just had an aha moment! The day my Mom's words rang so loudly in my ears is the day that changed my path for the next venture. I was at home and didn't have dinner ready. He had been working an eight to five, and when he got home, he was grumpy and hungry. Whoops. First mistake. (He didn't have lunch either, which was usual for him to not take care of himself in the eating department.) Then he complained that the house was too dirty. We replayed the usual fight of him thinking I sat at home and did nothing all day when things got tense again. As he was yelling and screaming in my face, my fight, flight, or freeze reaction kicked in. I froze first, then I ran and hid to get away from him and tried to make all the noise stop. I ran to the bathroom; he busted in through the locked door. So, I ran to the closet in the bathroom and curled up in a ball in the corner behind my panty shelf when he busted through this door, too. He kicked the panty drawer into me until I had to stand up to stop the pain of this plastic bin pinching me. When I stood up, he was yelling so loudly and close to me that he was spitting his words into my face. I could feel all the blood boil to my brain, and then I snapped. At this point, I didn't even know what he was saying. All I could hear were my mother's words repeating in my head, **"Get out before you don't have the energy to."**

It was 114 degrees outside. I was wearing some cutoff blue corduroy shorts, a tank top, no bra, no shoes, and I didn't have my phone. None of that mattered. I didn't even give myself time to think about it. My flight mode kicked back in, and I ran out the door as fast as I could. I ran for my sanity, my growth, my pain, my confusion, and my anxiety. I ran so I could have time to think and listen to my own thoughts and intuition. I needed to come up with a plan to get out, and I was thinking of my next steps for what needed to happen from here. As I ran, I could feel my feet burning from the hot black pavement. It didn't matter at the time, though. I wanted to get as far away from my house as possible. What the hell am I doing running away from my husband and my home? What kind of life is this?

I was searching for a place to hide and rest after about ten minutes of running. I needed a safe spot so I could catch my breath and get off this hot pavement. I needed to hide from all of my neighbors as well, because I knew he was going to be looking for me soon. My instincts told me to run, and then, told me to hide. I ended up finding the perfect bush that was so inviting. It was as if this bush had my name written all over it. It was around a corner, tall and easy to get in and nestle in the dark. I ended up hiding in this bush for over three hours. I watched my husband circle around the neighborhood while I stayed hidden in the dark corner. He was never going to find me here. Even his sister joined in on the manhunt.

I found myself happier in that bush than I was in my own home. My home wasn't safe anymore. I knew it wasn't what a home should be like. The realization that I was happier in a bush than I was in my own home helped me to make up my mind. I couldn't handle this marriage anymore. I was happier sitting with nothing in a bush, than in a home that enveloped me in so much pain within its confining walls. I would be fine on my own and could become humble without anything except my happiness. I could make it on my own. I didn't need this false love. I didn't need this pain. I didn't need this false sense of who I was. All of a sudden, everything felt so fake and wrong. I was tired of being weak and quiet. I was putting up with this abuse day after day because I felt it was what I deserved, when in reality, I would rather be alone. I didn't ever get the full "How to Love Correctly" manual, but I did know that the lines have been crossed and there was no going back on my decision to leave. Unfortunately, things had to get completely out of control for me to step up and make a decision for myself.

I walked back to that house with burnt feet and my mind made up after hours of regulating my nervous system. I only went back because I had to pee. I gave in after three hours of enjoying the peacefulness of that bush; that little bush helped to ground me back to myself and gave me an understanding of what a home should feel like. I also had to put an end to watching my husband and my sister-in-law frantically circling the block as they looked for me. I walked back in the house and went straight to the bathroom. When I got out, I demanded his attention when I spoke my next words. "I'm done being treated like this and I have to leave you." That was the moment that changed my life forever. I don't think I can ever remove this experience from my brain concerning our relationship, nor what he said on our honeymoon. He knew he fucked up too badly, to the point where I had to run away out of fear. I could tell he knew and was sorry, but it was too damn late. As he would say, "Action:Reaction." This was the result of him treating me the way he did. He got his heart ripped out that day, by himself.

I saw a glimpse of who I could be and what was important to me when I stood up for myself. I was protecting my energetic field and realizing my power by doing so. I knew there had to be something better out there for me; I could feel it. There is another path that is brighter for me; I just had to choose to walk down that road. Life wasn't supposed to feel this way. Love isn't supposed to feel this way. A husband or a home is NOT supposed to feel this way. I knew this. My heart wasn't happy here.

October 12th, 2011

Something had to change, and it needed to happen quickly. When my mother-in-law found out that I wanted to leave this marriage already, she strongly urged us to try counseling first. I was desperate to make my life better, and I figured I would give it a shot to see if our marriage was salvageable. Personally, this only stirred up the pot of drama between me and my husband. Lisa, our therapist, is also a hypnotist, and I decided to give it a try. Maybe I could unlock some hidden trauma from my past. I'm excited to get to the real source of my deep-rooted issues and pain. I don't want to be angry, upset, or stand-offish anymore. I want to figure out how I can heal and move forward from my wild past.

October 28th, 2011

Well, my hypnosis uncovered a few deep details that I was hiding. First of all, I had a lot of residual pain and trauma from being physically, verbally, and mentally abused at initiation into high school. I have carried around so much shame and guilt, but I also discovered there is a lot of pain from my sister not helping me out in that situation. I also revisited being raped by my classmate's dad. I wish he would've drugged me with something that made me not remember every detail instead of drugging me with something that only paralyzed my body. This is why I have a lot of intimacy issues, especially when a hand or mouth comes close to my vagina. I understand these things lie deep within my subconscious, and I don't even realize they are an issue until the issue is in my lap, screaming at me. I have come to an understanding that I need to become more aware when I start getting triggered. I need to release and forgive, so I don't carry this trauma into every relationship I have.

As far as the hypnosis's effects on my relationship with my husband, I feel like it's a step in the right direction. It's helped him realize that holding onto the past will destroy our relationship. He was so angry and filled with pain from holding onto everything. I think talking with our therapist is opening some doors of self-discovery for him. He saw how close he was to losing me when I ran away from home, so I hope he takes all of this to heart and puts in the effort to save our relationship, or I will walk away. I guess only time will tell if he soaks it in and makes an effort to change.

As far as I am concerned, after being hypnotized, I realized that I needed to find a way to honor, love, and forgive myself. My mother gave me art as a release when I was going through some hard times in high school, and I began to pick up this technique again. My heart was holding onto so much pain that all of this energy needed to manifest somehow. I've made some great pieces of art recently, though. I always make the most beautiful art when I am sad.

I needed to find closure in my past. I ended up writing a letter to the mean girls who initiated me and then burned it afterward. I went home for the weekend and told my parents about my classmate's dad that raped me (ten years later). That was hard news for them to swallow, and for me to say out loud, but I felt better after getting that off my chest. I also spoke with my sister and had a huge heart to heart about her not taking me home on initiation day. This should've happened years ago. Better late than never, though. I spoke my mind, and now I feel like I can move forward from here. My healing around this helped my family, as well. It helped my parents understand why I did the things I did, and it also helped my sister feel better about that traumatic day. I know she had a lot of guilt and shame for not protecting me.

As far as my classmate's dad who raped me is concerned, the only closure I got was finally telling my parents about it. This was the hardest thing for me to do. It had been ten years since it happened and I still could only just now be able to talk about it. It makes me cringe with shame and disgust. I thought about writing him a ransom letter saying I wanted $100,000 and I'll keep quiet. Keep in mind, he works with children in the health field and this could damage his practice, which is why I won't mention his name or exactly what he does. (Even though I feel like I should scream it to the news station.) Since it's been over ten years I couldn't do much about it. There's a statute of limitations of ten years exactly, where my case wouldn't hold up in court. It was enough closure at the time to tell my mom and dad what had happened and finally be able to speak it out loud.

It was an exhausting trip, but a much-needed one. My family is my rock, and my go-to when I need guidance, healing, or when I need to get away and breathe. I was able to relax, rest, and finally gain some strength from being away from my husband. I still haven't been able to grasp what's happening with us. It's like the therapy is opening up all the cans of worms and making us more unstable than before. I thought it could possibly help but it's showing me how much of this I don't want.

November 27th, 2011

I did it! I left my husband. I did this the day before Thanksgiving. I know it's shitty timing, but I just couldn't take it. Thanksgiving is a holiday to be around people you love and who love you, and that wasn't the case in my home. It was like a wave of energy that was gifted to me from a higher power told me to DO IT!!! I couldn't stand to be miserable when all I wanted was to feel love. After so much time of all of this bottled up inside, I was able to let my true feelings blurt out. I knew I had to do it to save myself. I need to regain my self-respect, courage, and strength. There's never going to be a good time for this kind of thing.

I have been emotionally checked out for some time now. I stopped having conversations with him, had a hard time even showing emotions, and certainly couldn't fuck him after all of the mean things he's said to me. All those degrading moments would replay in my head while he was trying to get laid. It became traumatic for me to try and force it. I couldn't hide it anymore. He knew something was up with me because he knows me well. I was staying with him to avoid an uncomfortable confrontation in exchange for my self-worth and love. I wasn't doing either one of us any good by allowing this cycle to repeat and repeat, like a nightmare. The ongoing "I promise I will work on being more respectful and not calling you a bitch" line was so overused by this time. I couldn't allow myself to go through that even one more time. Things would be good for a month, and then he would slip right back into those horribly degrading habits that belittled me and made me feel like trash. The doctors say he's bipolar, but I also think he's a gaslighter, addicted to drama and arguing that fuels his ego and fire. I have met people who get angry, but not the way he does. All the love and respect that I had for him flies out the window like a bird in flight headed straight into a fast-approaching plane. His bipolar disorder makes him almost lifeless when he moves into his limbic system. This triggers the fight or flight response as a way to protect himself when he's trying to justify his actions or when he gets jealous. I trigger him daily, and he always chooses the fight response. He loses control and can't remember what he says when he gets into the angry fits of rage. He doesn't care who it affects or who is on the receiving end. It was me most of the time, but it was also everyone he ever worked with, along with his family, and most of his friends.

One time in particular, he was staring at me with this creepy gaze at the foot of the bed. His eyes were pure black, glazed over, filled with emptiness and anger. I could feel the hate and couldn't bear to look into those eyes. The feeling of his energy was extremely overwhelming and heavy, like dark clouds that were suffocating my heart. As he was piercing my soul with his gaze, I finally spoke up. "This is not okay." It was then that I had the courage to say enough was enough. I scrambled to pack a bag and ran straight to my sister's house. She was conveniently living about two minutes away and I needed a house (not a bush) to hide in. It was perfect. She had an extra room in her and her boyfriend's house, and I knew I would be safe there, although it was right down the street. I couldn't breathe in my house. I couldn't stand to even look at my husband with his eyes filled with hate. I needed to take control of my life before I didn't have the energy to leave.

It's amazing how much marriage can change someone. I started to see this manic energy and extreme jealousy happen once we got married. I thought it would get better by declaring my love for him, but this only made him more controlling. If you ever think marrying someone will help solve your problems with insecurities, run the other way! It will only get worse, or you will feel like you're being eaten alive by always having to defend yourself. Don't marry in hopes that things will get better, because I know firsthand that it only gets worse and men become more possessive. If I remained with him any *longer, I knew I would wind up going crazy. I had to leave before I lost not only my mind, but also my self-respect and dignity. I know I'm not to blame. I should've taken off when he first pulled that shit about how he would kill himself if I left, plaguing me with guilt and conning me into staying with him. Abusive relationships are so challenging because you don't realize you're in the trap, and once you do, you become too scared to move or stand up for yourself. The hard part for me was the bipolar disorder. It was hard to say goodbye to the other side of him, the sweet side that was loving and wanted to make sure I was well-cared for. I'm also naïve and have a big heart that is trying to love unconditionally. So this, my friends, is a double-edged sword. What to do is mind-boggling and has been ever since my honeymoon when he told me he already wanted a divorce. Stay and support the man that I married for better or for worse, or save myself. Find myself. Love myself. It took a lot of thought in weighing out my options and making an exit plan. I didn't want to fall on my face the moment I left him. Now is the time to love myself first. Although it wasn't the best timing, I finally left him. I would rather be alone and grow into the human that I'm meant to be than to be with someone who draws out these feelings in me that are weighing me down.*

Sure, every relationship has its ups and downs, but that's what makes us evolve. It's important to take the gifts that you learned from past relationships and use them to grow deeper into the next relationship. My husband once taught me to, "Create your reality with the power of intention." Find the joy in practicing random acts of kindness and senseless acts of beauty, even if that means walking away from a toxic relationship to show that kindness to myself. I deserve respect and will not settle for anything less. I know what a beautiful creature I am, and I deserve an individual that can respect me on all levels. At this very moment, I take my power back. I don't know what the future holds, but I am able to envision many versions that will suit me. I entitle myself to fully embrace this pain and make it work for me.

December 1st, 2011

Tonight, my husband and I sat down and had a real conversation. It was good but difficult. I don't know how to handle my emotions around him yet. I was so full of sadness, anger, and frustration every time he talked about loving me. All I could think of was how badly he had hurt me, and that's not love. When he told me he finally understood, I was so angry! Why did it take me leaving for him to wake up!? I feel so sick to my stomach; I can't think about this anymore. To be continued.

December 2nd, 2011

Well, that was a rough night. Everyone has their own way of being lost in this world. For me, even though I'm lost, I find that the one thing I'm holding onto throughout this is my inner drive and determination about my potential outcomes. I'm looking inward for help, guidance, strength, and courage.

Right now, my husband is seeking guidance from all of his friends and longing for his wife to be there cuddling him. I think talking to other people is a good thing sometimes, but it also fills your head with other people's opinions, and a lot of mixed emotions can emerge. There he was, asking questions, searching, trying to find out where he went wrong and what to do next from other people instead of from his heart. I wish so badly he could look within and find his own answers. All the chaos swirling in his head is keeping him from listening to his own voice.

Currently, we are technically separated. Still married but not living together. I don't know if I will return to that house. I can't spend more than thirty minutes with him without getting annoyed or angry and upset. Who am I? It's like I know I have this tough shield that's no longer putting up with the bullshit and manipulative games anymore. In the time that we've been apart, I've gained strength. After thirty minutes, I can feel myself start to fade and drift away like he was sucking the energy out of me. I'm not happy, and I don't feel comfortable going back only to be disrespected by him again in the future.

How the fuck do I get a divorce? I'm 25. I shouldn't even need to be thinking about this. Should I get it over with so we can both move on with our lives? There's no point in dragging this out any longer. I've been gone for nine days now, and there's no way in hell I'm going back if I can't even be around him for more than 30 minutes! This madness inside of me, the anger and resentment, it isn't good for anyone. One thing's for certain: I'm not ready to give up on myself. I'm not ready to go back and have such low lows. I have a feeling this is going to take a long time to heal from. One thing at a time; do I get a lawyer or do I just walk away?

January 12th, 2012

Today is the start of a whole new life in a new year with endless possibilities! The grass is greener on the other side, y'all! I haven't written in a few days because I've had so much going through my head. My husband and I are still separated for the time being while I figure out if I want to struggle to make things work with him, or be set free to make a positive impact on others' lives. I know I have healing powers; I need to be in a good place mentally to have the energy to exert my gifts. No matter what, I've learned to hold onto my passions and allow the next steps to come from my heart. When I do the things I love, everything falls into place. The feeling in my heart will lead the way. Surround myself with positive influences and things that make me happy, and everything will begin to fall into place!

January 15th, 2012

I will totally recap this past month for you, but right now, I'm going to get a U-haul and begin to get my belongings from my house. I decided to file for divorce. The contract is being *written and we are going to sign the papers tomorrow. One interesting thing about getting a divorce is that women get to change their names, if they so choose. Some change it back to their maiden name, but I'm taking it a step further. My middle name was Brooke, and when I got married, I took that out. I put my maiden name for the middle name, and took his last name. Well, when I sign the papers, I am signing with a new name. This will be a new life for me. I have always had a strong connection with my Grandma Buzzy, even though I've never met her. I've always felt her presence guiding me. I found out through a psychic reading that she is my teacher guide, which makes sense because every time there was a lesson to be learned, a little bee would come flying around me and make itself known. I think of it as a signal to pay attention. In her honor, I'm choosing to replace Brooke with Bee for my middle name in memory of my Grandma Buzzy!*

As for everything else, I didn't get a lawyer, but he did. I didn't want anything from that marriage. I could've had half of a house and part of his lighting company, but all I wanted was out. Time to learn what it feels like to be happy again! It will be a breath of fresh air to be myself again. I can't wait to start a new life where I can walk on my own with my head held high.

January 30th, 2012

Okay! I'm finally slowing down from all of the excitement, and I have time to recap the past AMAZING month! Let's start two days before New Year's Eve. My friend took me to her friend's yoga class. I was excited, nervous, and anticipating what's around the next corner. (Remember, at this point, I haven't made a concrete decision if I was going to be set free or stay married. We were separated.) At the time, I was open to new adventures and possibilities. I should mention that my yoga teacher was this amazingly gorgeous creature. I've known him for over three years, but I have kept my distance due to the attraction I feel toward him. Plus, it didn't help that when a mutual friend introduced us, she was excitedly explaining how well she thought we would get along in front of my husband. She didn't even bother to introduce him or include him in the conversation. This was the major cause of tension between my ex and me, so I found it better to keep my distance. He was one of those fantasies that should stay a fantasy until I am open and ready. But, hey, since I was finally separated and open to see what could happen in life, I thought it would be harmless to take a yoga class! I knew I was playing with fire, but I had to investigate these feelings. I didn't care! I cared more about all the little things in life that brought me joy, rather than keeping my soon-to-be ex-husband comfortable. I cared about doing what I wanted instead of caring about my fears of his reaction. I was following my heart, listening to my spirit guides leading the way, and trusting in the path.

After the class, we decided to keep hanging out. My friend was right; we were getting along great! The only catch was, this beautiful creature wouldn't do anything sexual with me unless I finalized the separation, which I was so surprised by how easy it was to do. I finally had a good reason to say goodbye. This man ignited some kind of passion inside my second chakra that had been dormant for years. This was the push I needed to solidify my move and finalize the divorce. What a nice reward for having the courage to leave! If I had feelings this strong for someone other than my husband, I shouldn't be in this relationship. Cut the cords before you get the bed dirty!

February 5th, 2012

I had spent so many years with the wool pulled over my eyes. It was time to take a chance and go after what felt right. It's time to go into this world and enjoy life! I'm too young to be hidden in the dark and forgotten about. Time to live on the wild side and follow what was making my heart flutter and go pitter-patter, even if that meant going against everyone else's advice. I need to get loose, have some fun, and have some sexy, passionate love-making with someone new. I need to get lost to find myself again.

February 6th, 2012

It's official. The divorce is still being processed through the court (it takes about 60 to 90 days, but we only have about 30 to 40 days left). I figured our relationship is over, and I can't go back to that marriage. So, I decided to solidify my choice by having a super passionate night with the yoga teacher. I referred to him as "Mi Pantarito," or my little panther in English.

On our first night together, we turned into wild animals! It was beyond hot and passionate; It was filled with so many butterflies to the point where we would have to take breathers from each other. I knew I was in the right place because I could literally feel all my chakras come alive again. What I felt, I hadn't quite ever felt before. The sexual energy was mutual, but let me just say, he knows what he's doing. The sex was so fun and filled with new crazy positions and breathwork that only a yogi would know. He even had a ton of fun toys that we ended up putting to good use. One, in particular, was a yoga swing attached to a ballet bar that he had mounted on his wall. There was a ballet beam at about hip level, and then another one if you reached your arms up. (I'm guessing he does pull-ups and hangs from it. He took this hammock and turned it into a swing. OMG!) So, I sat in this swing, leaned back, and let my legs wrap around the sides of it, putting myself in the most vulnerable position, and I LOVED every minute of it! It was so freeing to be able to reactivate this dormant sexual drive inside of me. Friday the 13th, 2012, was officially the yummiest day of my 25 years of existence! This was the first day I was finally able to open up and have an orgasm from a man. All the trauma from my past has led me to be so closed up in that arena, that it's been difficult for me to climax during sex.

Let me tell you from my personal experience; upside down sex is a game-changer. If you haven't tried it, I highly recommend the adventure! Afterwards, though, be careful. I had a moment when I tried to stand up and I got dizzy, fell down, and hit my head. All that blood to my brain needed a minute to go back down before trying to walk.

There was something about this guy. I knew it. I'm so grateful it was all worth divorcing my husband for. Thank GOD, cause that would've sucked if the sex wasn't any good, but it was quite the opposite! He has this magic touch, and this smell, along with a natural calmness and coolness that I was so intrigued by. He was the polar opposite of my soon-to-be ex-husband.

After this experience, I felt like a changed woman. I saw a glimpse of what sex could be like: giving and receiving with passion and desire, returning to our animalistic nature, and letting instincts lead. Most of the time, we don't talk when I go over there. I hardly know anything about him. It's more of a feeling of knowing him and wanting more of him in a physical sense. I wasn't longing for his words. You could say we were practicing our telepathic communication to see if we could vibrate on that level. He spoke with his touch, and it is magic for my body! I can feel my orgasms as they start at the back of my neck and travel down my spine like it's activating my soul. This newfound territory is cleansing my soul, and I can feel an awakening happening inside of me.

I do have some guilt built up inside of me because I am still going through my divorce. I waited to the point where I knew I was done with the relationship and told him first before acting on my horniness. I only got physical with another person for two reasons: one, to solidify the divorce because I knew neither he nor I would get back together if I hooked up with someone else, and two, so I could FEEL again. I deserve it. I am figuring out now that having no sex at all or having this kind of passionate sex is what my mind, body, and soul need from me. I will not settle for less. I love, respect, and cherish my body too much to force sex with my husband or be with any person who doesn't activate me in all of my senses. As I'm going through all these emotions of sadness, excitement, pure bliss, extreme disappointment, and confusion, I'm trying to listen in and feel what I need right now. I'm trying to find my light again, and there is no way I am going to give my power away to a new relationship and miss out on the opportunity to focus on me now. In the past, I've jumped from one relationship to the next sex boy toy (or two) to another serious relationship. I never gave myself any time to heal or process my feelings from each person that had hurt me.

My vow to myself: From this day forward, I dedicate 100% of myself to finding my path, getting stable with who I am, and building my career.

I know I will get so much more done if I don't let boys distract me (or even girls for that matter). It's time to focus on Allison Bee Levy right now and figure out how to strengthen myself so that I can take on a whole new life.

February 21st, 2012

The universe works in mysterious ways. Mi Panterito told me to lose his number. I messed up pretty bad, so I kind of don't blame him. I got invited to a party and spent a good 30 hours tripping on mushrooms. So many mushroom chocolates were being passed around. It was such a good time and it was great to catch up with old friends that I hadn't seen in awhile. It made me feel alive again to be recognized and out at parties. People were shocked that I was out by myself. It was as if I was locked away and hidden in a secret cave for seven years.

I think people were also shocked when I first met Emily. She came walking in the room with about 50 other people in it, and my jaw dropped. I had a wave of needing to kiss her even before saying hello. I've never in my life done anything like this. I didn't even know I was attracted to girls outside of the strip clubs. It was a strong, passionate, and liberating feeling to follow my heart and do what feels good in the moment. People were staring at us in shock, either because of all the mushrooms or because we were so bold to be doing this. We left all our fucks at the door. I realized that night how much of a sexual being I am. If I want to make out with someone, I want to do it with the purpose of seeking pleasure. I don't need to hide it or put shame around it as I did in the past. I don't need to limit my love to only males, nor do I need to apologize to anyone for doing what feels right.

As the night went on and the crowd dwindled, I did not. I'm always one of the last ones standing. Here's the thing; when I get going, it's always hard for me to call it a night. I don't want the night to stop. It's as if I don't want to miss out on anything by sleeping. It was my friend's house, so I felt comfortable to stay over since I was still tripping pretty hard. That night, I realized that I don't have anyone to take care of me and bring me home when I get past my point.

This friend whose house it was is also a mutual friend of Mi Panterito's. One thing ended up leading to another that night while I was exploring my new found sexual energy. He happened to be the lucky guy that was in front of me at the time. We ended up having our own version of intimate exploration that was pleasurable in its own sense. It wasn't exactly what I would dream of, but I was craving the attention and needing to let loose. It was like a beast had been unleashed, and I was on a roll since my first sexual encounter back on the market. I should've known it would upset Mi Panterito. They were pretty close friends, and I stuck my neck in the middle of it all, fucking shit up!

I can live with losing him, though. He was pretty rude to me. He would stand me up and make me wait forever outside his house because he would fall asleep and forget I was coming. He wouldn't open up and have authentic conversations with me. It was just sex. I enjoyed the fuck out of it, but it never felt like it would last forever. Passion and intensity also fizzle out like an overheated light. I could tell I would get lost in him because it was more of an infatuation than anything else. Everything happens for a reason, so try not to be so hard on yourself and let the waves settle. There are so many more adventures and experiences to have.

March 2nd, 2012

"Follow your own truth, seek out your true soulmate, and trust your higher self to lead you to the balance you deserve and all aspects of your life will come together in perfect harmony." This is a quote from my transitional period reading from premiumastrology.com. This is what jump-started this huge breakthrough that I'm going through. I'm so grateful for this reading and the courage it gave me to seek out what my heart has been yearning for. This reading was so profound for me at this crossroads in my life. Writing has been something that has helped me so much, as well. It helps me feel better about my life and helps me to channel my higher self more easily. I hope one day this book can help others like it's helping me right now. This book has to have a happy ending! I'm determined to do the research and do what it takes to find my light so I can show you all the way to it, too! I believe in myself and in all the people who are reading this right now, going through their own challenges. I have it in me, and I know you do, too. We've got this!

March 4th, 2012

I keep drawing these three hearts on my left forearm with a red Sharpie lately, as my reminder to love myself first. I've been doing it for about two months now, and I think I'm finally ready to tattoo it permanently on me so it's always in my face as my reminder not to lose myself in relationships. It would be perfect! So, I made an appointment to get this tattoo done in a couple of hours. Until then, I'm chilling in the Greenbelt, sunbathing, and writing it out.

I have to admit that I feel guilt and shame all over my body and in my thoughts. My last sexual encounter is one that's haunting me. I hooked up with Mi Panteritio's best friend, who happens to be like the godfather of our group of friends. As a result, no one is calling me or answering their phones when I call. I always do this. Is it self sabotage, a cry for attention, or is this my way of not developing real feelings for someone by ruining it in the beginning? An act like this does nothing positive for the people I care about or me. Now I feel guilty, ashamed, and alone again. In the end, I only truly have myself. I would hope I could be happy with my own company. I guess it comes down to loving myself first and being comfortable with myself and who I am today--perfect timing for a perfect reminder tattoo.

I wish my thoughts wouldn't drive me crazy. My mind is disturbingly busy with chatter that I created for myself. I know that I need to 1) stay away from tequila, 2) do things I will be proud of, 3) get my life in order, and 4) venture away from everything and everyone I already know. Life is too short not to live the way you want to be living. If I only had one year left to live, I would want to travel and see the world. I want to have lavish memories of being able to make it on my own. Like I said earlier, all I need is myself right now. I need to learn to stand on my own two feet and succeed. Getting caught up in alcohol, drugs, concerts, boys, and drama keeps me moving in the same damn circle I've been going in for the past 12 years. It's time to change and take control over my life, but to do this, I need to do things differently. It is so much harder to implement this change in my life, but I suppose the first step is to recognize that I need to change. I need to practice abstinence so I can focus on going after my dreams. Phew, this is going to be a hard one!

March 7th, 2012

My ex-husband got fired from his day job today. This whole transition has made it hard for him to focus. I had a huge heart to heart with him about looking at this like a challenge rather than a problem. This is a test from the universe to see how he handles these hiccups. I feel like we can either have a negative, angry, hostile life, or we can choose to see the light in this situation and ask ourselves, "What is this teaching me?"

The negativity clouds your perception, like pulling wool over the eyes. If one chooses to stay in the negative world, negative things will keep happening repeatedly until one learns from it. It's all about perspective. See, if you are generally happy with yourself, your life, and your views on life, you will get that in return. If you look at life's challenges as a way to improve your life, you can grow as an individual. This allows you to practice using faith and trusting in the universe. All these difficult times are preparing you on your journey to make you more of a whole and complete person. You will never truly know these things about yourself until you jump off the safe side, and ride the tide life gives you!

Change is what has shaped me. From my observations, staying in the same place for too long, results in my light dimming. When I live within my comfort and never reach into the unknown, I'm not polishing up on my life experiences, which makes me feel dull and boring. In relationships, I become compliant, comfortable, secure, and stubborn in my choices. I thought I was happy when I was actually miserable inside. I wanted a simple life. I was just with the wrong guy, and I was blind to this fact for so long because I had lost faith in myself and my ability to be independent. Maybe it was the gaslighting or the everyday arguments that eventually knocked down my self-esteem.

Why is it that when we get comfortable in relationships, we begin to take things for granted? We begin to abuse the power, or the ego ends up hurting the ones we love the most, damaging the relationship. Then harsh feelings are made, battle lines are drawn, and impermanence slaps you in the face. Nothing lasts forever, right? No job, no relationship, no pet, and no materialistic thing will ever last forever. I feel like with the right balance and mutual respect, it could be possible to have a love that lasts forever (or until one dies). There needs to be room to grow and evolve as you age because people change. The question is, how can we change and grow together, and nurture the bond that ties us together? How can we not get too comfortable and destroy the best things we have in our lives? I suppose if it is meant to be, I won't have to try so hard, and if it's not meant to be, I won't be able to keep it.

March 29th, 2012

Change will always present itself to you when it's time to move to the next step. My sister and her boyfriend finally kicked me out of their place. They had their own issues, and I wasn't making it any better for them by invading their space. It was my time to go, but I couldn't put my name on a new lease somewhere because my name was still on the mortgage. Once more, I found a boy to take me in. This one's name is Ben. He promised a safe spot for me to stay for a couple months until my name is off the mortgage. I really like this guy! I met him at a party one night and I felt like I was talking with myself a little bit. We have so much in common and I am in complete bliss for the time being. Here we go again! Fallin' hard and fast!

I guess some people would call moving in this quickly "U-Hauling It." I'll go with it. We compliment each other well. He inspires me to tap into my creative side and I've been painting a lot more since I met him. He has a big garage, so it is easier to do my kind of messy artwork. It's nice to have a stable place to call home. I guess it goes back to the basics; having a roof over my head, a place to shower, and with someone who loves me. I care so much about this guy, and I don't want to fuck up my living situation, so I decided not to sleep with anyone else while we are together. This guy fills me with life! He brings so much laughter, joy, and intense feelings of wanting to nurture. I'm falling for him, and fast. Who knew once I set myself free that I could feel this kind of love again so quickly? It's almost like I'm chasing for that fulfillment to make myself whole and worthy. I guess this is what I need, because it feels right to my heart for the time being. I'm going for it and jumping in! Moving all the way in today and trusting that the universe has a plan for me. I know she does!

April 15th, 2012

Man! Life can get away from me quickly if I don't pay attention! I have been doing a lot of "work therapy" and busting my ass. I had originally planned to work hard so I could go out and get my own place, but to be honest, I don't think I have the credit to do so. Plus, I'm here in a much better place, and I need to slow down for a minute. I am working really hard for my event company and also for a gluten-free restaurant. I got a gig to make a bunch of floral arrangements for a wedding, and I have also carved out time to make and sell some artwork. I feel as if I'm in a flow and hustle state right now. Working this much, and this hard, is teaching me discipline. It's teaching me that I can do this. I can make it on my own without having a man pay for everything. My man doesn't have a job, so he can't pay for shit. I think I might overwhelm him with how much I work; then, when I'm home, I'm painting. I guess it's my way of dealing or not dealing with life. If I keep my brain busy, I don't have to slow down enough to deal with the emotions behind it all. On a brighter note, I'm super happy with the artwork that I've been spitting out. I could actually make some good money from these! I guess I have a good muse, along with a large garage to do my thing.

As far as my love-boat is concerned, we have had a few hiccups, but nothing major. He reminds me a lot of my ex-husband, which is kind of creeping me out. I could look at it as a red flag and run, or see it as a way to do things differently this time. I can't tell if this is my cycle and a lesson I need to learn from, or something that I need to stay away from. I don't know if I can handle another partner who verbally abuses me and puts me down. That's not the vibe I'm going for at this stage in my life. He's already said "fuck you" multiple times. I don't deserve that. Why is this happening to me? Do I just have the worst taste in men? I must have a sign on my head that says, "Sure, I'll be your punching bag of douchiness." I'm going to practice having a voice and standing up for myself this time. I think this is my lesson, and I want to regain my confidence in speaking my mind. We'll see where it goes. It would mean more to me to stay and do things differently than to run away and be a quitter. Maybe that's the Taurus in me. Maybe it's ignorance. Not sure yet, but I'll let you know.

April 24th, 2012

Oh, God, Allison! What have you gotten yourself into? This guy is great and all, but he totally brings you back to all of the men you've had in your past. He asked me, "Why do you always have to get the last word?" Maybe he's awakening me to my patterns and bad habits, but then the line was crossed again with a giant "FUCK YOU!" from him. This, I can't take! It sends shocks of pain down my spine. When these words are spoken to me, it sends a trigger response to my fight or flight and I want to freak out. That is such a low and degrading vibration and, in my opinion, so overused by men. This is why I hid in a bush for three hours and got a divorce! This is the second time in two months that he's said it. I've expressed how badly it fucked me up when my ex-husband behaved this way, so I'm hoping he gets the picture and cuts it out. Part of me is saying, "If you take it now, you'll take it later," but at least I tried standing up for myself this time. Let's see if he has enough sense to listen.

Maybe he isn't the charming prince I wanted him to be. Someone who loves me would never say such hurtful things. Maybe he doesn't really love me. I need to find my own place, so I'm not dependent on anyone else, and I have the space to grow my own light. Other people tend to dim my light and drag me down with drama. I can only look to myself for my happiness, and I know I need to protect my energetic field. I know I won't find my light in any other human because it is somewhere inside of me, but I can't reach it if I have people around me dragging me down.

*I think all relationships have good and bad moments, but it should never come down to verbal abuse. That's abuse, too. And it is **NOT OK**! This life of mine has so many cycles. This man brings up all the cycles all the time. It is time to face my problems and move past them with this man. I have spoken my mind, and now I am giving him the opportunity to grow from it. I can't help but have the question in my head: "Should I pay attention to the red flags and run again?"*

I hope the answer comes soon, though. We decided to get a joint birthday present and get a wolf cub! I know, right? I might be crazy for doing this when we have our problems, but I was practicing going with the flow on this one. Maybe it would help our relationship. I've never had a dog before, only cats, so this would be new and fun for me! He said he had a wolf cub before, so he kind of knows, but I'm not sure what happened to it. I'm hoping he knows what he's doing because I sure don't.

We found this little cub on Craigslist. He was only $300, and I already put half of the deposit down for us. I will pay the other half when we pick him up on May 6th. He's the eighth generation of a domestic breedline and ninety-six percent wolf and four percent malamute (Alaskan Grey Wolf and White Arctic Tundra). We got the first choice because Ben was on the ball with getting in touch with the breeder first. We picked the one that had the cutest marking and smiling face. I'm so excited to meet this little guy! This is going to help me stay put for a little while since I am working full-time, and he isn't working at all. He can be at home training him while I'm at work during the puppy phase. Kind of nice to have him be a part of a team *and help out. Maybe this will help keep him on good behavior. Nonetheless, this will be a huge test for our relationship.*

April 30th, 2012

Today would have been my one-year anniversary being married with my ex-husband, and my Grandma's birthday. My teacher guide (Grandma Buzzy) is so present in my life and I am so grateful for this connection. Getting married was honestly the biggest lesson of my lifetime by far. I feel her when I'm learning, when I make mistakes, when I take leaps of faith and trust in myself. It's as if I can feel her holding my hand, showing me the way, or comforting me when no one is around. When I fall and pick myself up again, I can feel her presence saying, "Come on, Honey, you got this!"

Even though I am not where I thought I would be one year after our wedding, I know I'm meant for more than whatever that was. This is building so much character inside of me at a crucial time in my life. I'm 26 and have so much life ahead of me that I'm so excited to see. It's not the life I pictured, but I know this is where I need to be, learning the lessons that need to be learned right now in this lifetime.

June 18th, 2012

Since I last wrote, we got a wolf pup! His birthday is March 30th, and I got him at six weeks old. We picked him up May 6th and oh, my goodness!!! He is my WORLD! It was supposed to be a split birthday present for Ben and me, but so far, I have paid for all of it and the vet bills. So, there's that.

This little guy has helped bring so much joy into my life! I never knew I could love something so hard! He's teaching me, even more so, to have a voice. I can't let this wolf run all over me, because he is going to get big quickly and I need to make sure that I maintain control and the "alpha" mentality. I named him Chi, after the energy that flows through everything. I saw this calmness in him that made me feel complete. Ben also felt super balanced, and Chi was exactly what we needed. We found Chi from a breeder in Temple, Texas, who was a sweet old man. Chi is my spirit guide here to save me. I can feel it. I now have a walking angel to be in my life to show me the way when I can't see. I feel so blessed right now. He's teaching us both to work on our weaknesses; mine would be to gain a voice, and Ben's would be to work on patience and managing his aggression. Since I work most of the time and Ben doesn't have a job, he's home with Chi helping to train him. He came to us already puppy-pad trained at six weeks old. This little fella is so freaking smart; did you know that wolves are ten times smarter than the average dog? I could use some of this in my life, and I can't wait to grow old with him. They live to be about 18, so we're in it to win it for the long haul.

Side note on my relationship with Ben: I have been on a mission since last August to step into my own and find my light. I get to doing well, up until a relationship enters my life and knocks me off my course. Maybe this is all a sign that I'm not supposed to be in one, and that's why it isn't working. I tend to give my everything to another person and forget to invest time and energy into keeping myself balanced. I could be doing so well if I poured this energy into myself, but it seems as if I don't know how. You would think I would know how to love myself, but I guess I missed this part growing up.

I feel like if they are good, then I'm good; therefore, we're balanced. I need to ask myself, "Am I good?" This is the whole reason I put this tattoo in plain sight on my forearm--as a reminder to LOVE MYSELF FIRST! Good thing I can't ever forget it now. This lesson is one I hope to accomplish in this lifetime. The drama that comes with relationships is the part that I can't handle. The emotional tug of war is simply exhausting if you keep on running in the same circle. I have to break out of this cycle somehow before it tears me down again. It's as if I can feel it creeping up behind me.

July 8th, 2012

So we did it. Chi and I left Ben (repeat of my life.) I had to. It wasn't safe for us there. Remember when I said earlier that Chi is helping Ben control his anger? Well, something happened. I came home one day from work and was hanging with Chi in the living room. When Ben walked in the door, Chi ran and hid in the bedroom and was totally freaked out. I started questioning, and he ended up confessing that he hit Chi, an eight-week-old wolf. I was outraged! I don't want a crazy fucking wolf attacking people because he was beaten as a puppy. I can't handle that for 18 years.

I asked him why he hit Chi, and his response was, "I tried to get him to do a trick, and he wouldn't do it, and he went after the treat anyway, and he bit my thumb!" And so he hit him? I couldn't do it. I should've seen the red flags when I mentioned he was helping him control his anger. No way around it, I had to leave. So I left as quickly as I could. Once I finally had everything packed in my car, Ben stole Chi and took off with him while he was howling out for me to help. I called the cops, and they did absolutely nothing. There was nothing I could do. I left for the night, not knowing what the fuck I was going to do or how I was going to get my wolf cub back. I needed Ben to sober up before I even tried to talk to him again. He's too scary when he's angry and drunk, and he has a gun that he has whipped out in this state before.

I waited for him to finally come back later that night after he cooled down and ended up leaving him first thing in the morning. I explained it wouldn't be fair for him to keep Chi because he had no job and no way to care for him. Plus, Chi chose me. I was his main caretaker, and it was obvious that Chi would've been happier with me. I paid for everything anyway, so he had no room to speak. He's mine. End of story with this man. I left there calmly and graciously, with the single-most important thing in my life, Chi. I am now officially a wolf mother, and I wouldn't have ever thought this would happen.

This is the reason why I was with Ben in the first place. Chi was meant to be in my life and what a great teacher he is, already helping me finalize my decision to leave this guy. If I'm going to pour my heart into anything, it's going to be this wolf. I know it will come back tenfold when he's older and loving me unconditionally. I am going to give this boy all the love that I have and cherish our bond. I may be bailing out of this relationship with Ben, but he gave me Chi, and I will be forever grateful for that. See, everything does happen for a reason.

Funny enough, the one place I knew I'd be welcome, the one person I could still rely on, was my ex-husband. It was the only safe place I knew I could go with Chi immediately. I'm grateful we can still be friends and that he's letting me crash here while I get my feet back on the ground. I moved in with my ex-husband when I moved out of my parents' house at 18 and never knew anything else but to go to him for help. I know he loves me and will always be there, but I think it's also a plus that he loves Chi. It's impossible not to.

It's not the same in the house, that's for sure. I'm staying in the guest bedroom, and my ex has a new girlfriend who is a stripper. Go figure. It's fine, though. I'm happy for him as long as he is happy. I can handle it for a short time until I'm able to find a new home. Plus, it's not anything I want to see or be around, so this will give me the push to get my act together. It's a whole new story finding a home with a two-month-old wolf. Not that many people are keen or know how to live with a wolf. I need to consider Chi and make sure that the new roommate will be able to handle him. I need a yard and someone with patience and a kind soul. I know it is possible. I'm sending it out to the universe that the perfect living situation comes my way. I do need to take my mama's advice, though. "Don't shit where you sleep." Meaning, don't sleep with my roommate or move in with another boy that I'm dating.

On another note, being single again has opened up the opportunity for me to feel free. I cherish the freedom to be my own boss. I admire those that are independent and strong, and I feel like I gain this by being able to take control of my life and surroundings. That feeling I was craving when I left my ex-husband is back in my life. I don't know why I do this, but when I get into a relationship, I lose myself. I become so codependent and I lose my sense of self. I don't know how to stop it. Maybe there's something wrong with the way my brain has been wired as a result of all my traumas. I forget about my passions and am left feeling drained, dull and weak. I suppose these are signs of unhealthy relationships, but I get so lost and blind to them when I'm deep in it. When I become single, it's as if the fog has been lifted and I can see clearly on my path again. I wish I could be happy being single for long periods of time so I could get comfortable in my own skin.

I have a theory on how to find your light that was sparked by a conversation with my ex-husband. My theory is that when you are in a codependent relationship, you have no room to be yourself and continue doing what you did before the relationship started. Forget about "you." It becomes only "us." We begin to look to others to fill our happiness tanks, but in the end, it isn't their responsibility. We have to fill our own reservoirs. Is it possible to be independent in a relationship without the ego getting the best of you? Is it possible to be without jealousy or the constant wondering of where they are, driving you crazy when they don't respond to your message? How can you still shine bright, if not brighter, and be in your own power and truth in a relationship? I'm on a mission to find this out. It seems that when I lose my power, it is when I am in a relationship. Maybe it is because I never gained my power and truth on my own, so I don't even know what that would look like. I've been in relationships since I was in seventh grade, and now that I am a grown adult, I don't know how to have a relationship with myself. I need to learn to be alone, which I am terrified of. I have faith that I can hold steady in my power and master my own light. It might take some time, but it is then that I will meet someone who lifts and brightens my light to another level. I know he's out there growing and learning, just as I am right now.

My ex-husband also shared another brilliant idea. He told me that before he does yoga, he sets an intention. His intention was to beam with light out of every inch of his body. I thought that this was so beautiful because I was the one who taught him yoga and brought him to his first class. This is the perfect way to manifest what you want to create for your world. If you believe in the power of intention, you can shape your world through the vibrations of your thoughts and what you put out into the universe. Good and bad. Send out the vibrations that you would like to manifest, and watch them appear in your life. You can do this, I can do this; Anyone can do this. We are worth it, and we deserve it; you have to believe you are worth it and deserve it. If that's what you want, then make it happen for yourself. In the end, all you have is yourself, and you are the only one that can create this for yourself. No one else can do it for you; you have to want it. It all starts within, and the vibration you put out.

My MANTRA: I open my mind and heart to all possibilities.

CHAPTER EIGHT

A WHOLE NEW CAN OF WORMS

At this point in my journey, I finally found a home on the Greenbelt in Austin that had three acres and two neutral roomies. I found them off of Craigslist and just went for it. It was the first thing that felt right, so I followed my heart. I had to get out of living with my ex-husband and his crazy lifestyle of bringing girls home from the strip club. I was getting beyond grossed out by it. I think he kept doing that to push me out of there and to be honest, it worked!

I found my first little home living with strangers and working as a bartender in downtown Austin, off 6th Street. That time of my life was a blur because I started to drink almost every day. This was when my writings stopped for a few years. I got lost in a spiraling tunnel, and life became a constant party. Working as a bartender can easily cause a big drinking problem; it can get the best of you if you're weak and have a hard time saying no, which I do. I was the employee that wasn't allowed to drink on the job because there were too many nights when I would get too fucked up and couldn't do my job or drive myself home. Everyone else did a good job drinking responsibly; I didn't know my limits. This was the beginning of when I would lose control, and something else would encourage me to keep drinking when I really shouldn't be having another sip. Anyway, I was cute and brought them business, so they kept me around for a little while longer until they finally had to fire me for drinking too much on the job.

I started working at a pub in the neighborhood called the Black Sheep Lodge. This is where I fell fast for a Mexican Marine named Juan, who also had a bad drinking problem. Together, our crazy was our kind of crazy. We were the wild, loud couple that was always the life of the party. What came with that was a whole lot of out of control behavior. This was when I truly became an alcoholic. I knew I had a problem when I got fired from the bar off of 6th Street, but this was when we would regularly have a flask of Jameson on hand, and we were typically the last ones standing. It's safe to say we were both functioning alcoholics. He was a personal trainer, and I would regularly work out with him and his sister, and then rage it hardcore afterward, downing a bottle of Jameson at least three times a week. I moved into a tiny little duplex with him after my roommates kicked me out for getting too wasted and behaving disrespectfully. Let's just say he had a negative impact on my conduct when I was living with my new roommates. Once more, I found myself in a state of desperation, and moved in with another man (another cycle of my life) and did this for about a year and a half. Hence, this was why I haven't written. When I am with a man, I get too distracted to sit down and write, and so I end up neglecting my book. *Where's the balance, Allison?*

I always had a feeling he was cheating on me, but I never had proof. I assumed that if I felt that way, he probably was, so I felt like I should cheat on him so it wouldn't bother me as much. I cheated on him a lot during the last six months of being with him. Not proud of this, but I did. Most of the time, it was with my best friend and her boyfriend. He didn't even know to be suspicious of my best friend. He would get to the point where he would pee on the walls in the middle of the night because he was too drunk. He got aggressive and pretty scary sometimes. It became repulsive after a while, and once more, I needed to escape.

My best friend and I discovered the magical power of dabs, which is a super-concentrated version of Mary Jane that got me so high. I would run away to their house when Juan was too drunk to handle, or if he was scaring me, which was quite often. They became my safe space and also the place where I could score some feel-good substances, which, in the end, led to curiosity and sexual encounters. Dabs and Molly were around quite often, and I had a hard time turning them down, so I didn't. The drugs got me to the point where I couldn't drive, especially if I had been drinking beforehand. I wanted so badly to escape from reality, so I turned to drugs to relax and let go.

Juan would get physical and throw me around. He fractured my wrist one night while we were drunk downtown off 6th street. He picked me up and threw me; I had on heels and couldn't catch myself. He was a former Marine with a bad drinking problem; together, the combination was so unpredictable. The result was too scary to deal with, so when it would get to this point, I would run away for the night to my best friend Katelyn's house and wait for him to sober up before I went back. He knew I was with my best friend; what he didn't know though, was that I was fucking my best friend and her boyfriend. I felt like if he ever did find out, he would probably seriously injure or kill me. This guy could snap in a heartbeat. I had to find a way out of this relationship, and quickly. I was with him for a total of two years at this point, and it was starting to go south. The ball had been rolling with this guy for long enough, and I was searching for a way to get out. I had to time it perfectly because I didn't want to be around for the rage that would come from the aftermath, that is if he ever found out what I was doing.

Chapter Nine

My Escape Route

Amanda, my other best friend, moved to Costa Rica to be a teacher and was getting married to a local out there in December of 2013. She needed some help with her wedding, and I was so excited to leave the country to help her. Honestly, it was perfect timing! I needed to get out of Dodge for a while. I arrived in San Jose, Costa Rica, and was picked up at the airport by Amanda and her fiancé, Arturo. I spent most of my time there in San Jose, where she lives, preparing for the wedding. To be honest, it wasn't what I expected Costa Rica to be like. The city was crowded; the traffic was scary with motorcycles driving in between the cars, weaving in and out at fast speeds. I didn't see many tropical trees or anything lush in the city, and most people didn't speak fluent English. It's hard to get around in San Jose if you didn't speak their language.

We ended up venturing out to Manuel Antonio for Amanda's bachelorette party. That part was beautiful and way less stressful. More people in the beach towns have adopted English as a second language to make money off the tourists. Manuel Antonio is a beautiful little beach town that is about four hours from the city. Here, we were able to relax and get massages, take walks on the beach, and forget about all of life's distractions. I fell in love with this country once I was at the beach and in the jungle. I was in my element, and visions kept coming to me of different events I could do there. They were about three years behind the USA when it came to new, cool, hip things to do, so it was easy to figure out what they were lacking and what I could bring to the table. I was pumped and could sense that I was supposed to be there. I could picture myself making it there, and I was trying to figure out how I could make that possible. Someday, somehow, I wanted to live there. I knew it!

We succeeded in creating a wonderful wedding at a fancy house in the middle of the city in San Jose. The wedding was beautiful and Amanda and Arturo were beautiful together. Being so close to my best friend since the sixth grade was refreshing as well. Getting away from my life back home was a welcome break, as I was avoiding the fact that I needed to leave my boyfriend. I knew that I would have to leave him when I went back. I would be without a home once more, but it would be better than being in an abusive and toxic relationship. It was sad that I only had a week to stay in Costa Rica, but I left with dreams and visions of coming back and making a living as an event planner in this country. This trip gave me hope that I could create an alternate life reality for myself, like Amanda had done. It was inspiring to travel and see another part of the world. I left there with a sense of curiosity and excitement about what life could be.

On my flight back to Austin, I had a conversation with the gentleman sitting next to me. I told him of my aspirations to go back to Costa Rica to be an event planner. I mentioned a few different event ideas that I came up with and was beginning to get really excited about the possibilities. Apparently, while I was doing that, a man three rows back was listening to our conversation. When we got off the flight and headed to our connecting flight in Houston, he came up and asked me, "Do you really want to be an event planner in Costa Rica?" My response was, "Is this a trick question? Are you kidding me? I would LOVE TO!!!" He kindly and confidently replied with, "Well, I overheard you talking to the man sitting next to you on the plane, and I own a small boutique hotel on the beach there. I'm in need of an event planner. I have two events coming up that are in the books. I have a bachelor party and a wedding coming up in three weeks. I'd love to talk more with you about the position, and possibly hire you to work for me in Costa Rica."

My jaw dropped. I didn't know if this was a hoax or if I'd stepped into another dimension, or what had happened. I was in shock. *Was this actually happening? Was I so powerful of a human that I manifested my dream job in my dream location almost instantly?!* This had to be too good to be true. I wanted to know more, so I sat with him on the connecting flight to Austin from Houston because he, too, lives in Austin. I picked his brain some more about the position for two hours during our flight. He told me he would need me to be there in three weeks to prepare for the events that were already booked. I just met this man and was hesitant about jumping right into anything. Still, I was also so interested and invested emotionally that I couldn't let this opportunity slip through my hands! He offered to pay for my flight out there, and he would house me at the hotel until he bought a house where I could be the property manager. He told me it would only be a couple of weeks of me at the hotel because he was in the process of debating on which house he was going to buy. His goal was to eventually have me manage his property and assist any of the hotel guests with their events and private parties. Let's get this straight. He offered to pay for my flight there, give me a job, and cover my living expenses, and all of this was promised before we landed back home. I had to think about logistics. *What about my wolf?* I couldn't leave him behind. If I was going to Costa Rica for my dream job, I would have to bring my bodyguard and best friend with me. That was part of the package deal. I told this man I wouldn't do it if I couldn't bring my dog, and he said it would be fine once he had his property; then Chi could stay at the house. We could both stay there. Until he bought the property, I would have to house Chi with Amanda in the city. I had to think about this one for a minute and try to figure out how I could make all of this work. If you dream hard enough, anything is possible, *right*? I had to make a decision quickly, though, because time was of the essence.

One week later, I met with this gentleman at a Starbucks to feel it out and see if I could get him to sign a contract. His response was, "What if you suck, and I'm stuck with you?" Valid point, as he's never seen my work and what kind of events I can produce. He didn't even know me, yet he was taking a risk as well. I kind of saw this as a red flag, but I ignored it because I wanted it so badly. I overlooked all of the warning signs and the feeling that it might be too good to be true. I mean, if I chose not to go, that would haunt me for the rest of my life. I didn't want to spend my life wishing I would've done this. *This is my dream job in paradise!* The hotel was in a town I didn't get to visit, but I knew where it was. The name of this town is Jaco. We had to pass through Jaco on our way to Manuel Antonio for Amanda's bachelorette party. She would be about two hours away from me, and I could still easily go to the city to see her or vice versa. Plus, this was the perfect exit strategy to get away from Juan. It would be on good terms because I was moving away, and I would still be able to do this before the word got out about me cheating on him. This was the perfect escape plan that had been gifted to me, with a beaming light at the end of the tunnel. I saw this as my only way out with this guy. I also saw this as an opportunity to chase after my dreams. I'm not going to find it in the comfort of my bedroom or the vicious cycle of Jameson and hangovers. This was a chance of a lifetime, so I told my new boss that I would be ready to fly out in two weeks.

*Side Note: When an opportunity like this presents itself, take it. It's the universe's way of steering you in a different direction. Ask yourself the question, "Will I regret this later on?" If you can't decide, it's better to try and fail than to let it slip away and never know.

CHAPTER TEN

JUMPING OFF THE CLIFF BLINDFOLDED

Now that my mind was set on this new position and the big move, all I needed to do was tell my boyfriend and my family. Let's just say, my decision completely blindsided them. Most everyone I told was shocked and thought I was crazy because it came out of nowhere. I had two weeks to prepare for a life-altering move and say all of my goodbyes. My boyfriend was shocked but didn't put up too much of a fight. He was probably happy that this was happening, so he didn't have to break up with me. Like I said, I felt like he was cheating on me, so there wasn't a lot to hold onto in the first place. We both knew the relationship was over. I was thrilled that his reaction was supportive of me chasing after my dreams and making something of myself.

As for my dad, he played the "what if" game over and over with me about everything--half of which I couldn't give him a good answer to. He was terribly nervous and didn't think it was a good idea, but he saw me getting a job in the field that I went to school for, so a big part of him was proud and supportive. My poor mother took it the worst. She felt in her heart she was never going to see me again. It was heartbreaking. She was still there to support me in whatever decision I made, but I could see the sadness in her eyes. Those wonderful humans are my biggest cheerleaders and wanted to see me succeed so badly. They are the kind of souls that would support any decision I made, even if it killed them on the inside. They did what they could to help get me ready for what I was about to endure, but I don't think anything could have prepared us for what was about to happen.

It was going to cost me about $2,000 to get Chi to Costa Rica. It cost that much to fly him in a crate underneath the plane in the cargo space. Brainstorming, I came up with the idea to have a fundraiser to gather money to bring Chi with me as my bodyguard. There is a program online where you can design shirts and sell them to raise money for your campaign. The goal was two grand, and I met that plus some, thanks to one of my best friends from grade school, Jeremy. He was finding success working in the oil industry, and he wanted nothing more than to support his friends living out their dreams. I'm so grateful for this man and our friendship that we've maintained for a lifetime. Without his support, this would have been way more difficult for me to start a new life in another country. I also had a huge "selling my life away" party, where I sold most of my paintings, fur coats, my bike, and everything I owned that I couldn't bring with me. To be honest, that part was super cleansing. Letting go of all of those material items that I didn't need was such a freeing feeling that I had never experienced before. This was a good practice in being humble and living with the bare minimum. I raised a little more money from that event, yet I still didn't feel like it was enough. Time was of the essence, and it started to get critical. *How will I have enough money to get by and be okay for a bit until I get adjusted with my new position?* I mean, I also took out a loan for $2,000 from the bank, but I still didn't feel like that was enough.

I reached out to my best friend (yes, the one I cheated on my boyfriend with) because I thought maybe I could join her at work for a bit before I left town. She worked at a strip club on the outskirts of town called The Yellow Rose. I didn't do this for a living, but it sure is a good way to make a lot of money in a little amount of time! I worked a total of seven shifts before I left for Costa Rica. I was making $400-$700 a night having fun and dancing with my girlfriend! It was the easiest money I ever made because we would tag-team the guy groups and bank. Never have I seen that much money coming in so quickly. I blacked out nearly every night from drinking too much. I felt like I needed to drink to be able to do something like this. It was my mask, and I was wearing the shit out of it. I was still living with my boyfriend, so I had to be sneaky about doing this. He would flip his shit if he found out. Luckily, he was too lost and drunk in his own world to notice what was happening. I would say I was spending time with my best friend before I left, and he never questioned it. My last week in Austin was spent hustling, doing everything humanly possible to have some stability in the midst of the unknown.

The hardest part about trying to figure out my journey to Costa Rica was getting Chi there. The airlines are super particular with what breeds they carry. There are restrictions on the type of crate, and he could only fly at certain times, so we had to make sure we were booked on the same flight, not to mention all the shots and medical records that I had to get for him to even be able to board the flight. If I didn't have my bases covered on all of the requirements, he wouldn't be able to come, and I wouldn't go. He goes where I go; he is the determining factor in my life. I busted my ass to ensure a smooth move for both of us after hours of meticulous planning.

The day came when it was time to leave for the airport. My flight flew out of Houston, so I spent the last night with my parents so that my dad could drive Chi and me to the airport early in the morning on January 20th, 2014. My mom couldn't bear the extra suspense of me leaving for the car ride, so she decided she would stay home. As my dad pulled down the driveway, my mom stood there in tears as we drove off. The saddest part about all of this was when we reversed out the driveway, mom came running after us, reaching out for me with her hands. She thought she was never going to see me again, and it was as if I was being ripped from her arms. I couldn't stop crying because I honestly didn't know if I would ever see her again, either. Anything could happen, and being that far away without an exit plan to come back, left us all feeling unsettled. It was almost like watching your child die in front of you, and there's nothing you can do but let them pass along gently and with the support of your full, loving heart. My dad had to be the strong one and try not to cry the whole drive there, especially after driving away from mama like that. I don't know how he did it, but he remained stable and steady enough to keep the mood uplifted for the three-hour drive.

We got to the cargo space with Chi and his crate to go through a full examination of their standards. I was hoping I did everything right for the airline so we could pass this part of it. I wouldn't think they would let a wolf into Costa Rica, so I lied and called him a husky. Luckily, it worked. He was getting super freaked out and could sense some things were about to go down. I fed him some allergy medicine so he would stay nice and calm during the flight, as recommended by the vet. Once the inspection was complete, I left him in the cargo area for loading under the plane. I had another three hours until my flight took off, and then it was about a seven-hour flight from Houston to San Jose. He stayed in that crate for over ten hours, which makes me cringe to think about. We never used a crate with him as a puppy, so he wasn't used to being caged like this. I felt so bad forcing him in there; I had to pick him up and wrestle him to squeeze him in. Walking away from that was hard, too. I felt his anxiety and uncertainty, and I sure had plenty of my own as well.

It came time to leave my dad's side for my drop off. He asked me one last time, "Are you sure about this, Al?" I couldn't back out now. I have now adopted a mindset that I need to prove to everyone that I can make it on my own, especially myself. I needed to prove that I was strong enough to take charge of my own life and be successful at it. I was ready to grow up and have an adult job and travel the world. As sad as it was, I told my dad, "I can do this! I promise!" and gave him one last hug, as tight as I could, for as long as I could. I took in one last big inhale of his cologne and stared into his tearing eyes and told him, "I'll make you proud, Daddy!" After that, I had to make a quick break, because if we dragged it out for too long, it would've ripped our hearts apart. I turned back and gave him one last smile and wave, then disappeared into the crowd of people at the airport. Well, here we go. It's all or nothing at this point, and this was me giving my all for the change and growth I needed. I had to prove that I could do this for myself. My goal was to live in Costa Rica for one year to see how it goes. No pressure that way, *right*?

CHAPTER ELEVEN

PURA VIDA

My flight to Costa Rica was smooth sailing until it was time to pick up Chi. This is when I found out firsthand the meaning of *Pura Vida*. In English, it translates to *pure life*. I quickly learned that for me it means *I didn't mean for this to happen, but I guess I have to be okay with it*. It's hard to be upset about life's shit storms when you are in paradise. My first experience of this term came when it was time to get Chi from the cargo space. Two police-like officers were standing with their arms crossed in front of Chi as he was whining in his cage. They were demanding $400 cash, or I wouldn't be getting my dog.

I argued that there was never a tax fee mentioned when I was doing my research on how to get my dog there. That's when they replied with *Pura Vida*. That is the situation now, and there's no calling the cops on this one. Amanda and Arturo came to pick me up and were helping to translate with the guards over this. Chi was getting even antsier and more restless in the background. My friends said if I called the cops, they would probably add another "tax fee" to the

$400. I couldn't believe it! I had no way out but to pay these guards the money. I didn't mean for this to happen, yet I had to be okay with it. Over in Costa Rica, they can do that kind of extortion with Americans. This was my first experience and my welcome present into this country. I felt so naïve and taken advantage of, but I had to learn quickly that this was a thing here. There was no way I was leaving there without my dog, so I paid them off. I only had $600 cash with me; luckily, the rest was in my bank account. I ended up paying more in "tax fees" to retrieve my dog from customs in Costa Rica than I paid to get him as a puppy. Nonetheless, he was my bodyguard, and he was coming with me. There was no debating that.

The first two nights, I was staying in San Jose with my best friend. We had agreed that it would be better for Chi to stay with them until I got my feet on the ground, and my boss bought the rental property that I was going to manage and stay at. My boss said it would only be a week or two until he purchased the house, so we would wait until then.

The third day in Costa Rica, I got dropped off at the bus stop and was on my way to Jaco with my life on my back. It's about a three-hour bus ride, depending on traffic, to get there from the city. Keep in mind, I never rode the bus in the States, so my first time experiencing riding a bus was in another country. Amanda assured me it was safe and easy to get around, and she even asked the bus driver to help remind me where to get off. I was quickly learning the ropes of how it's done there. Nervous and confused, this was the first time I was actually on my own without the help or the guidance of anyone else. I was told we had arrived in Jaco, and I got so excited waiting at the front of the bus with all my bags. I wasn't sure which bus stop to get off at because there were so many, so I risked it and got off by the highway. I got my feet on the ground and quickly realized this wasn't the right stop. I was at the other end of the city with all my bags, lost, with no way to call a taxi. Luckily, Jaco had a plethora of taxis driving by, and it wasn't too long before one picked me up. Then, I had to figure out how to tell the taxi where to go because I didn't have a physical street address to give him. I told him the name of the hotel, and he didn't recognize it at first. The address is a description of where it is compared to landmarks and measured in meters for blocks. There aren't street signs with numbered addresses. I had no WiFi or phone yet, so he called the number on the website to speak to someone to help give instructions on how to get there.

I finally got to the hotel and was welcomed by the man I met on the plane, along with a super sweet Costa Rican concierge girl, Nella. It was an epic moment for me to sit in the hotel where I now worked and enjoy my first smoothie in paradise. It was picture perfect, and I was feeling so blessed. I knew I only had a week to plan things for the wedding, so as soon as I got to my room, I started trying to figure out how I was going to make it all happen. I had no time to waste at this point. *I'm in a new city and have to make contacts with a floral company, find a hairdresser, and find someone to do the bridesmaids' nails.* I knew I could do it, but I also had to squeeze in some relaxation time for me, so I made a plan to go jump in the ocean and get a good night's rest so I could go out in the morning to accomplish my goals.

I headed out in the morning looking professional in khakis and a nice blouse because I wanted to look presentable as an event planner. The hotel was far away from everything, but I ended up walking into town to try to save money and get to know the city at the same time. I didn't realize how incredibly hot and humid it would be. After this day, I cut off about three pairs of pants into shorts. Since most places didn't have any AC, it was constantly hot. But, *PURA VIDA, right*? I found two glorious spots to cool off in the heat of the day. I found out the floral shop had a cooler where they stored all the flowers to keep them fresh, and then there was also the Mas X Menos grocery store. Once I got the flowers confirmed, I had to figure out how to make money off of them. Since my boss isn't paying me separately for the services, I had to tax it into the bill for the items found from my vendors to my client. I would have to charge a finders fee to my clients for arranging it. The hairdresser and mani-pedi vendors were a little harder to find. I felt like I had completed one mission, and that was enough for one day. Plus, I was at a point where heat exhaustion and my jealousy of people on the beach became overwhelming, so I had to add in some play-time to make this experience complete.

Time to surf, baby! Nella offered to take me out to see if surfing was my jam or not. Coming from the middle of Texas, I had never surfed before. I had no idea what I was doing, but my friend did a good job walking me through how to paddle out without getting too smashed up each time by the waves. I didn't catch any waves that time without wiping out, but this sport planted a seed in me that made me crave more. I was hooked, and I was determined to learn this sport. Honestly, my favorite part about surfing is sitting out in the ocean, getting a tan, floating on the board, and watching everyone else strutting their stuff on the waves.

Later that evening, my boss, Jack, decided to take a crew of us out for a night on the town. Oh, boy! I was in for a treat on my first night out in Jaco! Nella came along, too, and there were a couple of other ladies who I didn't know. They were pretty, but I didn't think anything of it at the time. We had a lovely dinner and then decided to get a few more drinks at a couple of the hot spots in town. We were sitting at one bar drinking Chiliguaro (a local drink similar to a bloody mary shot with their local liquor, *Guaro,* which is similar to vodka but with more of a burn), when all of a sudden, I locked eyes with a gorgeous man. He had huge brown eyes that were piercing my soul with curiosity. It was like a signal straight to my vagina! I couldn't keep my eyes off of him, and he couldn't stop staring at me, either. It was somehow as if we knew we were meant for each other to experience. He was with his group of friends and they were leaving the bar in a hurry so he gave me one last look, saying "bye" with his eyes, and then disappeared. I followed him out because I didn't want to miss my chance to speak with him. I overheard his friend shout out, "Hey Felipe, wait up!" and boom, I had his name! (Name was changed to protect his identity.) Without any hesitation, I followed up after his friend caught up to him and said, "Hey, Felipe!" He turned around, surprised as to whose voice that was and looked at me with this gaze that made my heart melt. He was also confused as to how I knew his name. Gotta admit this was a pretty sly move on my part. He was instantly engaged and in shock. He didn't know if we had already met somewhere or if I was a stranger. The cuteness in his confusion made me even more drawn to him. The chemistry between us was unreal! We hadn't even had a conversation yet, and I had already fallen head over heels for him. *What was this?*

I got lost in his big brown eyes. He had long hair up in a man bun, the body of a surfer, and a penis that was so big that you could see it through his pants. Total package before any words were spoken. His first question to me was how I knew his name. When I told him, he was instantly impressed by my bold move to take charge. He asked if I would like to join him and his friends for the rest of the night, and I couldn't resist. I ran back inside and grabbed my purse, and told my boss and co-workers that I was going to part ways and go with this dreamy man for the rest of the night. There was no talking me out of it, and I didn't even give them a chance to respond. Jack looked upset and confused, but he didn't say anything to try to stop me. I thanked them kindly for dinner and then I was outta there. I was so overly excited to experience falling in love with a surfer boy in a new country!

He waited for me to return and then we took off to another bar, or three. I was freshly there and had a good amount of money saved in my bank accounts, so I bought all the drinks that night. I didn't quite know how much the currency difference was into colónes, so I was blindly, and drunkenly, spending money. After a few drinks, money no longer matters to me. This money was supposed to last for a while, though, because after this wedding and bachelor party that I was planning, I had nothing else on the books for the future.

We ended up at this one bar called Le Loft. It was a super happening place, packed full of people like a tin of sardines. I noticed a lot of pretty girls dressed extremely sexy, American men, and some locals sprinkled in there. What a great place to do some sexy dancing and exchange sweat! I was so excited about what was about to happen between me and Felipe. I could feel how excited he was as he was dancing and rubbing up on me. I wasn't sure if dry humping was ever an accurate way to judge how it would be in the bedroom, but with this guy, I could tell it was going to be a good time. He was packing a pretty big punch down there!

I was beyond in my element, soaking in how horny this man made me and how much fun I was having! It was exactly what I needed--to let loose and enjoy life for a moment after the stress of the move and the new job. I had no idea what I was feeling; I had never been that attracted to someone so quickly. Was it love at first sight? I didn't know, but I was going to find out one way or another. He was also sharing the best cocaine that I had ever had. My senses heightened, and the urge for sex escalated after a few small bumps. I had never really dived into cocaine in Austin. It wasn't ever good and always gave me a headache, but this coke was so pure that I experienced a whole new level of raging. I could drink like it wasn't even affecting me and dance harder than I ever had, all while having intense waves of horniness and sexuality.

Bars are typically open till 2 am there, except for a couple of places open till 4 am. It was around 3:30 that morning when everything was getting a little wild. We ordered two more shots at the bar during the last call, and then reality hit me. I paid for the drinks and had my wallet on the bar in front of me. I turned around behind me to give the shots to my new fling to hold for me, and when I turned back around--my wallet was GONE! WTF! It was only my second day in that town and my wallet was stolen! *This can't be happening.* I had no idea who was standing next to me because that whole bar was so packed, and all of it was a sensory overload while I was so intoxicated. I tried to tell the bouncers, and they weren't the most helpful. They told me, "*Pura Vida.*" (Once more when the timing couldn't have been worse.) I gave them my number, but I hadn't even purchased my Costa Rican phone yet, so we also gave them Felipe's number to call if they found it. There was nothing I could do at this point but cancel my cards before someone steals all my money. Luckily, I didn't have my passport on me, only my driver's license, a credit card, my debit card, and about $20 cash. I couldn't let that ruin my opportunity to be with Felipe that night, so I played it off like I was okay, and it wasn't that big of a deal.

At that moment, it was game-time with Felipe! He took me back to his home in Hermosa, which is about a ten minute drive up the mountain and out of the city. I was down for the adventure and wanted to also get my mind off of what had just happened. When we got back to his house, it was time for us to ravage each other and experience each other's bodies for the first time. We couldn't wait for it! We ran upstairs and locked ourselves in his room while his friend and his girlfriend stayed in the living room next to us. They were in town from another city, so they had the honor of being kept up all night by us. I had never made that much noise in the bedroom in my life, but I had also never experienced a dick that big either!

I was amazed by his golden tan, hair longer than mine, and his huge brown eyes that made me melt! I would happily be his toy and let him do whatever he wanted with me. We didn't even talk about protecting ourselves with condoms. It all happened so fast, and we didn't even care; we knew we would be together after this night. I wanted all of him, and he wanted all of me. We must have had sex over eight times that night; we couldn't stop! I don't know how he did it, but he was like the energizer bunny that could keep going and going. It was hot, passionate, wild, animalistic, and had so much intensity! I remember a distinct moment in his bedroom that is ingrained in my memory. I was standing up, leaning over his desk that had a window opened on the other side. We were up on the second floor, so this window was overlooking the palm trees and the beautiful pink, purple, and yellow sunrise. I was listening and admiring the howler monkeys and birds singing their early morning songs. He came up behind me, held onto my hips, and entered my soul. I was so wet from this guy that it was such a natural feeling to have him inside of me. I felt like this man was perfect for me in every way. We fit together like a glove, and that made my serotonin levels soar. He reached deeper parts of me that hadn't ever been explored before, and I was in a state of complete bliss as I joined the songs of the howler monkeys. (His neighbors and friends made sure to tell me they heard it all the next day!) I never was a moaner or made a lot of noise while having sex before, but this man was knocking the sounds out of me. I was soaking in this moment so it could last forever. His beautiful dick, so deep inside of me, woke up an urge and a desire for this to never end. At this point, I didn't know if I loved Felipe, or his dick.

This was the beginning of my addiction to sex, drugs, and this man. Little did I know, everything was about to change because I fell for Felipe. I was right about him and knew that he was going to be in my life; I just had no idea how much my life was going to change from having him around. All I knew was that I wanted more of what he was giving me. I spent the next three days locked up in his house having wild, animalistic sex over and over and over. Nothing else mattered except his dick inside of me. It was as if I became punch drunk in love with his potion, and forgot about anything else in my reality. I didn't even go back to the hotel that much, except to change and freshen up before going back out for another exploration of the nightlife in Jaco. Nella, the girl at the front desk, warned me about this boy and told me to be careful. I took her warnings with a grain of salt because I was already addicted and ready for my next fix.

CHAPTER TWELVE

CHOOSE YOUR BED WISELY

By day five of being in Jaco, I realized how harsh and heavy that town could be. I was making a trip back to the hotel to change my clothes when the owner of the hotel stopped me and pulled me to the side. He didn't look happy. I gently asked him if everything was okay. His reply was, "No. It's not okay. You made your choice as to what bed you were going to sleep in. Your decision is clearly not mine; therefore, you need to get your things and get out of my hotel. Also, after these two events, I won't be giving you any more." I was so confused! This man could've been my dad, and he never even hinted that that was his motive. If he had, I would have turned down his offer! No wonder he didn't want to sign a contract! He wanted to have sex with me in exchange for a job? *Is this how this world works over here?* I was outraged and also felt like my whole world had crashed on top of me. I lost my wallet with all my connections to money, then I got fired for not sleeping with my boss, and became jobless and homeless my first week living in Costa Rica. *What the fuck?* I wanted to know what he was thinking, flying me out, and doing this to me. His reply was, "Look at me as a catalyst to get you out of your comfort zone so you can experience life. You're here for a reason, figure it out and just enjoy it. You made this bed; now you have to sleep in it. I have a group that has booked out this hotel this weekend, and I need you to get your things and leave by today. I'm sorry I can't help you anymore."

That was a wake-up call from the world, if I've ever had one! I felt so tricked. I didn't see any of this coming. *Universe, what the fuck are you trying to teach me right now?* It's time to either sink or swim, and I wasn't going to sink! Not yet. I promised myself I would make it for at least a year, and I am standing strong behind my decision. This felt like a nightmare, but hey, *PURA VIDA*! I swear, that saying hits my heart every time I hear it, or say it to myself. I couldn't let this all drag me down. Yes, I have been completely stripped of everything and now am in survival mode, yet at the same time, this also helped to keep things in perspective. I was dropped out of nowhere in a beautiful country, with a beautiful man, who kindly opened his home to me. I had nowhere else to go, and I don't think he minded that his booty call became a permanent fixture in his home. I had no way to get a hold of any money because I canceled my credit cards so that no one could take the money out of my accounts. The cash I did have was running low, and I had to find a way to make it stretch until I got a money order from my parents. I found out the hard way that if you cancel your credit cards, they won't mail new ones across country lines due to fraudulent activity protection. I was stripped of everything a normal person would need to survive. *How the heck was I going to keep swimming on my own?* I wasn't. I was going to be swimming with Felipe until things smoothed out.

Once more, I found myself in my cycle, depending on another man to help me survive. I had no choice, though. It was either that, or I'd live on the street in a third world country until I figured out how to get my credit and debit cards back in my hands. To be honest, I probably would've lasted a week. I happily took the invitation to stay at his place, not thinking about the consequences of U-hauling it into his home. I mean, I only knew the guy for three days. How well do you think you could know someone? I was willing to take the risk and see where it went. He helped me get all my things from the hotel and took me in. I can't even guess what I would do if that situation was turned around. *Would you let a stranger come live with you out of the blue?*

Not realizing what the impact would be on this relationship, I went all-in with no time to waste. It was a hot and messy little honeymoon phase, and I was soaking up every minute of it! I then officially became addicted to sex. I never saw myself as that kind of person, but this guy woke up something in my second chakra that I couldn't let go of. The grasp of his embrace took me to another world. It was either that, or the alcohol and cocaine, that took me to another world. To be honest, it was probably all of it. We would wake up at the crack of dawn and have wild, loving, and passionate sex. The next step was to get ready for the beach so he could catch some good waves to surf before he had to go to work.

I tried to learn to surf with him in Hermosa when he would go out, but it was too scary to learn to surf in. The waves come in quickly, and they aren't beginner-friendly. I felt intimidated by the pro surfers that I was out surfing the same waves with. They made sure to let me know that I was going to get hurt, or hurt someone else. They were loud and clear that I didn't belong there. It was their playground, and I was just a visitor there. Honestly, there were a few times I would try to paddle out, and I would only get slammed by the waves and couldn't even make it out to the break. Hermosa was definitely not a place for beginners to learn; that was in Jaco. So I chose to hang out on the beach and get a tan while I made friends with the locals and smoked lots of weed. It was one of my favorite things to do in Hermosa; wake up early to get coffee on the beach, watch the surfers, the sunrise, and the waves, while smoking a joint. *I could get used to this kind of life.* I would take a walk down the beach to the grocery shack and get the best pupusas! *¡Qué rico!* Everything was within walking distance once you were on the beach. It was such a cute little town that felt like paradise.

After that, we would go back to his home, which was three miles inland, in the jungle. It was there that I would spend most of my time. I would do some chores and relax until he got home from work 12 hours later. We arranged that since I wasn't paying rent or for food, I would be in charge of cleaning and cooking to help maintain the household. Once I was living there, he encouraged me not to work and to sit back and enjoy the simple life. I had been working since I was 14, so I happily agreed to his terms. Plus, I didn't have papers to work there, which made it hard to make a decent living. It was a little outdated to keep the woman at home to tidy up, and it was definitely not what I was used to doing. A huge part of me thought it was peaceful, quiet, and tranquil at the beginning. Life was easy. It was simple. This was the *Pura Vida* kind of life I was happily willing to try. *Why not?*

I went back in time. I had to wash all the clothes out of a bucket. Even the bedsheets, which we had to wash quite often because we were constantly making a mess! That was the hardest thing to wash. I had to tie one end of the sheet to the door-knob handle and then go outside and wring it out and try not to let it drop on the ground. We hung our clothes out on a line in the yard and let the sun dry them. I had to get used to using their detergent. Every time, it would feel starchy even though I rinsed the clothes so many times. Maybe I was using too much. I'm not sure. There was no such thing as a dishwasher there, so all dishes were done by hand. The cooking was a challenge for me, too. I never learned how to cook. I mean, I can cook a mean steak and potato, but that isn't what they eat in Costa Rica. Plus, we were on a budget, and the meat there was not that great for the price. There were a lot of rice and beans, pasta, and filler food that we would eat. One of my favorite things to do would be to go outside and pick star fruit from the tree in the front yard so I could make starfruit juice. I felt like an animal, hunting and gathering my food, and it was amazing how plentiful they were. I also had a mango tree and an avocado tree in the yard, so we were set! I truly loved that life. I loved how simple and beautiful it could be. I was escaping reality and hiding out in paradise while I was running away from all of my problems. I was now unable to make any of my credit card payments, my loan payments, my Victoria's Secret bill, Express, and The Limited bill payments. I didn't have the money to do anything since I didn't even have a job. I had come to terms that I was going to be sent to collections, but a big part of me thought it wouldn't matter anyway if I was living in Costa Rica. I straight up fell on my face, and this beautiful man grabbed me right before I hit the ground. I was surviving, safe, happy, and free. Nothing else mattered to me at the moment; it's safe to say that this is the time in my life when I lost touch with reality.

Felipe would normally work 12 to 14 hour days at a gambling and gaming company call center. I didn't ask too many questions about what he did, and he didn't like to talk about it. He would take the car and leave me stranded in the jungle at his house during the days without any way to get around other than on foot. I didn't have a bike or anything, so if I wanted to go somewhere, I would have to walk or hitchhike about three miles to do so. Never thought I would be hitchhiking, but it was the thing to do over there because most people didn't own a car and most people were friendly. The town we lived in was so small that most of the people wouldn't pick me up because they knew I was Felipe's girlfriend. He was pretty standoffish to most people and was known for having abusive relationships with his girlfriends. I could see why, after some time had passed. They didn't want to piss him off because he was the overly jealous type. Around the second month is when it all started to show. I tried to avoid his jealousy at all costs because I was a visitor in his home, and I wanted to be respectful. I was also so in love with him that my eyes weren't even on anyone else. I wanted to make him happy so our home could stay happy. So, I did as I was told and stayed home most of the days doing things to contribute to the household. I didn't have WiFi, but I would read, watch movies on his laptop, sit in the hammock and watch the beautiful sunsets, listen to the sounds of howler monkeys, and still have time to do something on his list.

Once he'd get home, we'd usually go out on the town and strut our love for each other, dance like we were in his bedroom, and party until 3 a.m.! We had so much fun, yet did so many drugs that I could barely remember any of it. Looking back, I wonder if I still would've had so much fun without all the candy up my nose. Night after night, we would go to one bar, then the next, depending on what night it was and where the free drinks were. It was so easy to get drunk if you were a girl in this town. No matter what night it was, there was some kind of ladies' night happening where I could drink for free.

Jaco didn't have a good wine selection except at a few fancy restaurants, which is what I prefer to drink. Without this option, my drink of choice became a double shot of whiskey to sip on. My favorite was Jameson, but that was also a hot commodity, so I settled on Jack Daniels as my second back up option. My man wouldn't pay for my expensive taste, so I found a way around that by meeting people at the bar. It was easy to meet people since there were so many tourists that would come through the town. About nine out of ten times, they would offer to buy me a drink with an exchange of a little conversation. It was almost too easy. As a pretty female in a party town where prostitution is legal, all the guys had their minds set on one thing. I wouldn't ever let them get too far, but I will admit that I flirted my way into getting a drink and then left them to return to my man. I guess that might not have helped with Felipe's jealousy issues, but when

I am drunk and desperate for another drink, this girl did what it took.

Something changed after about two months when his jealousy started to get the best of him. Maybe it was me being in his space and seeing all of the sides of my personality that had him on edge. We didn't have WiFi at the house, so if I did get online, it meant that I was out of the house. Felipe could see when I was online (and not at home) because he was at his computer all day for work. If I got online, he would immediately call me and question me about where I was. Most of the time, he would throw such a fit that I was out, and cause a big fight between us, to the point where all I wanted to do was go home and hide. There were times when I went to the beach to lay in the sun, and I would catch him in the distance spying on me. Since this town was so small, any time I would go out of the house, one of his friends would call and give him the heads up. Things started to get weird, and I felt the noose around my neck begin to tighten.

Felipe told me that he had to go on a work trip to the city to help his bosses find another office in San José. At this point, I barely knew him or his work, so I took his word for it and said my goodbyes. He said he'd be back in a week. I spoke with him a couple of times on his trip, and his stories were not lining up. I didn't think much about that trip until after he returned home. This is when things started to go south between us. I was using his WiFi off his phone one day to check in on Facebook when I stumbled upon a tagged picture of Felipe with this strange chick in Santa Teresa. It was taken a few days before, when he said he was in San José. This is how I found out that he was cheating on me (*thank you, social media.*) No wonder he was so jealous before this; he was the one with the guilty conscience! That's one of the things about having a relationship with someone from Costa Rica. It's as if they don't know how to commit because there are so many tourists that pass through and then leave. It's too easy to cheat. Felipe and the strange chick do this every year when she comes back to this country. I caught him red-handed in a lie, and there was nothing he could do to prove me wrong.

So, what the fuck do I do now? He lied and cheated on me with another girl in another city and hid it from me. I was living with him and had nowhere else to go. I didn't have a job, so I had no money saved up to move or pay rent anywhere. My parents didn't have any money to send me, and I still didn't have my new debit cards. I was stuck in this mess with a broken heart. The girl he cheated on me with came and left. *Maybe now I can have him all to myself, or maybe he's going to do this again to me. I'm the one stuck with the pain of his decision as he tries to play it off that everything is going to be okay.* He tried to explain that with me living there and being in his space, it became too much, too quickly for him. He needed to get away, and he chose this opportunity with his friend to do so since she was paying for everything. He ran without even considering what would happen if I ever found out. I didn't know how to handle this. I had no money, no real friends there besides his friends, and I had nowhere to move. He didn't want me to leave, either. He felt horrible when he saw how badly I was hurt and how much I did care for him. He was trying for weeks to cheer me up, but it wasn't the same in the house. I tried to live with it and make the most out of what we had, but our trust was broken, and now both of us were jealous and more on edge.

It came up on the three-month mark for when I needed to get my passport renewed, and I had a game plan in mind. I finally got my credit and debit cards back, and the first thing I did was buy a plane ticket to Miami to try to get some work. This was going to be a business trip for me, working at a strip club to get another load of money stashed up and saved. *Hey, if I could work for eight days and be set for three months in Costa Rica, why not?* It seemed like a good idea at the time, and honestly, I felt like there was no easier way to make that much money in a short amount of time. There was no better time to do it, as I needed a break from that house.

*Side Note: If they cheat on you once, they are most likely going to cheat again. If the trust is broken, especially early on, it's more difficult to make a clean recovery. Get ready for a bumpy relationship if you do decide to stay.

CHAPTER THIRTEEN

CAMILLE

I booked my flight in a hurry and took off to Miami without much planning. I flew into a city that was about an hour away from my Airbnb, so my taxi ride there took an outrageous chunk out of my funds. I made it to the Airbnb, exhausted, and my next step was to figure out what club would let me work for them for a week or two. Miami is a huge party city with countless strip clubs. It was hard to know which ones were safe and which ones were sketchy, especially since I didn't know anyone to ask. I had to go to the clubs myself to check out the vibes. I hopped in a taxi and drove across town to the first club. They turned me down, so I walked to the next. At this point, they were all somewhat nearby and close enough to where I could walk. I went to about three places before I stumbled upon the club I would work at.

They accepted me, but the outfits I had didn't meet their requirements. The shoes I had also didn't meet their standards, so I had to do a little shopping before I was able to work that night. With a club willing to take me in for a week, it was game time. I got in another taxi and got dropped off at a lingerie store so I could buy some new outfits that looked more like a "Victoria's Secret Model." Shoes had to be over four inches high and have a platform under the toes. I went through and got about six different outfits, one good pair of shoes, and then I headed back home to shower and get ready for the evening's events. I was nervous and excited and felt alive again! My adrenaline was pumping as if I knew I was about to get into trouble. I was processing the heartbreak from Felipe, but I was excited to experience my own version of getting away. I went out to work, but also had another motive for hustling like this. For me, stripping was empowering when I could make money off of my looks. My name was Camille because I felt like I had to be like a chameleon and adapt to my surroundings. It seemed as if I was in control and had a way of building these powers that would pursue and tempt. I seemed to feel this power when I had a handful of cash in my hand. I felt sexy and wanted; I felt alive. I knew it wasn't the healthiest way to get attention or money, but it was paying for my ride in Costa Rica for a bit longer, and for that, I would do almost anything to succeed.

I felt so fancy in my new clothes. I made around $700 to $1,000 a night in Miami, depending on my mood. I have to admit, I'm not proud of some of the things I did there. There was a room upstairs that people only went in if the guy paid $1,000. The girl would receive $700, but the catch is, you have no bodyguard. There's no bouncer there watching over you to make sure you're safe. It's pretty much a staple that anything goes in that room. The guy I went in there with was actually pretty cute. He seemed like someone I would consider dating in the outside world. Viewing it this way helped me to get through what I was about to do. I needed to not give a fuck for a moment. When we went up to that room, anything went, and I was on my own. Lets just say, I walked back down those stairs with shame and guilt written all over my face. I'm not proud of that experience, but the truth is, I did it to survive. Working in that environment, you have to be somewhat outside of your body to be okay with what happens there. Therefore, I made sure to get heavy doses of whiskey throughout my shifts. It was empowering to earn that much money at once, yes, but it's also a strange environment of which I can only take so much at a time. I got lost in its seduction, manipulation, and greediness, and I definitely would wake up in the morning with regrets.

This job can be draining, especially when I would pick up other people's heavy energy; it can be a dark place. Good money, yes, but an extremely dark world. I did this for a total of eight nights. In between, I made sure to have a few days to rest so I could regain my power and humility. It was hard to be able to put on a show when I wasn't in the right mindset or when my body was sore and killing me. It felt like I beat up my body and soul in a trainwreck at the same time. I had days where I slept the entire day to process what I had done to myself.

I knew that I also needed to make sure to pamper myself while I was there. I was walking around shopping one day in Miami, and apparently there are a few blocks around 100th Street that are extremely dangerous. I didn't realize this at the time, but I had no business walking around there alone. There are a lot of drugs and sex-slave victims that go missing from that area since it's a port city, with easy connections to other countries. No one ever mentioned anything about this, so I was trying to save money on taxis by walking around on my own. As I was walking down the street, a man suddenly came running out of a motel parking lot chasing after me. He was yelling at me, "Hey, girl! You want to make some money? I got a guy in a room ready for a pretty girl like you! Whatchu need? You need weed? You need coke? You need crack? I got it!" All the while, I kept briskly walking down the street to get as far away from that motel as possible. I shrugged him off with a "Naw, I'm good," and continued moving farther away from the motel parking lot. He then followed me down the street even though I told him I was fine and didn't want anything from him, and he replied with, "Well, where are you going?" I pointed in the direction I was going and made something up, "I'm going to a CVS store or a Walgreens." He said, "Hey, I got you! Let me give you a ride!" At this point, we were about two blocks past the motel, and I was starting to get scared. He wasn't giving up or leaving me alone. It was as if I had a huge target on my back, and I was being hunted. I had to come up with something to get this man away from me. When he offered me a ride, I said yes without thinking it through. When he turned around and ran back to get his car, I took that as my opportunity to make a run in the opposite direction into the middle of traffic to flag down a taxi. A taxi stopped, *thank God*, and I jumped in before the man saw what I did. I told the taxi to go as fast as he could in the opposite direction until I figured out what to do next. I didn't care where we went; I just wanted to be out of that area. This taxi driver was the first one who told me of how dangerous it was in that area where he picked me up. Later that night at the Airbnb, the host also told me the same thing and felt bad for not warning me.

Not wanting to go straight to my rental home, I decided to lay low at a Starbucks for a while and charged up my phone. I had enough action for one day. After that experience, I was ready to get back home and hide. I wasn't in the mood to dance or be looked at like that anymore. But, I came out here to work, and I still needed to put in a few more days of hustling before heading back to Costa Rica. The show must go on. I spent the next three days working to earn the rest of the money, but it felt more forced and it wasn't enjoyable anymore. At first, I was doing it because I wanted to, and by the end of it, I was doing it because I had to. I ended up spending more money in Miami than I planned to, and my mood got worse, so I was walking with less money each night. The taxis were taking most of the money I was making, on top of paying off three months of unpaid bills. I wasn't even making that much money after that, and the cost of the clothes and shoes added up. By the end of this trip, I looked haggard. My whole self-esteem and self-respect was out the door. My bank account had more money in it, but it wasn't enough to last me a very long time.

The whole time I was in Miami, my family didn't know what I was doing. They couldn't make sense of why I would go there in the first place, knowing that I don't know anyone there. I was there for a lengthy amount of time, and I only talked to them after I was nearly kidnapped, so it left them with the feeling that something was off. They would question me about it, and I would bypass the question by saying I had to get my visa renewed, and I'm visiting friends that they didn't know. I was processing a lot of shame and guilt about what I was doing to myself. I wasn't ready for my parents to find out my mischievous ways of making money, but I wanted to keep in contact with them and let them know I was okay. I hated keeping secrets from my family because I was so close to them, and they could tell that I was up to something. Plus, I'm a horrible liar, and anyone can see right through me.

After Miami and working at their clubs, I went through a shock phase. In Austin, working at the club with my best friend was a blast; I had so much fun and felt so alive! Miami, though, was dark--really dark. I think it could've been because I stripped for a longer time, and I had to keep making money because I had to keep spending money. The work felt like a lock and chain around my throat. It wasn't ever good enough. I still felt like I could've made more money, but as a stripper, if you're in a shitty mood, no one will want to interact with you. That's how you get your money, and some nights I didn't want to play that game. I wanted to be left alone and was overly picky about who I let in. Most of the people I would let in happened to be the ones who only wanted to talk without paying for my time. At the time, I needed that for my mind and soul, but not for my wallet. I guess that's the balancing act you have to play in life with anything, though. I was ready to go back home. Felipe knew what I was doing in Miami, so it was nice not to have to explain myself to him. Over there in Costa Rica, it's a cultural thing that they understand. Prostitution is legal over there, so most men understand this kind of work; they might not like it, but the get it. I suppose it was the oldest profession for women, and it is still prevalent there. I was ready to be back in his arms and have him hold me, and he knew that.

I returned to Costa Rica with my spirits low. I stayed in San José for a night with my best friend, who was also watching my Chi boy! Any time I am with him, I notice my mood instantly lifts. I missed him so much and now, more than ever, was one of the moments when I was glad to have him in my arms. I made sure to give her a little money for dog food and for taking care of him, but it wasn't nearly as much as what she deserved. Amanda had been so sweet to watch over him this whole time. My first three months in Costa Rica didn't turn out the way I had planned, yet I was so grateful for Amanda and her family for watching over my baby and making sure he was safe.

I was ready to have him come back home with me and be by my side again. Felipe came to pick us up from Amanda's and took us back home. I was just hoping that my dog and my boyfriend's dog would get along. He had a female American Stafford, which is like a pitbull on crack. She could be sweet, but she could also snap in a heartbeat. It's how that breed reacts. A lot of Costa Ricans had this breed of dog and would use them as security guards to protect against anyone trying to rob the home. To my surprise, the two of them got along well enough for it to be manageable. The only person Chi didn't get along with was my boyfriend, of course. Felipe had his reservations about Chi and made sure not to get too close. Chi is a wolf, which most people in Costa Rica had never seen before, so he was pretty intimidating. The first night Chi slept with us, he hovered over on Felipe's side of the bed and watched him sleep. It was as if Chi was saying, *don't fuck this* up. *I'm watching you.* I personally thought it was cute how protective Chi was, but Felipe thought otherwise.

After about a month of Chi living with us, things started to get pretty bad between Felipe and me. He started to dislike Chi because he was shedding a lot of hair and had a musky smell, until eventually, he didn't want Chi to be in the house at all. Chi loved being free in the jungle and on the beach, and he would prefer that over going inside the house most of the time. It was like he knew he wasn't welcome inside by Felipe, so he would keep his distance. As time passed, it was difficult to get Chi to stay around the house, and he would take off and be gone for hours at a time. It made me go crazy as a mama; I wanted to make sure my baby was safe and didn't get lost or attacked by another dog, but this is when I had to have faith that he would always come back to me. Sometimes they say when you love something or someone, it's best to set them free. If they want to stay, they will stay. After a while, it became hard even to get Chi to come inside. It hurt me so much that I had to do this with my dog, but it wasn't my house, and I didn't have any other option without an income to get my own place. Chi was causing a lot of stupid arguments between us. Whether it was my dog's slobber in his car dripping on his arm, or the smell that Chi had, or the hair all over the house--there was always something. It was obvious that our relationship was a rocky one, and we needed to figure out how we could make it work between us. With our trust out the door from his cheating escapade, the tensions were high, and we needed a way to rebuild our bond.

Felipe figured he could fix this situation by taking me on a surf trip to Nicaragua. His boss, Ricky, needed to get his passport renewed, so Felipe invited Ricky and his girlfriend, Stephanie, to join us on this double date adventure vacation. I thought it sounded fun, and what better way to get over things, than to explore new places together? The neighbor agreed to watch Chi and Felipe's mom watched his dog while we were gone, so we had that figured out. It was only going to be a short three-day trip, so he should be fine. I was always down for an adventure, and since this was a spur-of-the-moment decision, I said, "Fuck it, let's go!" I didn't let anyone know where I was going except the neighbor; I packed a small bag of the essentials, and then we headed out in the morning.

CHAPTER FOURTEEN

NEVER WOULD HAVE SEEN
THIS COMING

As we headed out of town, Felipe and Stephanie were speaking intensely in Spanish. They seemed flustered, and I had a feeling they were up to something, and sure enough, they were. They were trying to get a hold of their dealer before we went on our surf trip so they could stock up. Apparently, it was going to be a fucking party! Felipe, his boss, and this Tica (Costa Rican female) all pitched in and ended up getting two quarters of weed, a bag of Molly for all four of us to split, and four individual coke bags. It was insane. I wasn't sure about this at all. I was the only one in the car that didn't want to bring all this to the border, but I was outnumbered. I kind of started to freak out about the situation, but also at the same time, I trusted Felipe and was following his lead. I tried not to worry, but my mind couldn't stop thinking, "What the fuck am I doing?" Felipe convinced me that this would work. He had a good stash spot in his car, where he stored everything for our drive. He stuffed everything all together in a sock and placed it in the secret spot. It was under his steering wheel, deep inside the car. He told me that he had done this plenty of times before and not to worry. So, I went with it.

I should've known the universe was trying to warn me through my initial intuition. We ended up getting a flat around Uvita in the palm fields. It was pouring rain, and we had to wait it out until it lightened up. Things weren't going as planned, and it turned out that I wasn't a fan of this Stephanie girl I had to share the backseat with. Maybe it had to do with our personalities clashing, the language barrier, or how she spoke. Everything started to get to me, especially when we were stuck on the side of the road. After nearly three hours, we were finally able to get the flat fixed and be on our way. It was a seven-hour drive to get to Nicaragua. We had one police checkpoint in Costa Rica when we made it to the beautiful Guanacaste area. It's normal for them to set up roadblocks to check in on most of the cars. That one went smoothly, but we also knew it was coming up. After this, we decided to camp out at the beach before making the rest of the trip to the border. Felipe knew this surf spot in Playa Grande that he had to check out before we passed through it. We had an overnight stay there to rest and enjoy the beach before we continued our drive.

Nicaragua was only an hour or two away from our camping site. We set out early in the morning and made our way to the border with all of our party favors stashed in the steering wheel. As we approached the border, my heart began to race. I didn't know what to expect because I had only crossed borders in and out of the United States at the airport, and not in a third world country.

I was putting out the intention that we would get away with this and be on our way to San Juan del Sur for some surf, or at least that was what I was trying to manifest for us. As we approached the border, it got to the point where we needed to pull over to use the toilet and get something to eat. Those borders are filled with vendors and their carts of mangos, mamons (a local fruit), and other nut mixes. Not only that but these borders have some sketchy restaurants that reminded me of a cafeteria-style buffet that must have violated health codes; none of which I wanted to eat at.

When we all came back together, we ensured everything was in the stash spot, and the car was cleaned out before we proceeded to the checkpoint where our car was going to be searched. As we got closer, it became more crowded with traffic, and we got boxed in. There was a guy outside our window who was trying to help us prepare for the checkpoint process. I thought he was a part of the border help because he was giving us tips on what line to get in and how we should go about this process. He was a younger kid without a uniform, and I noticed that there were a lot of other guys out doing the same thing. Maybe they were looking to get a tip or any donation for the help they provided to the border crossers. He was helpful and informative, letting us know which lane was the best to be in. As we approached the border crossing point, he somehow picked up that we might have something in the car. We were all looking around for evidence, trying to do one last search. He told us if we have anything in the car when it is getting searched, it would be found. He told us that there were going to be eight cops at the checkpoint searching our car. This young gentleman kindly reminded us that Nicaraguans and Costa Ricans don't like each other; therefore, this car would be getting searched more carefully than the others. The kid recommended that we take whatever we had in the car and give it to a person to put in the bag as they stood off to the side while the car was getting searched. Felipe turned to me without even hesitating and said, "I'm going to give it to you; stash it in your purse. You'll be off to the side. The car is getting searched, not you." Let me just tell you guys, my purse was small and already so full. This sock of paraphernalia was literally hanging out the top of my bag. I didn't want to do it, and I told Felipe that, but he somehow convinced me that it would be okay. The kid that was helping us also saw Felipe give me the sock, so it was known that we were suspicious. My stomach began to turn into knots with the fact that I was actually about to do this.

I ended up hiding a quarter of weed in my panties because it wouldn't fit in my purse. I had now found myself as the carrier of everyone else's drugs across the border when I was the one that didn't want to do it in the first place. *How did this happen?! What did I sign up for?* Everything felt so wrong, and I knew this wasn't going to end well. Blindly in love and feeling like I didn't have a choice because of this peer pressure from everyone, I found myself being a sitting duck. I felt like I had bombs strapped all over my body, and if I messed up, we were all going to blow up.

At this point, the car had been dropped off in the middle of the checkpoint to get searched with Felipe, and the rest of us were waiting on the sideline. As we waited, I figured I would go ahead and get a bottle of Jameson at the duty-free store. I had to pull the sock out of the bag to get to my wallet, and I could feel my face turning bright red. I felt like this process took forever because the cops were searching extra hard to try to find anything to bust us with. I didn't know what to do with my time, so I paced to the bathroom and considered leaving the bag behind the toilet while we figured this part out. I could leave this sock behind, and there would be no problem. No one has caught us yet, and no one would ever know. I contemplated it, but then I realized, it wouldn't have been completely hidden. The next person behind me would've seen it. I was starting to get overwhelmed and didn't want to get caught dropping this off anywhere, either. I went back to check in on the process, and the car was still getting searched.

By now, Felipe was looking frantic. He started to sign and make movements with his hands for me to run away. I was frozen and confused as to why he was asking me to run. We had everything out of the car, or so I thought. *Where would I run to, anyway?* I was scared and lost and didn't know where to go, so I ended up staying off to the side without heeding his warning. The cops had found a few roaches from some joints in the car and now began to pull out our luggage and throw things around; they were searching so hard, they even felt the inseams of each piece of clothing. When they pulled out all of our bags, Stephanie suddenly remembered that she forgot her personal stash of cocaine in her luggage. *WHAT THE FUCK, WAIT, WHAT?! Are you serious? After we all stressed multiple times about getting that car clean, you just NOW remember!?* They were sure to find it! This is it. It was only a matter of time before we were asked to come and join the car. Sure enough, the cops found Stephanie's drugs and summoned us over to the car. I was searching for a spot to dump this sock real quick before walking over there. I tried to be smooth and drop the sock off in the trashcan before making it to the police. The kid who was helping us cross the border saw what I had done and mentioned it to the cops. So, this kid that was helping us was actually working *with* the cops. The cops went to the trash bin and retrieved the sock, then forced us all into the center of the checkpoint area where the car was.

I tried to stay calm as I approached the police officers, but I felt like I was about to shit in my pants. I had never been in trouble like this before. I couldn't understand anything they were saying because all they spoke was Spanish. They had us sitting down and watching them as they pulled out everything in that sock and placed it on the hood of the car. The cops made us stand by the hood of the car once it was all laid out so they could take a photo of us for the daily paper. This was a big bust for them, and boy were they proud! The border cops told us that we had to wait for the captain of the prison to come to the border to see if he would charge us or let us go. At this point, our fate was in the hands of the infamous captain, and all we could do was wait. The chances of us getting out of this were slim to none.

There was a police station at the checkpoint where we were waiting to be strip-searched. This was not my day; I still had a quarter of weed hidden in my panties. I asked Felipe what to do with it, and his reply was, "Just wait." Felipe offered to go in first so he could see what they were doing in the search and buy me some time to figure out a game plan. There was this desk I chose to sit on while I was waiting in the dock area. After Felipe got out of the search room, he saw me sitting on the desk and told me to open my legs so he could slip the weed into the drawer. *YES--This was such a sly idea!* With his help blocking the view of some policemen, we waited for the perfect time to sneak that bag out so we could stash it in the police desk drawer. This was a close call, but I was able to get the bag out in time before they called me in to get strip-searched. I went back to get searched, and they found nothing. Once we were all cleared, we had to wait, and wait, and wait. I felt like it took hours for the captain to come. During this time, we had some hope that somehow we were going to be walking away from this. Felipe somehow convinced me to stash the weed back in my panties just in case we were let free, and also so the cops wouldn't find it while we were there waiting. I don't know how this man convinced me to do half of the things on this trip, but somehow he had this power over me.

As we're waiting anxiously for hours, I finally overheard some of the policemen say that the captain was coming to take us to jail. I got nervous again and once more wanted this weed off of me. I was tired of feeling on edge, so I went to the bathroom to pee and dumped the weed in the toilet. To my surprise, the toilet wouldn't flush. This was my kind of luck! Over in third-world countries, some of the toilets needed to be filled with water in the tank for the pressure to pull everything down the pipes. I had to leave the room with the guard outside the door to get water from behind the building in a bucket and bring it back around. Before I went out to grab the water, I did my best to grab most of the weed out of the toilet by hand and throw it in the trash can (just in case the police walked in there.) I nervously got the water and came back into the room to flush the toilet. Thank God it worked and got everything down. Now I had urine on my hands, and sure enough, there was no soap! This is, by far, the worst day I had ever experienced. About ten minutes after this bathroom experience, the captain pulled up after four hours of waiting.

The captain had finally arrived, and he reminded me of a man who hadn't had sex in over ten years. He was short and had a permanent frown on his face that was so intense that it made him look like a super unhappy fish. He evaluated all of us and our situation, then, without much thought, decided that we needed to come with him to jail. All four of us rode in the back of Felipe's car while the captain and another officer rode in the front seat. I kept my bottle of Jameson close and kept taking sips from the bottle to comfort me in such a distressing time. I was scared and didn't know what else to do. Alcohol was my coping mechanism and how I dealt with stressful situations. Felipe reminded me that it would be wise not to drink too much because he wasn't sure when I would be able to use the bathroom again. That's when the magnitude of the situation hit me. I saw the fear in his eyes, and that's the moment I finally got scared. I put down the bottle and sat in silence for the next hour and a half as we drove to Rivas, where the main jail was located.

It was beginning to get dark when we finally arrived at the jail. The gates surrounding the grounds opened up, and it reminded me of a junkyard with tons of cars jam-packed in a small space. Three small concrete buildings made up this jail that were all along the edges of the parking area. We were told to grab a towel, some snacks, and a change of clothes, and that was it. By this point, I was mentally exhausted from our day, hungry, and slightly drunk from the whiskey I slammed in the car.

We were told to wait outside on the steps of the middle building while we waited for processing. It was here where I began to freak out. All the men inside that jail were barking like angry pitbulls about to fight as a way to intimidate the new people coming in. The barking was so loud, and it went on for what felt like forever. I had never heard of anything like this, but apparently, the people inside the jail got word that there was a Costa Rican outside, and they were trying to scare him. I curled up in a little ball on the ground and hid under my towel in the fetal position, not knowing what was about to happen to me. I felt like I was about to be fed to hungry sharks, raped, or thrown in a fire pit. The guards made me get up and said I couldn't lie down for some reason. My whole body felt heavy and shaky from being emotionally drained and terrified, but I did as they demanded and felt like a puppet on a string. They would only speak to me in Spanish, so I was slow to respond, which frustrated them even more.

After we waited outside for an hour of madness and barking, we were finally let inside to the holding cells. It was here where we were separated into different holding cells that were tiny and had no bathroom. There were these two holding cells outside of the main jail, along with a small dull desk with a guard where people were held before processing. Felipe and his boss went to one side, while Stephanie and I were shuffled to the other. There was a little window with bars on it at the top of the cell where we could still see each other, but we had to stand on our tiptoes to do so. We could stick our hands through and still be able to touch one another. The guys in the main cell were a few feet away on the other side of a gated door, and we could hear all of them cat-calling at Stephanie and me, and trying to pick a fight with Felipe. It was such a heart-sinking night that seemed to last forever. More men filtered into the guys' cell and their tiny space got even smaller with each person entering. They must have packed about eight men in that tiny cell throughout the night; I suppose they were either waiting to process them in the morning, or keeping them overnight until they sobered up.

I needed to sleep at this point and all I had was my towel to curl up with on the ground. It was the longest, most painful night I had experienced in a while. My bones were poking out into the ground, keeping me from getting too comfortable. I had to toss and turn throughout the night to keep from bruising my hips and also because Stephanie was hogging most of the space, making it even more uncomfortable. The noises in there throughout the night were haunting. I felt like if I went into that main part of the prison, I would be eaten alive. All of my worst nightmares were playing in my mind and in my dreams. There were so many people overflowing in that prison that the conditions of the heat and the smells made me sick to my stomach.

I started to get thirsty when the early morning came around. I then realized how alone I was. I begged for water; they refused. I asked for a phone call. Not even a question as they laughed at me. I started to panic at this point when I knew any rights that I did have were completely disregarded in Nicaragua. The police can do whatever they want, and there are no repercussions. Most of the time, you could pay them off, but if I had gotten caught in the US with what I had on me, I would be in jail for a good ten years, at least.

I couldn't understand Spanish fluently because I had only lived abroad for four months, especially when they spoke fast. I had to keep asking Felipe or Stephanie to interpret what they were saying because I felt so lost. Felipe told me the guards were laughing at the fact that I thought they had international calling. He also said we don't get any water or food unless we have friends or family to bring it to us. They don't have the means to supply the prisoners with these things.

My heart sank into my stomach. My mom didn't even know where I was! I didn't have WiFi at the time, so I lost track of keeping up with everyone or checking in on social media. I never told my parents about this trip because it was such a last-minute decision for Felipe to make it up to me for cheating on me. It was supposed to be three days of fun and surfing and exploring the world. I was regretting that I loved his dick so much to the point where I would almost do anything for that guy. I became so completely blind to all the regular, natural, RED flag warnings from him. Most people would have run away long before this, but it was as if he put me under a spell and completely knocked out any common sense that I did have. I had to take some responsibility at this point. Now, we were both criminals living a nightmare of a life together.

Later in the morning, they pulled me out of the cell and told me to walk with them outside. I was running through all the scenarios as to why they would pull me out separately, and the only reason I could think of was that they were about to rape me. We walked outside of the jail and entered into a different building. I was unsure of what was happening because they hadn't pulled any of the other people out to do this; I was the first. I was praying that my angels would take care of me and help get me through this. They were speaking in Spanish, and I couldn't understand them. I had my head held low and followed them outside down a hall. I thought they were taking me to a separate room to pass me around for all of them to share. My heart was racing, and I was trying my hardest to make sense of what he was saying so the fear would subside; but it was almost impossible.

As we entered the other building, we walked up to the captain's desk with a big book in front of him. He simply asked for my signature and to date it for the records. That was the only record of me being in that prison. After my signature, the guard walked me back to the holding cell, where he asked for everyone else to do the same. I was just the first to do it.

My fears were beginning to get the best of me, and I had no idea what to expect. This experience was by far the scariest situation I had ever found myself in.

I had a Xanax prescription in my luggage in the car that I asked the guards if I could get because my anxiety was practically unbearable. I was having a constant anxiety attack, and it was getting worse as the day went on. Thank God they allowed this, along with my birth control. As they went for my bags to get my medicine, they seemed to have a plan as well. The guards asked for us to show them all of our money and everything in our bags. They were adding up the total of all of our money combined and rummaging through our things to see if they wanted any of it. They gave us our toothbrushes but first cut them in half so we couldn't use them as weapons. We had a total of around $700 between the four of us. It wasn't much, but we thought we could try to bribe our way out of there. Sometimes people can do that with police in Nicaragua and Costa Rica. Felipe was the only one who could strike a deal because he knew the best Spanish. I wouldn't want to depend on Stephanie to do anything, especially strike any deals involving my life. Felipe attempted to give them all the money so we could get out of there. At least for the time being, he was trying to pay them to feed us. We pleaded with them over this for a while, but they coldly refused without thinking twice. Money couldn't buy our way out of trouble this time.

After they searched our bags, they moved Stephanie and me into the main jail cell. This was when it got surreal for me. As I walked in there, all of the men welcomed me with whistling, blowing kisses, and hollering cat-calls my way. I felt like a new wrestler going into a boxing ring to fight a giant. I walked in with my head held low and kept to myself in a little ball in the corner where I was blocked from the men's view. As I walked into the women's cell, I could tell they were all sizing me up. Most of these women looked sweet with only about two bad apples that were gawking at me like the guys were. The cell was packed with 18 women, and there were only four beds. Literally, the cell was over four times maxed out. There were about nine cells for men and only one cell for the women. The men had it even worse by being packed in a six-bed cell with 22 people in it.

Terrified, I didn't know what to do except stay in a small ball and cry to myself. I would cry for hours as the men kept calling at me and wishing me to stop crying. The women tried to comfort me, as well. I could tell that they were sweet, and most of them, like me, didn't belong there. As the ladies were standing around me and placing their hands on my shoulder, they were saying something to me that I will never forget. They were telling me, "Have faith and not fear. The more you cry, the longer you will stay."

As I sat in the corner in my ball, I realized I was even farther away from that exit door and falling even deeper into the darkness that was starting to overtake me. I couldn't help but size up everyone at this point. It was turning into survival of the fittest now that I was lumped in with everyone else. One girl ran over to me and started acting like she was hitting on me. Funny enough, she was the only one who could speak some English. She was pretty forward, and so was I, as I denied her requests for intimacy and immediately told her of my boyfriend who was out in the holding cells. She offered to keep me warm at night, and she was going to make sure to sleep next to me to protect me. She was the worst out of all of them, but it was nice to speak English for a change. There were three girls who seemed like they were meant to be in there. These girls were troubled girls that needed some discipline, not girls who have been caught for murder. The other people there didn't seem like they should be in there at all. There was a super old grandma who was having a hard time moving around. Later, I found out she had multiple dislocated ribs and vertebrae. She was one of the eldest and longest-held prisoners in that cell, so she had acquired one of the four beds. She was the one who watched over us and maintained order. Then there was also a nine months pregnant woman in there. She was so sweet and soft-spoken and literally about to burst at any moment. She was in there with her mother, father, brother, and sister. Her brother brought home drugs, and once he entered the house, the police took in the whole family for possession. Then there were other girls who seemed sweet, but were caught in the wrong situation at the wrong time, like myself. If one person in the car had something, everyone in that car would go to jail. The same went for homes, so there were a lot of families. At least they had each other in there; my family didn't even know where I was.

I spent most of this day crying. It was a good excuse to be in my own world; people wouldn't try to talk to me because they knew I needed to get it out of my system. I was in culture shock and was feeling displaced. I was in an overcrowded, third world country prison, and nobody even knew where I was. In a heartbeat, I was stripped of any American rights, all things material, my family, my freedom, my life. I was ripped away from any sense of normalcy. I was in the process of shedding the layers of my identity with my tears. I wasn't even sure of who I was when I had nothing to my name.

It came time for dinner. Since they wouldn't take our money to release us, we offered to pay them again so we could eat. It had been 24 hours since we arrived and we hadn't had any food. To our surprise, they ended up giving us smaller half portion plates of food. We got a tiny piece of chicken with some rice and beans, and that was it. Other people's plates were twice the size of ours, but it didn't matter. We were starving, and we weren't going to complain.

I could still see and communicate with Felipe by sticking my head against the metal bars on the door and looking to the left. He was still in the holding cell with about five other guys in there with him. We mostly talked with our eyes because we were supposed to be quiet in there. I thanked him for finally convincing them to feed us. That night, we saw the fear in each other's eyes. *So, this is how it's going to be. Begging to be fed. Maybe they will, maybe they won't. It all depends on how they feel that day, I guess.*

That night was the second-longest night of my life. I was so exhausted from crying all day, but I had to keep on guard because I felt so uneasy. *How are all of us going to sleep when there are only four beds? There are 18 of us.* The alpha females (one was the grandma) were the ones who had the beds because they had been there the longest, or they won the privilege through intimidation. The rest of us had to pack in on the ground side by side, basically spooning each other in between the beds, and along the tiny walkway into the bathroom area. I chose to sleep underneath one of the beds, thinking it would be better. No one was doing that, and I saw I had space to do it, so I did. Once I got under the bed, it felt like a coffin after everyone laid down for the night. I became trapped, claustrophobic, and filled with anxiety. Above me was concrete, below was concrete, up against the wall had everyone's water bottles, and then on the open side, there were feet and heads from other inmates closing me in. Little did I know, the ants also loved this little spot because of all the crumbs and trash that got hidden underneath the beds. I was having a panic attack stuck underneath the bed in a coffin I made for myself. I don't know why I thought that would be comfortable, but to be honest, nothing was comfortable about any of what I was going through. At least that lady wasn't going to touch me under there.

Once more, I cried my eyes out until I was numb and worn out enough to escape in my dreams. I was able to get a couple of hours of sleep under there until the ants began to bother me, and then I couldn't take it anymore. I could barely scratch my legs because I didn't have enough space, and I felt like I was being eaten alive. I freaked out and began to scream as I pushed people's feet and legs out of the way so I could get out to breathe. I practically woke everyone up as

I was crawling out from that tiny space. I was trying to find a spot to sit down so I could collect myself. I would have been torturing myself by attempting to remain there any longer. I ran into the bathroom because no one was in there, and I had a moment once more, where I felt my life crashing down around me. No one can save me now. I had nothing and was in the worst possible situation you can find yourself in while abroad. I felt like I was on that show, *Locked Up Abroad*, living out everyone's biggest nightmare. I couldn't understand how I could've let this happen to my life. It was hard for me to face the fact that this was my new reality.

I was also having withdrawals from alcohol, cigarettes, weed, and cocaine. At this point, this was probably the clearest I had been in years. There hadn't been a day when I didn't try to alter my brain to numb out the world since I was thirteen. I was feeling everything, even all of the things I never wanted to feel. I felt trapped, weak, stupid, lost, scared, angry, confused, hopeless, and alone. I found myself balled up in that same corner of the bathroom I ran to when I first entered that cell. I was pretty much right next to the toilet, but I had space, and that was all that mattered at that moment. I stayed there, shaking and scared, nodding in and out of sleep as I was squatting in the corner until the women began to awaken early in the morning.

The second morning was surreal. Everyone got food except for us. I couldn't understand why they would starve us. The other women felt bad for us and shared what they had on their plates with me. I tried to teach them some English in return for sharing their food. I remember this was the first time I ever experienced this certain type of cheese; I called it squeaky cheese. I'm not sure what the actual name of it is, but it was a fried cheese that was salty and would squeak as you chewed it. It made me smile for the first time since being in there. After breakfast, the ladies cleaned the area with a small hand-held broom to pick up all the crumbs and trash so the ants wouldn't take over the space. It was a morning ritual to start the day. I was at the point where I needed a shower, badly. The other girls were having the same mindset, so I stepped back at first to see how the girls were doing it. One girl had to hold a jug of water over the other while they showered as they stood over the toilet area. (The toilet was a hole in the ground that you had to squat over to use.) I didn't know how to feel about being naked around a stranger, but I had to get over it. There was no way I was asking Stephanie to help me with this. I tried my best to stay away from her and avoided getting into a conversation with her altogether. So, I kindly asked one of the girls I had been trying to communicate with if she could help me shower. She agreed, and I couldn't have been more grateful. She also shared her shampoo and conditioner with me since I didn't have any. *How is it that these people have nothing, yet they are the most giving people I have ever met?* I felt so blessed to be around such a sweet group of girls. It was as if they were taking me in as their own, just like family that I hadn't seen in many, many years. That was starting to be some kind of comfort for me. Most of the other girls ganged up on that one girl who was trying to hit on me, so I knew they had my back. I couldn't say the same about Stephanie. Since she was Costa Rican, most of the Nicaraguan girls kept their distance. In addition to her lineage, she was annoying everyone there, including me. She would get up next to the bar door and scream to her boyfriend, "I love you, Ricky! Ricky, I love you baby!!!" over and over again. It was over the top and against the rules. It only made the guards mad and it riled up the other men in the cell. It was extra attention that we didn't need and she could cause us all to get punished, so we gave her the cold shoulder. I didn't know her from before, and I sure as hell don't think we'd ever make good friends, so I chose to befriend all the other girls in the cell instead. I guess my survival of the fittest mentality was kicking in.

On visitors' day, all the family members would bring in supplies and check up on the inmates. Everyone gathered in the courtyard outside, bathed in the sun, and got their presents and hugs from their families and friends. Once more, my life flashed before my eyes. I felt like the world was crashing down on me as I was the only terrified and lonely American girl, curled up in a ball in the corner, crying while wishing for my family. I couldn't help but think the worst. *I am all alone. No one even knows I'm here. I'm never going to see or hug my family again. My family doesn't even have passports to come to visit me if they did find me. How would they even know where to begin searching for me?*

I got so thirsty sitting in the sun; it had been days since I had any water. I saw a water faucet that fed the plants, so I went to try to take a sip from the hose. The guard saw me and yelled at me to stop me from proceeding! I was desperate and begging for something to drink, and his response was a firm and rude, "NO!" It felt like a nightmare that wouldn't end. I'm sitting there scared and alone once more, with nothing to my name. There I was, without anyone to comfort or help me, feeling so utterly lost and in a place where I didn't belong. Still no phone call; it wasn't even a question. There was no way to reach the outside world. I could be stuck forever, and no one would even think to look for me here. As I observed everyone else's gifts as they walked back into the cell, I saw this one man who had a bottle of juice. I went running up to him in hopes that I could have a little sip of his juice. I was so thirsty, and he must have seen the desperation in my eyes. To my surprise, this kind man ended up giving me the whole bottle of mango juice; I couldn't believe it! His family had brought it him, and he gave it to me without hesitation and without even opening it. My jaw dropped as I thanked him; I was shocked by his kindness. I had a moment of hope when this was happening. I saw the kindness in the people's hearts who were trapped in there, who were just like me. This was gold to me at the moment! Now I had something to trade with the girls for different supplies. It worked quite well and the girls were so pleased with the tasty beverage I gathered for them.

These people in this prison were starting to make an impression on me. I would never have thought that this was how it was going to be, especially not in comparison to their barking calls when we arrived and were waiting outside. I was starting to see their hearts because that was all they had to give. I started to get all this attention from the men trying to please me and keep me from crying. They would make me little bracelets out of plastic bags that were so intricate and beautiful. They would pull plastic bags into thin strips and then braid them. It was a delicate process that was extremely impressive. All the bags in Nicaragua were wild and fun colors, and there were plenty of them because everything came in bags. Instead of trashing the bags, they got creative with them. Silverware was also a hot commodity, so one man saved a plastic spoon and decorated the end of the handle with my name on it. It was crazy how they started showering me with gifts once I opened up. A couple of the men could speak broken English and would try to talk to me all day. I felt bad for Felipe because the men started to yell out, "We love you, Alli!" just to make him jealous, and because they were entertained by me. They hadn't ever seen a young, pretty, white girl in there.

All this time, Felipe and his boss were still in the holding cell by the front desk. They didn't have a bathroom and sometimes there would be up to eight people in that tiny cell. The people they were holding in the same space were Nicaraguan and were threatening to beat him up at times. He tried his best to stay quiet and lay low so no one messed with him. I felt bad for him, but the fact that they were still up-front in the holding cell gave me hope that we would be released soon. They weren't booked in the main prison cells yet, so the officers in charge had to have something planned. I kept asking them what was going to happen to us, and they responded with, "One more day," everyday. No answer they gave us ever answered any of our questions. It was a twisted game of *How we can keep them scared and begging?* They liked to keep us on edge with nothing but fear and confusion swimming in our brains. That's how the guards had control and power over us. It was sickening to witness this kind of inhumane treatment, but this was my new reality and I was beginning to get used to it.

On the third day, I talked to one Frenchman and he told me his story about how he arrived in prison. He was walking down the street, smoking a joint when they caught him. He had been in there for seven months without a phone call or anything. He told me he was trying to get a hold of a lawyer from one of the other inmate's families reaching out to his family, but nothing had happened yet. He had a joint, and he had been stuck there without a way to contact his family for the past seven months! He told me once the lawyers get involved, it could take years to work with the embassy to get him out. That is, if he could reach his family. *What does that mean for me, then?* What we had was way more than a joint. We had a half-ounce of weed, Molly, cocaine--cocaine in four separate bags, might I add. We even had to take a picture for the newspaper. My stomach sank. I thought I was going to die there. *My mom was right; she might not ever see me again.*

I feared the worst and I began to panic once more. With no room to move and nothing to do but sit and wait, I could feel myself starting to lose it. Day three was probably the hardest because I was fighting and resisting all of what was happening to me. I was creating this tension within myself as I sat there, trapped in one hell of a mess. I cried the majority of this day, too. The guys in the other cells were trying to cheer me up by making bracelets and handing out cigarettes to calm my nerves. I had one guy buy me a burger and fries when it came time to eat dinner. It was strange because no one else got burgers that night, only I did. This guy seemingly ordered from a special menu or paid the guards to go to a store to get this. I had this overwhelming sense that everyone was starting to care about me. I was fragile and so out of my element in that prison, and it showed. Everyone could tell I was innocent and didn't belong there. I was like them; in the wrong place, at the wrong time, with the wrong people. The ladies kept telling me every time I cried, "Have faith not fear. The more you cry the longer you stay." I couldn't understand having faith at the time. I couldn't understand how not to have fear, either. I didn't know how to do anything. It was a reprogramming of my brain waves with a whole new territory that I hadn't yet discovered. Growing up, faith was a confusing subject. My mom and dad have different beliefs, so religion was always confusing for me. My parents taught me to believe in something bigger than me. *How can I have faith right now when these men aren't giving me any answers?* They are laughing at us and getting pleasure from keeping us in a state of panic. I was nowhere closer to a phone call to my parents. *How can I have faith when I feel so lost and hopeless?* This was my rock bottom, worst-case-scenario, besides death. *Might as well be dead, because I am dead to the world right now. I'm lost and no one would ever find me here. My dog is expecting me any moment now and I'm not going to be there.* My neighbor was watching Chi, and I didn't even know how he's doing. I knew my neighbor was reluctant about watching my wolf in the first place and I was wishing and hoping Chi was okay and safe. It takes a strong alpha person to handle a wolf, and I had my doubts about my neighbor. I wished I could hug him so badly at this point. I cried myself to sleep once again, but earlier in the evening. The older grandma in the cell offered to share her bed with me since she knew the night-time was the worst for me. It was the size of a twin bunk bed, but it was a way better sleep than on the floor with the centipede spooning train. It was probably the best night sleep I had gotten since I arrived there.

I woke up on the fourth day, and it all started to hit me. This is now my new normal. The girls woke up, ate breakfast, and had their coffee. Next, they started cleaning, taking their showers, and we would sit and try to teach each other different languages. I bummed cigarettes off the guys in the cell next to us so that I could have one with my coffee; it was almost as if everything was on repeat. It was the same thing, different day. All the while, Felipe and Ricky were *still* stuck in the holding cell up in the front of the jail. *Why would they keep them up in the front for so long?* I guess the jails were already too crowded? Or maybe it was the fact that the guys in the main cell would probably beat up Felipe for being Costa Rican if they let him in. I don't know, but I felt bad for them, yet it kept the hope alive inside of me that the guards had a plan. They had no beds and no toilets, all while being stuck in an even smaller space than we were. The guards continued to tell us, "One more day," and they wouldn't give us any real answers. It was a circle of questioning and then they ignored us, bypassed having to answer us. It was like they enjoyed keeping us on edge.

All we could do was wait. I could drive myself crazy like I had the first three days by thinking of all the things I was missing out on and how badly I wanted to call my mom, but that wouldn't get me anywhere. If anything, it would make me cry again, which I didn't even have the energy to do anymore. I did that for the past three days, and it was miserable. I was tired of fighting all the emotions that were raging through my veins. It wasn't until I finally came to terms with where I was in my life that things started to shift. I began to try to be okay with my new normal. *What else was there to do?* I was tired of fighting it. So, my perspective started to change, and I was finally able to relax into where I was. *This is my life now. I can choose to fight the fact that I can't do anything or give into my fate and be okay with where I am.* I'm the kind of person that is usually happy and goofy. I missed that side of me and knew that this was still inside me somewhere. It was hard to be okay with losing my freedom and any chance at a regular life again, but they couldn't take away my peace or my personality, and I was refusing to let that happen.

In the afternoon, a visitor came to the prison. It was a priest who came bearing a sweet and refreshing gift for us. He brought us coconut water that was packed in little sandwich bags that were tied at the end. We had to tear a little hole off of the corner to sip it out of the bag. This immediately caught my attention because this was the sweetest thing someone could do. After the coconut water was distributed to everyone, the priest started to sing songs from the bible, and everyone else began to join in. The songs were all in Spanish, so I couldn't understand what they were singing, but I could feel the message. I sat next to the gated door and had my feet sticking out, enjoying the little bit of sun peaking through the ceiling on my toes. I wanted to be in the middle of everything that was going on at the moment. I was mesmerized by what was happening in that prison. I wasn't sure what was happening, but I was captivated by it and was soaking up every minute of it. As I said earlier, faith has always been unclear to me, but I could feel a higher power in the jail cell vibrating off of everyone. It was pure magic, and I was witnessing it firsthand. The energy in that prison completely shifted, and a peaceful choir of voices massaged my soul. I had a moment when tears of joy filled my face. My heart was warming, and everything became okay again. I was able to find my peace. *This was what I wanted to feel this morning.* I could close my eyes and feel magic pulsing through my veins. Some part of me must have known this time was coming. Something in me shifted, and I felt at home within these walls.

After the priest left, the whole jail cell became calm and quiet. Everyone felt rested, blissful, and still. The vibe was hopeful again. I was in shock as to what I had just felt and experienced. I had never been moved by God, the Holy Spirit, or whatever you would like to call it, so I wasn't sure what was going on. All I had was time to let this soak in, so I let it. I sat up on one of the top bunks and stared into space for a long while. I was observing the feeling of being at peace as if I was in meditation. I began to listen to my inner voice telling me, *I am okay. I am alive.* I was grateful for that experience and the stillness in the prison that followed it. I finally had stopped the mad voice in my head that was fighting my reality. I was in this present moment, feeling grateful. Life was simple for a moment, and my heart was full. It was in this moment of stillness and calmness, that I had the greatest a-ha moment of my life. After my mind became clear of harmful thoughts, something profound spoke clearly to me. This voice inside me was as clear as day, almost yelling at me, "*Move! Do yoga! Do your practice! You have that! No one can ever take that away from you! Move, do your practice, MOVE, GET UP, DO YOGA!!!*" It was so loud and continuous that there was no pushing it aside. I tried for a moment more to sit there and question why I was hearing this so loudly, but it was as if all of my angels were screaming at me at once to do this! I had no choice but to get up and move! I was also super excited that I had something that they couldn't take away from me. This practice was mine and lives inside of my heart. I knew it well enough as a student to do my own version of it on my own. No one could take away my knowledge or what I could do with my body. It was exactly what I needed to do, so I did it!

I hopped down from the top bunk and asked the girls to kindly move over so I could do my yoga practice. They did so out of curiosity and began to sit along the side to watch me as I did my practice. I ended up going to that same corner spot of the room where the men couldn't see me. They gave me just enough space in the walkway towards the bathroom, and they all sat around on the floor and the beds to watch the spectacle. I started to do my practice on my own, doing some Sun A's and Sun B's to myself, and then I began to do some core work as always. I didn't know a lot, but I did know that moving the body helps with anxiety and depression. I was moving my body through what moves I could remember.

I had been practicing yoga for about four years before that. It helped me get through a divorce and this was my choice of exercise in the US. I could practically close my eyes and feel like I was back at home. I knew the practice strictly by repeating the poses over and over again throughout the years. I simply imagined what my teacher would be saying and then allowed my body to recreate the class. Everything finally felt right. I felt safe; even better, I felt alive! I never realized how much movement is medicine until I was locked in a tiny, overcrowded cage, unable to move or stretch for days at a time. It felt so nice to let that energy flow out of me and feel unstuck for a moment. I could feel the stress, anger, and frustration melting off of me. It was liberating to be able to get out of breath and break a sweat. This was the most comforting feeling that I had felt since I had been in Nicaraguan jail, and I was the one who created this kind of peace for myself.

The other girls watched and witnessed the magic of yoga, and what it can do to brighten one's energy. Doing my practice sparked something in all the other girls that made them curious. I wasn't more than 15 minutes into my practice when the girls stopped me and asked me to teach them, too. They wanted to learn and I was more than happy to teach them. *I mean, what else am I going to do here? This can be my way of giving back to them for sharing what little supplies they had with me.* I didn't have much to share, but this was the perfect gift to give them. This was the first time I ever taught anyone yoga, so this was an epic moment for me as well. I never saw myself in the teacher role, but it came naturally. The girls lit up as I taught them! I could only teach them one at a time because there wasn't enough room for more than one person to practice. I also was able to partner the girls up for some fun core work that they could play around with. Basically, it became a party! Most of the girls lined up, waiting for their turn to learn the practice and get my advice on their form. The movement soon became their medicine as well. They all started laughing and smiling and bringing such a joyful energy to our cell after they too, were able to move.

I probably did this for over an hour, and the guys all started to get curious as to what the girls were up to. Since the jails required all of us to be quiet, the girls started to use sign language to talk to their husbands, brothers, cousins, dads, and friends that I was teaching them yoga! Soon after that, there was a shift in that prison that extended beyond the women's cell. Something magical and unexpected happened. Since I had made the girls happy, it made the men happy because the women were happy, and the noise level began to get louder! It started slowly as the guys began thanking me for teaching the girls and lifting their spirits. Then, they started to scream out how much they loved me and thanked God that I had come in there! Not only were they screaming, but they were throwing notes and food, swinging their towels, and all around getting wild! I had never seen anything like this. I was in shock from the positive response to something that felt like fun to me. These people were cheering for me like I was a saint or some kind of a hero. I was overwhelmed with joy that I created these smiles in others, but I started to get kind of scared after it went on for about an hour.

The captain started to get super upset that he didn't have control over his prison. He was walking around staring into each cell with this super pissed-off look on his face. I remember distinctly looking into his eyes when he came across the women's cell. He glared into my eyes as I stood there: tall, strong, sharp, and scared as can be. Right when we had this interaction, Stephanie threw a note and it hit the captain right in the cheek. His face got red, and he kind of growled at her before storming off to look into the next cell. I was so scared that they would take me away and lock me up somewhere where I couldn't cause another riot. Technically, they could've done whatever they wanted to me there; no one would ever know. I was terrified as to what was going to come next with my punishment. Scared and wanting to hide, I decided to cool off in the shower and chill out of sight for a bit while the riot died down. I could hear all the screams of, "I love you," "Thank you, God," and people chanting my name as I showered.

I was in the middle of my shower, when all of a sudden, all of the women came rushing in to tell me something. They were super excited and jazzed about something, but I wasn't sure at first why. I was in shock when they were saying, "Estás libre!!! Vamos, vamos, vamos! Tú eres libre, tú eres libre!!!" *Wait, that means "You're free, you're free, GO GO GO!"* I was confused, but they continued to pull me out of the shower and over towards my things. They were jumping with joy, and I was standing in a towel so utterly lost. The guards were telling me to hurry and get my things before they shut the gate on me. I ended up giving most of my stuff away to the girls because they had been so kind to me. I could get more "things" once I was out. I'm not going to lie. A part of me was sad that I was ripped away from all the girls that fast. I had bonded with them and finally became okay with where I was. There was also the other part of me that was ready to run out that door and never look back. I gave away most of my clothes and gave my favorite loose top to the one girl who was about to have a baby. All the other girls were grabbing for my things to help me, but also to ask if they could have it. I basically ran out of there with my flip flops on and my towel around me (I had more clothes out in the car with my luggage.) I couldn't believe what was happening. I was free in the blink of an eye, and so were the rest of my trip companions. The guards finally took all of our cash, which was around $700 and kicked all of us out because I taught the girls yoga and made everyone happy in prison! *Was this real? Did yoga really just set me free from Nicaraguan prison?*

Yes; it was real. I was given a second chance at life. I was given my freedom again, and the world around me became so much brighter once I stepped outside. Yoga had set me free from Nicaraguan jail; I couldn't believe it. They didn't like that I was able to make the inmates happy and gain control over the guards in there. So, instead of locking me away in a private dungeon secluded from everyone, they released me back into the world so I couldn't impact anyone in the prison anymore.

I immediately called my mom the moment I was released. I saw a bunch of messages on Facebook from her, wondering if I was okay. I started the conversation with, "Don't worry, I'm safe now!" and then proceeded to tell her about my latest adventure. This kind of thing was every mother's worst nightmare! As I look back on it, I realize that I was more excited to tell her than nervous about what she would think. I had made it out, and that was the important part of the story. She had a feeling something was going on because it had been a while since I checked in with her, and because she wasn't able to sleep during those nights. Normally, my mother is always on point at sensing when I need help, or when I'm going through a hard time. She knew something was wrong, but it was her nightmare, knowing she couldn't do anything from so far away. She was just glad I was okay, and for the moment, we bypassed the magnitude of the situation. It was music to my ears to be able to hear her voice again. I thought I was never going to speak to my family again; I thought I was going to be a lost soul on this planet forever.

Then I called my neighbor who was watching my dog. I was missing in action for an extra day, and we were going to stay in Nicaragua that night because it was getting late. Not only that, but we needed rest after what we had been through. That phone call didn't go as well as with my mother. I knew my friend didn't know how to handle Chi and that she was somewhat scared of him before I left, but I didn't realize how severe her fears were. He can be hard to control at times, especially if you don't claim that you're the alpha in the situation. She told me she was scared of him because he wouldn't listen to her, but she would still do her best for the next couple of days. That call had me unsettled, but there was nothing I could do. I didn't have any means to get back to Costa Rica on my own that night, so I waited nervously.

I was going with the flow with my boyfriend and his friends and still tried to make the best of our one night on vacation--our first night of regained freedom! As soon as we got our hotel room, we ended up having passionate sex like wild rabbits to get it out of our systems. That night, we went balls to the wall with excitement that we weren't in jail anymore! We finished that whole bottle of Jameson between the four of us that was left in the back of the car during our stay in prison. After that was finished, we went out on the town in San Juan del Sur looking for more. That night was filled with a celebration of freedom and wild, intense sex! It was almost as if we had a newfound appreciation for human connection. Both of us couples were locked in our rooms, making crazy love all night because we could! We all had thought we were never going to be able to have sex with each other again, so we made the most of our time and enjoyed every minute of our evening.

We drove back the next morning without even making it to the beach to surf. We were too hungover, and the waves weren't even that great, so we ended up driving out earlier than we planned. I was starting to worry about Chi, but I couldn't get us back home any faster. When we finally made it to the house, we opened the door to a horrific scene. Chi bolted out the door as fast as possible, and we looked inside to see why he ran so fast. There was poop, diarrhea, and pee all over the house, like bombs spaced three feet apart, upstairs and downstairs. My neighbor friend got too scared of Chi because he wouldn't listen to her, and he wouldn't go back in the house without growling at her. So, she decided to keep him locked in there for the last three days out of the five that we were gone. This was the moment when I realized I couldn't leave Chi with just anyone. It was a nightmare cleaning all of this up after such a long and exhausting trip. I had to bring the hose inside the house and scrub the whole house down on my hands and knees. Felipe couldn't handle it, so he left to go to the beach while I cleaned. The downstairs was mosaic concrete, and it took a scrub brush broom, tons of water, and house cleaner to get the smell and feces out. Felipe was not happy at all and grew an even bigger hatred for Chi after this. His reaction showed me how it was going to be if I were to stay with him. He was pissed and screamed at Chi and me relentlessly. We were both traumatized. After this, Chi wasn't allowed in the house anymore. Chi knew as well; he was even scared to go in that house. I felt so bad for Chi. He knew something was wrong and could feel that I was in trouble. I'm glad I wasn't in jail for a longer amount of time. I felt so bad that Chi had to go through this, and I was feeling even worse with Felipe screaming down my throat. From that point on, I had to get used to Chi being a free wolf. I know it sounds completely irresponsible, but that was the way it was at the time. I couldn't afford to get my own place and I had all the faith in the world that Chi wouldn't run away from me. He would always come back, and that was all I needed to know in my heart. If anything, I was worried about the other street dogs attacking him, but I knew he was strong and could take care of himself. He would find ways to cool down in the heat of the day by finding mud puddles in the cow fields and rolling around in them. He was stepping back into his wild nature and would come back looking like a totally different dog; but the important thing was, he would come back. There would be mornings when I would wake up and freak out because I couldn't find him anywhere. After giving up the search, we would arrive at the beach to our usual surf spot--and there he was, just waiting for us. It was scary because he had to run down the highway for a bit, but he had his mind set that he wanted to go to the beach. He was free to roam and explore, but it scared the shit out of me! To top it off, the locals didn't enjoy this because most of them were scared of dogs, especially one that looks like a wolf. Chi would get into trouble sometimes, but I had no choice. I should've left Felipe after I found out he cheated on me, or when he took me to jail, or after seeing how he treated my dog. I was too weak, addicted to his dick, and codependent on him to know better. His dog was allowed in the house, but not mine because of what he did while we were away. Chi also had a lot of hair that he was shedding, and he didn't get many baths because he would always find water or mud to roll in. I felt like most of our fights from there on out were about Chi. I wished I had the means to leave this man and be a more responsible wolf mother, but I was only doing the best I could do at the time.

*Side Note: Don't cross borders with drugs or with people that you don't know. I also found that the minute I relaxed into this experience in jail, I was finally freed. It isn't until we become accepting with our surroundings that we can find the inner peace that lives within each of us to get the answers we are searching for. When we finally give up resisting that which is causing us pain, we will see other doors and opportunities arrive. My recommendation--take time to be still. Allow yourself to feel all the feels so you can begin to understand them better. In the stillness of it all is when the true self and answers arise. Have faith and not fear that this world is working for you, and for your highest good.

CHAPTER FIFTEEN

TOO TOXIC TO KNOW BETTER

This relationship with Felipe wasn't all hot and heavy in the love department after a while. I felt like I had become a burden to him, weighing both of us down. The passion, spark, and intensity started to fade between us, and the spark of the new relationship energy began to fade. It took about four months of me being in Costa Rica with Felipe for us to start getting under each other's skin. I jumped into living with him and never gave him a choice about me entering his space. I felt so codependent that I didn't know how to stand on my two feet in that country, nor did I have any money to do so. All of my funds that I made in Miami were depleted and I was back at ground zero. It didn't help that he wouldn't allow me to work because he was too jealous of me possibly meeting other guys.

We played the same roles day after day, with him working, and me cooking and cleaning. We seemed balanced, but it wasn't in my eyes. I began holding a grudge; I felt like I was his slave, and I started to feel trapped, just as I was in prison. I would spend many days waiting for him to come home, sometimes over 14 hours. I didn't have a car or even a bike that I could take to get out to the beach easily, so I ended up staying locked away in the mountains. We were addicted to sex and would still have sex first thing in the morning and then about seven more times that night, but we were *not* happy. We were simply going through the motions of addiction. He made me a list of things I could do around the house to improve it and keep myself useful, and I would chip away at this list as the days passed. There were many days where I would be too depressed to even get out of bed. During the rainy season, things can get very nostalgic and sometimes the days would blur together with darkness. The only time I was happy was when he was inside of me and when no words were spoken. I literally was so addicted to his dick that I would wait around for him and do everything in my power to please him. I couldn't think about anything else. I was punch drunk in love with his penis and didn't care about how unhealthy and unbalanced all the other aspects of that relationship were.

We drank and partied a lot to drown out all the noise of us not being a good match for each other. I knew he had cheated on me, and it made living with him even more challenging. To top it off, he hated my dog and made sure to let me know about it daily. Felipe began to leave the house for longer periods each day. He told me he was working overtime because it was their high season, but I knew he was lying. He didn't want to come home or be around me. At first, I enjoyed the simple life of disappearing into the jungle with no way for people to reach me. Then, I started to go stir crazy when I wanted it all to stop and I wanted my normal life back. I felt like I was trapped. I became so unhappy and would spend my days wondering what the hell he was doing out there without me. I eventually started walking about four miles to the beach to get away from the house for a while, or I would go for long walks in the mountains to clear my mind. If I went to the beach, it was inevitable that I would get in trouble with Felipe, so most days I chose the mountain route. By getting in trouble, I mean that I would meet new friends (boys), maybe smoke with them, and that would get back to Felipe somehow, and he would freak out. Even if I didn't talk to anyone, I would get in trouble for leaving the house because one of his friends would notify him I was out, then he would get upset that I wasn't doing chores at the house to help out.

One "friend" in particular that I met one day on the beach became a game-changer for me. His name was Gustavo. I began to develop feelings for him quickly and without any guilt. Gustavo soon became my Venezuelan lover who would always find a way to cheer me up when he came into town. I met him one day after watching him surfing with his friends in Hermosa. I fell fast and hard for this one. He lived in Pavones, which is at the other end of Costa Rica, and he would pass through town every once in a while for work or to surf. I noticed him there once before, but I lacked the courage to speak to him. I felt like *if Felipe could have his fun, why couldn't I?* I saw this as the perfect opportunity to even out the playing field and give Felipe a taste of his own medicine. No other girl had done that to him in the past; he was always the one to cheat. Gustavo became my new pursuit, and he quickly won my heart over! I thought he was American at first, because he spoke perfect English. It was easy to talk to him compared to the language barrier that Felipe and I experienced. Gustavo knew I was with Felipe, and would always encouraged me to get out and find something better. He warned me about Felipe, and only wanted the best for me from the beginning. He was friends with Felipe's ex, so he knew how Felipe treated the girls he dated; he hated to see Felipe repeating the same patterns of manipulation with me. I knew I needed to get away from Felipe as well, but I was scared and didn't know how. I tried to hide my relationship with Gustavo at first, but it became obvious to everyone around what was going on. It was no surprise to anyone after a while, that anytime Gustavo would come to town, I would find a way to escape or "break up" with Felipe to be with Gustavo for a few nights. Everyone knew us both and they witnessed us strutting our stuff together in town, without a care in the world. *It was a small beach town, and everyone knew everything anyway, so why try to hide?* Felipe hated this, but for some reason, he would still take me back when Gustavo left again. I knew Felipe was still cheating on me too, so I wasn't overly concerned about his feelings. I had my own way of dealing with being cheated on, and that was to cheat back.

Gustavo had a way of taking away all of this pain and bringing pure pleasure in the moment. Gustavo had impeccable timing, too. Every time he passed through town, it would be when I needed some cheering up. This relationship with him worked perfectly for the capacity that I had in my heart at the time. He was there for the moment, and then he would leave; it worked out this way. Sometimes, Felipe made sure to make it impossible for me to get out of the house when he knew Gustavo was in town. I was shooting myself in the foot because I was still living with Felipe and putting up with his manipulation. I don't know why Felipe never kicked me out after this; his reaction was the complete opposite. Every time I would try to pack my things and leave, he would scare off the taxi drivers and threaten them to go away. I couldn't understand why Felipe was still trying to hold onto such a toxic relationship with me, but maybe he was just as addicted to the drama and sex as I was at the time.

This was the time of my life when I stopped caring about myself. The only thing I cared about was sex, whiskey, cocaine, the party scene, and a tan. I mentally checked out to continue this vicious cycle of unhealthy habits. I wasn't making good decisions for myself or my body and mind. I knew I was falling into an addiction with drugs and alcohol, but I continued down this path because I was lost; I only found happiness when having sex, or when my mind was altered, and I was numb to the world. My life was spiraling downwards like a tornado out of control, ripping up my foundation. My relationships with Felipe and my family declined rapidly, making my world filled with darkness and emptiness in my heart.

I was going in circles with the same stupid mistakes again, but in another country, and without the support of my family being so close. This was when I learned I can't run away from my problems; they will come into my life no matter what side of the world I'm on. I was repeating getting lost in alcohol and the party scene, along with another cheating war that seemed so similar to the one I had back at home. *I was running away from all of that in the States, yet I am doing the same damn thing over here. Why? Why do I keep doing this?* It seems like insanity. Well, here I was again. Only this time, I was so far away from my family and friends, or any support group I had back home. I would break up with Felipe only to realize I would fall on my face, and then I would run right back to him and the control that he had over me. I had no real friends in Costa Rica because I wasn't even allowed to get out of the house. The insecurity and the jealousy of his *machismo* attitude became apparent, especially after Gustavo. I was a sitting duck, abusing myself in this relationship by not respecting myself enough to leave. My confidence began to dwindle back down to nothing and, once more, I felt weak and helpless without any energy to do anything about it. My light was diminishing as I became this rag doll toy that he had ultimate control over. I knew Felipe wasn't happy being with me, yet I couldn't figure out why he wanted to keep me around. *Maybe in a weird way he does really care about me.* I suppose sometimes we find ourselves dependent on the drama to fuel us in relationships, whether it is good or bad. We only know what we know. It's a lot harder to start all over again with something new than it is to stay comfortably uncomfortable. I couldn't find the strength to leave him, and he didn't want to watch me walk away, so we found a way to deal with it.

One day, Felipe came up to me in the morning before he left for work and said, "Don't you dare walk outside the house today!" I wondered why he was acting so harshly. He knew I had to walk his dog at some point, but then I understood why. I heard Gustavo's voice laughing over at the neighbor's house. Gustavo and his girlfriend were in town, and they happened to be staying next door for a day and a night because they were friends with our neighbors. I wondered if Gustavo planned this to check in on me. He's never stayed over there before. It had also been about two or three months since I last talked to Gustavo because Felipe kept me on a tight leash after my cheating escapade with him.

A huge part of me wanted to go over there so badly, just to say hi and give him a hug, but he was with his girlfriend, and Felipe would've been so pissed if I had. I didn't want drama for Gustavo, nor did I want drama for myself, so I obeyed. I stayed in the house all day, listening for his laughs and daydreaming about our time together. I sat upstairs on the outside patio in the hammock, being still, so he didn't notice me. I would sit there with my eyes closed, listening to Gustavo talk, wishing so badly that he was talking to me. He knew I was in that house. I could feel how close he was and the curiosity that was running through his brain. That day was torture for me. I stayed inside all day, so depressed, crying my eyes out. I wasn't in prison anymore, but I had made my own prison cell here with Felipe. I was trapped and felt like I had no control over my life. *What was I doing to myself?* I had no idea what my next moves were going to be, so I froze and did nothing but cry.

I had done all of this to myself. If I wasn't promiscuous, if I hadn't gone and messed things up even worse, then I wouldn't be in this untrusting kind of relationship. *Why didn't I get out when we got back from Nicaragua? Or when I found out he cheated on me the first time? No matter how good this dick is, I need to find a way to say goodbye.* For the seven months we had been together, we had broken up a total of ten times. I had my bags packed at all times. It was like we knew it wasn't meant to be, yet we tried to hold onto what we wished it could've been if we both hadn't screwed it up so badly.

*Side Note: You can *not* run away from your problems. They will come back to haunt you until you have faced them and have figured out how to heal from them, no matter how far away you run. These are our bad habits, our cycles of pain that keep repeating in our lives; they make up our shadow side that lives within each and every one of us. The first step to unlocking the healing is to recognize the patterns in your life so you can be more aware of when they come up. It might take years or even a lifetime for you to learn how to break the chains and try another route. The key to unlocking them can only be broken with your permission. In the end, it is your journey and your path--therefore, you are the only one that can make the change and confront your shadow side. Also, if you are addicted to the dick, that isn't love. It's infatuation, which can lead to some very unhealthy tendencies. Be cautious of drama-driven or trauma-based relationships.

Chapter Sixteen

Sink or Swim

There were my rebel days when I'd get fed up with being in that house, and I would go to the beach anyway, regardless of Felipe's demands. One of those days, I met these two girls from California. They were a breath of fresh air! They had just moved to Costa Rica, and they lived right down the street from me. *How perfect!* They were fun, creative, and so easy to talk to because they were from America. *Finally, I found some girlfriends here.* I had one other friend from the States that I had met, named Emily, but I finally found a couple more. (The local girls didn't care for me too much and gave me the cold shoulder.) It didn't take long for them to realize what was going on with Felipe. Most of the time, when they'd invite me to the beach, I'd be too afraid to join them and it became hard to hide his manipulation and the control he had over me from others. Instead, I would say I needed to catch up and do some chores or come up with an excuse that I didn't feel good. Finally, they came up to me and had a talk with me. They told me they couldn't watch this happening to me anymore. This wasn't right, and they were willing to help me come up with a plan to get out. It was like a weight had been lifted off of my shoulders when they offered me a cot in their room that they shared until I could get on my feet again. This was the exit plan I was searching for, and one that had a promising outcome for stability. All the other times I tried to leave, I ended up falling on my face and running back to Felipe, but not this time. I was determined about this change, and now I had the support of my new friends that saw what was going on.

We made a plan to get all of my shit out of Felipe's house while he was at work. I had to do this the right way this time so he wouldn't come home in the middle of it as he had in the past to stop me. It had to be right after he left in the morning because he wouldn't be back till around lunchtime, maybe, if he did come back. The night before, while he was mysteriously still gone, I packed up my things in preparation for a quick and easy exit. I noticed as I was packing that something strange began to happen. It started with a few chirps, and then it became apparent that about five bats were swarming around in the house. We would leave the windows open so a breeze could come through the house because there was no AC, but we've never had bats fly in here. They were darting all over the house and were confused about how to get out. All the while, I had to keep ducking so they wouldn't fly into me. I was freaked out by them, but also saw this as a sign from my angels.

I followed my instinct and looked up the meaning of bats. "The bat teaches us to face the darkness and find the light seen in rebirth. You must face your greatest fears and begin a new chapter in your life. Face your fears so that you may overcome emotional barriers that are holding you back from taking this physical or spiritual journey. As a shapeshifter, he inspires transformation. It is time to follow those new ideas, hunches, and emotions you may not be familiar with. Embrace the possibilities the universe has in store for you. Bat serves as a reminder to let go of our ego so that we may pursue our spiritual growth, and renew thoughts and beliefs on a regular basis. He helps us with inner work, loving our enemy in the way you love yourself and nurturing personal growth in all of its forms. Bat brings gifts of insight, renewal, and increased perceptual skills. Trust your intuition and instincts. He will help you discern the hidden meanings in the words of others. You will be able to hear what is not being said." (I found this at https://www.spiritanimal.info/bat-spirit-animal/)

Wow. I mean, how on point was this for my life right now? It was my confirmation from the universe that I was doing the right thing. I knew it in my heart as well, but this helped to solidify that I was on the right path. I find it super helpful to ask questions to the universe and then let synchronicities and signs be what guides me. This always gives me direction when I'm lost. With a little investigation of following my intuition, I got the answer I was looking for. As I was packing, I was asking myself if this is what I wanted to do, and then this happened. *Now I have no choice. I can't let my own fears stop me from stepping back out into the world and trying to survive on my own.* I could do this! I knew then, that the universe had my back, and I was going to be okay.

The next day, the neighbor helped me pack my things and bring them down the street to my Californian girlfriends' house. It was a small two-bedroom apartment that now had four of us living there. It was tight, but temporary. Their roommate agreed to help me for a bit of time until I found a job, especially after he found out about the situation I was in. I needed to readjust to getting back on my feet so I could get myself out there, find a job, and eventually move out on my own. This was my first time hunting for a job since I lived in Costa Rica. It was harder than I had imagined! Since I didn't have papers or a work visa, I was viewed as an illegal trying to work. If I did land a job, they would have to pay me under the table, and it was less than average pay. The locals are strict about this and don't want to offend anyone in their town by hiring a *gringa* (American girl), so it became a challenge. They like visitors, but it's different when you live there. It becomes personal when you begin to take their jobs and their men. I tried to get a job teaching English at a Montessori school in Hermosa (the one and only school in this town), but I didn't have all the qualifications needed to be a good candidate, nor did I want to do that.

I searched for some restaurants in town and found one that would be opening soon, and they were hiring. It was a little restaurant and bar in Jaco that was owned by American men from New York. They seemed nice, but I always had my intuition telling me something wasn't right about them. I was waiting for this place to open when I also found a second job as a waitress for a home catering service, owned by another American man. It provided a gourmet, in-home catering experience. This was a great little gig because I would get big tips for working one night. However, that was the problem; it was only about one night a week. I had to find another stable source of income in order to make it. I felt it was only possible to get to a job interview if the business owners were American. Since I didn't know fluent Spanish or have papers to work there, the owners of the businesses could get a fine for hiring an illegal immigrant, so it was a huge risk that they had to take. Even though it was illegal for me to work there, I did know customer service, and I was very good at it. Most people in Costa Rica are all on "Tico Time," which is basically whenever the person feels like doing things. They don't rush and they don't care how long it takes; it is ready when they are ready to do it. This would be a good example of the *Pura Vida* kind of life. Yes, it was frustrating, but that was what set me apart from the rest. I knew I could get a job at the new restaurant/bar in town, because I walked by and talked with one of the owners; he was adamant that I returned when they were hosting interviews.

I eventually made enough money doing catering to get my own little cabana on the beach in Hermosa. This room sat on top of a hostel space. It was similar to an attic, or a small triangle room that had the bare minimum. It had a bed that came with sheets, a small nightstand, and that was it. The bathroom was shared with the other hostel guests, and there was a communal fridge that I could store only a small amount of food or drinks in. The owner was also an American man that sought refuge in Costa Rica. This man was so sweet that he was running his business into the ground by being such a kind soul. He always wanted to be there to help others out, and I found this so admirable because, honestly, I needed the help. My rent there was supposed to be $100 a week, but I was never able to pay him that. I think I gave him $300 to move in, and then after that it was always so hard for me to pay on time. I would give him half of everything I made when I did make money. This was the only way I was able to make it on my own at first. It was such a struggle to earn a decent living, and the money was never consistent with my catering gig, so it was hard to budget.

This little triangle room was perfect for me, though. I would fall asleep at night listening to the waves crashing just feet away as I felt the breeze of the ocean coming through my screened window. I was typically found walking around on the beach and had so many options of things to do and people to see and meet. It was a sensory overload of always being in the mix of everything. These were my prime years when I was my wildest. This was when I became a surfer boy magnet. I was fresh meat on the market, and I was always out in my bikini, looking for an adventure.

My mom made a bunch of feather jewelry and sent me a feather extension kit so I could get resourceful. I began to sell these offerings on the beach to the tourists, and even locals, to help me make money. I never thought I'd be one of those beach hustlers, but times were tough, and in order to make money, I had to get creative. At least I didn't have the typical sunglasses or bracelets. Not only did I sell the feather jewelry, but I could also install feather extensions straight into your hair so you could always have feathers in it. Costa Rica was further behind the States when it came to fashion, so I jump started this revolution over there. I also made a bunch of swimsuit cover-ups out of the surfer boys' old t-shirts, which made nice take home gifts for the girls. I would cut them up and braid them and make them into a short dress or a bathing suit cover up. The other girls in Hermosa saw this new trend and started gathering their boyfriends' shirts and asked me to do custom pieces for them, too. It became a sentimental piece that was like a badge of honor for the girls to wear.

I used most of my earnings on rent, cocaine, dog food, and whiskey. I didn't use much money to feed myself. At times, I would go days without eating. I didn't have much of a fridge, so I winged it and adapted. I would wake up and jump in the ocean, and then begin my search for someone smoking weed. Then, I would find some tourists and see if I could help them find anything during their stay in town so I could make some quick money, or score some free drugs. I would hunt for bachelor parties because they were a goldmine of opportunities for me. I would walk along the beach and look for Americans, in hopes of a free party or maybe some food. It was insane the amount of treats they had, compared to the offerings of my humble life. Plus, it was nice to find Americans so I could speak in English. I soon became good at greeting and finding the tourists that needed a little tour guide to show them around. I met some pretty cool people that way, but also some douchebags. Nevertheless, everyday was a hustle. A hustle to find more parties with drugs and alcohol, a hustle to eat, a hustle to pay what rent I could, and a hustle to stay afloat. I had Chi with me during this time, and he was such a trooper! He followed me around wherever I was going on the beach. I personally think he loved being wild and free like I was at the time. At times, he wandered off and disappeared for a while, but most of the time he could sense when I needed him back. He was the best at finding me at the bars at night, telling me it was time to go home, like he was my dad! He would always follow me to the parties or the bars and wait so patiently for me outside the gates. If I went out to try to surf, he would wait at the edge of the water, following and watching me. I couldn't have asked for a better partner in crime to come with me on this trip. He was my angel, my bodyguard, and my best friend in all the ways I needed him to be. I wish he wanted to come to stay up in the triangle room with me, but the staircase was super sketchy. He had a hard time jumping up the stairs because some of them were broken; it was even harder for him to get back down. So, if I wanted him in that room with me, I had to carry him up the stairs, and he wasn't a fan of that either; but I would still force him sometimes.

One night, I was able to catch Chi and tie him to the stairway at the bottom of my cabana. I woke up in the morning to a horrible sight when I looked downstairs. Chi was tied up, and something was terribly wrong with him. He had thrown up all over the place, and the smell was so pungent that it was unbearable to be around! He had been poisoned with rat poison or something of that nature. I looked closer at his vomit to investigate, and it had tons of little plastic squares, the kind you would use to mark an underground pipeline. I couldn't make sense of any of it. A little surfer boy came by and said my dog had been poisoned by a man who lives down the beach. He gave him a bunch of meat that had poisoned bags inside of it, intending to clog his intestines with it. *Why would anyone do this to Chi?* The reply was they were scared of him running free on the beach, and they thought he was eating their chickens and livestock. I suppose seeing a wolf running down the beach was kind of scary to some people, especially those that are scared of dogs. It was more often the case that Costa Ricans were terrified because of all the aggressive guard dogs that they breed to protect their homes, and the overflow of street dogs.

I hoped and prayed that he would make it through this. I felt so bad for him. He threw up all around the hotel grounds that day. I tried to clean up as much of it as possible, but it still left this smell of death. I don't know if I could've made it without Chi. I felt like such a horribly irresponsible mother at the time. I knew Chi wasn't safe there anymore and had to make the hardest decision to let Chi go back and stay with Amanda in the city until my life became more stable, and I could get a better home for us. I never realized it would be so hard over here in so many different ways. I was so lucky I had her as a friend to help me out with Chi. I thought I could do it with him, but I found it to be harder than I could've ever imagined. The challenge to find a good home, have enough money to feed him, and be able to have a fenced yard was proving to be more difficult than I expected. I didn't have a yard, he wouldn't stay with me in my room, and I barely had enough money to feed myself. I would share all of my food with him and he also found a way to gather the food from the rich neighborhoods. Some people caught Chi digging through the trash because they would throw away perfectly good catering food, like it was nothing. He was resourceful enough to survive, like me, but I still felt like a complete failure. I was fucking up my own life, and I didn't want anything else to happen to Chi. I knew he would be in good hands because Amanda and her family had fallen in love with him when he stayed the first time. Luckily, they had a car, so they were able to come to Hermosa and pick him up to take him back to the city. One of the hardest things was to say goodbye to my spirit guide and best friend, again. I knew it wasn't for forever, though, and I knew at least he would be safe.

I came to a lot of profound realizations while living there in that triangle. I was searching for my light and trying to find out what would truly bring me happiness. I wanted it to be love, but to be honest, I was too wild for anyone to love at that time. I wanted and needed the love of friends and family, yet, they weren't there. The friends I did make were tourists, but then they would eventually leave. My idea of searching for happiness was when I found the attention. I craved it every day like a drug. People thought I was the life of the party, and I thoroughly enjoyed being the center of attention, but the local females did not. I had the attention of most of the guys in that town, and even some of their boyfriends tried to pursue me. Half of the time, the guys I would meet wouldn't even tell me they had a girlfriend, which made matters more tense than they needed to be.

Soon after all of this, I got a tattoo on the side of my stomach that says *Dying to Live, Living to Love.* I was looking for love in all the wrong places by trying to live each day to the extreme so I could feel alive. I was killing myself, trying to search for anyone to love me. All I needed was to turn my mindset around and begin to love myself again. I was disillusioned with the idea of what love really was and what I needed for myself. I never gave myself the chance to feel my emotions and work through my issues. I went to Costa Rica to find myself, and I ended up losing myself in paradise. I separated myself from anything familiar to me by moving so far away from my comfort zone, and now I didn't even have my dog by my side.

I did find one thing that felt familiar to me, and that was the party. Not caring became familiar to me. I learned that I have no limits or willpower when it comes to calling it a night. I would always be the last one standing, fiending for more drugs or alcohol as the sun came up. I was terrified to end the night and have the euphoric feeling of the cocaine and Jameson in my bloodstream fade away. I would spend a lot of my nights unable to sleep due to my anxiety about where I was in my life, or what I had just done with "what's-his-name." It may have stemmed from how lonely, depressed, and horny I was, but it was most likely due to all the cocaine I was putting in my veins. I would have a lot of a-ha moments when I was in this state of mind, going a thousand miles an hour. I documented most of these moments in my handwritten book, but to be honest, going back and trying to make sense of some of my entries during this time frame was a challenge. I would get super emotional and scribble my writing, or I would end up channeling something else as I wrote, and most of it didn't make sense. But sometimes I would pop out some gems. Here are a few of my entries during this time to give you guys an idea of where I was.

July 23rd, 2014

Learning How to Love

As babies, we come into this world with the instinct to love. We have no ego; we have no jealousy or any outside influences to cloud our judgment. For most of us, we are surrounded by family and people who love us unconditionally, tending to our every need and desire.

Throughout life, I feel like we are searching for the same euphoric feeling of pure love. We can search for a lifetime, but it isn't until we are ready to accept all parts of ourselves that we will receive full acceptance of others. To truly love yourself and all of your imperfections is a hard feat to figure out. To do this, I think it takes being able to love yourself and nurture yourself and your temple; you must know yourself and trust yourself. Get to know your strengths, your weaknesses, your goals, your temptations (because we all have them), and recognize when these patterns arise. If you know yourself, you can understand how to nurture and love yourself, this can be what you attract. When you can be in your light and live with integrity of what feels right for you, then things will start to magnetize towards you.

You can search your whole life for the one person to love for the rest of your life, but who knows if it's forever, or for a period of growth in your life? Whether for a lifetime or a moment, when you love someone, you can feel it in your veins and in your heart. You can say, "I love you," but it doesn't mean anything until you live this kind of love through your daily actions. You're not supposed to lose yourself or your focus on your goals and dreams when you fall in love. When you are truly sharing your aspirations with someone deserving of you, you will have the support you need to flourish.

Knowing how to love is natural by birth. It's all the issues, traumas, and abuse that make the haze over the heart heavy to bear, and hard to love. Knowing how to love is a process that I'm determined to figure out one day. It involves trial and error and putting your heart on the line. Learning how to do this with complete loving-kindness is not easy, especially if you're trying this with someone you aren't supposed to be with. Nothing good worth having in life is ever easy to get. Stay focused if you want it, show it in your actions, believe it can be possible, and be willing to have it all crashing down in a heartbeat if it goes that way. Loving someone has no beginning or end date set in stone. Don't try to plan for the future; don't dwell on the past. Love comes in the now--in the present. Don't run when it is in front of you. If you want to be loved, you have to first learn how to love yourself. This, for me, is the hardest thing to understand at the moment. I want to get it so badly, but I keep having this repeat of failures and disappointments. I need to learn how to be happy on my own and just fucking marry myself!

Trust, respect, and freedom are key to having a healthy relationship for me. This is what I know is important. If that person can't love me for who I am, then that's not the kind of love I need. Maybe it will be only lust, or maybe it's infatuation, or maybe it's because I feel the need to have someone next to my side with the hope that they will change or get better. Loving yourself is key to knowing who you are, what you are worth, and what you deserve. It's a hard road learning how to love and discovering who you are, but follow your heart and instincts; they will ease the tension of the learning curve. Eventually, I will open my eyes and heart to find the light and truth within myself.

August 17th, 2014

BREATHE!!! It's hard being so far away from my family, friends, and wolf right now, but I'm learning more and more about *myself everyday. I am stuck in Costa Rica, and I've come to terms with feeling lost at this point in my life. I'm accepting and surrendering to it instead of fighting it. If I had to go home right now, I wouldn't be able to do it. I don't even have enough money to buy a plane ticket home, nor am I able to get my wolf back with the $2,000 it cost me to get him here. My parents declared bankruptcy and have no extra money to send me to help get me home. I have no savings or credit cards because I wasn't able to pay my bills and fell on my face when I got here. Totaling it all up, I am about $7,000 in debt with collections back in the States because my dream job was a scam. I couldn't go back now, even if I wanted to, and I have to come to terms with it.*

I am happy here, though. I've become content with living a humble life with no WiFi, no mail, and no connection to my old life. Everything here is fresh and lush and the animals are so vibrant and plentiful! Costa Rica is my new beginning to a laid back and simple life. Work is the only hard part about living here.

After a long break, I ended up going back to Felipe because I was once more without a job. I don't know what I would do if it weren't for him. He has helped me so much, taking me in, feeding me, and giving me rides around town. He has truly been the closest thing to family for me here, even though we don't always get along. We fucked up our whole relationship from the beginning, but there is this underlying need to love and care for each other, even after we saw our ugly sides come out. For me, it was so much more of a bumpy road when we weren't together. I barely ate; I was wild, and had no limits. I felt lost on my own even though I tried to find my way. It was more like I was in a blacked-out dream that was out-of-order and constantly hungover. I am so grateful to him for opening up his home and his heart to help me once more, especially after what I did the last time we broke up.

I had a bad scare with one of my rendezvous one night when I went to the city. I felt somewhat off during the days that followed, but I had never gotten an STD before, so I wasn't sure if it was a yeast infection from the heat and humidity, or if I had picked up something. A foolish decision on my part was to sleep with Felipe before knowing what was going on with me.

One morning, I was uncomfortably walking his dog in the neighborhood when these three American Staffords came running into the street to attack us. These dogs were massive and seemed like they were pitbulls on crack. Felipe's dog got too close to their fence and they all three went wild and squeezed out underneath the dinky chain-linked fence. It was such a brutal attack that has left me scarred for life. These dogs were aiming to kill his dog, and I couldn't let that happen, especially after I might have given him an STD. I did my best to protect his dog and was grabbing these dogs by the back of the neck and throwing them off her like Hercules. I had these mama bear instincts kick in, I suppose. All the while, there were six Costa Rican men fixing the street three houses down with shovels, watching us; doing absolutely nothing to help me! I'm screaming for help as I'm trying my best to intervene, and then the alpha dog saw what I was doing and decided to try to attack me. He ran around the side of the fight and jumped up to bite the left side of my face and neck. I had some angels lift my arm up right in time to put that in his mouth, instead of my face. He then proceeded to lock his jaw on my upper left arm and pull me to the ground. I was terrified. I had this dog's piercing eyes staring into my soul, and if he went in for another bite, it was going to be my face. Luckily, at that exact moment, the neighbor opened up their gate and it made all the dogs scurry off in different directions. His dog ran home, and I was dragged into the neighbors' house to keep me from fainting. So much blood was gushing out of my arm from three tooth punctures. It tore one of my muscles open and it was a gaping wound. The neighbors called the owners of the dogs, and they took me to a private clinic where I received antibiotics and a pain shot in my ass, after they gave me stitches.

I guess that was a blessing in disguise because I needed antibiotics to cure the STD that I picked up. My last adventure was to visit my dog in the city. I met a musician at the bars and ended up going home with him that night. Well, this stranger ended up giving me chlamydia. I didn't realize it until after I had already slept with Felipe. It was two days later when the dog attack happened and I got super strong antibiotics, yet Felipe was the one left with the symptoms of bumps and painful urination. It was humiliating that I brought that back to him and felt so horrible. This dog bite was my karma for doing this to him, but it also helped to keep me around because I saved his dog. He ended up being nicer about it than I expected him to be. The only thing he wanted me to do to fix this was go into town to buy the medicine to cure it. Thank God!

*A huge part of me feels so guilty for bringing my dog to another country and not even being able to be around him. I'm so lucky, though, because if Chi would've been in that dog fight, I wouldn't have been able to afford the vet bill. At least he's safe with my best friend in the city. I'm so lucky to have her helping me with Chi. It makes me feel so guilty to give Felipe's dog all the love, though, and not my own. A piece of my heart is missing without him close watching over me. Felipe's dog I are sitting here, healing our wounds and bonding after our experience together. I have to remember to **just breathe** when I feel like this. Be patient, and everything will work out the way it is supposed to. It's in these moments when you sit back and trust the universe. It's hard when you feel like you're walking with a blindfold over your eyes, and nothing seems to be going right, having this faith in these moments and believing things will get better will be worth it. Just remember, keep breathing*

October 2nd, 2014

So, I'm sitting at the house alone again, waiting for Felipe to get home. It's been over 14 hours since he left. I wonder if he even wants to come home to me. The other day he called me a, "Disgusting Bitch" because of what happened when I went to the city. His niceness soon faded to anger. I didn't mean for that to happen. I might have been a little crazy when I first got here, but there is no need to call me names like that. I can't get past it when someone says such hurtful things. Every time he tries to touch me, I hear his words diminishing me, and I'm left feeling full of anxiety and sadness. I deserve better. Once the name-calling begins, it's hard for me to open up my heart and legs to someone. I learned that in my relationship with my ex-husband.

So, I've recognized another pattern here. Noticing what the pattern is, is the first step to changing it. I get myself stuck in abusive relationships and living situations where it's hard to get out. I choose to be comfortable with what I know, even if it is an uncomfortable situation. I'm too weak to leap into the unknown because I don't understand my limits or how to say no. I live with my boyfriends, and when it ends, I end up homeless and back in a state of desperation once more. I fall for the savior type, as I play this helpless victim role. It's more convenient and affordable to live together, and I fall in this trap. In the process, I lose my identity.

It's also the slow season, and no one is hiring at the moment. The restaurant in town I was going to work for isn't open yet, and now it's a waiting game. I have no work, no money, my dog isn't even with me, and I am on the verge of a failing relationship that I only came back to because I had no other choice. What the fuck am I doing with my life?

I need to learn to rely on myself first. It's a lot harder for me to pull up my pants and do it. I came here to learn something about myself and grow as a human, not to repeat my past and lose myself. I guess only I can change my reality; I can't and run from myself and my past. If I want my life to change, I need to be the one to change it because no one else is going to do that for me. I have one more month before business starts to pick up and I will be able to see money flowing in again. My *bags are still packed over in the corner, and I am not planning on ever unpacking them. There's no point when I know I'm not supposed to be here. Once it's high season, I will be able to have more control over my life and be able to change my reality. So, what the fuck do I do in the meantime? Practice patience and understanding, I suppose. All I do at the moment is sit at home waiting for Felipe to get home, cook, clean, walk his dog (even though now I am traumatized to do so), and watch movies. I guess life could be worse. I could still be in Nicaraguan jail. I don't dare leave the house to go to town or to the beach anymore; it isn't worth it. Honestly, all I want to do is to hide from the shame that I created for myself. I need to reserve my energy for what's about to happen to me and avoid unnecessary fighting. I can feel myself losing what little bit of light I have left and my strength in myself; it's time to lay low and recharge. The past will continue to repeat itself until the lesson is learned. It's time I choose a different route to get a different result.*

October 10th, 2014

I have three months left before I have reached my one-year goal of living in Costa Rica. That was how long I gave myself to figure out if this is the life for me. If I went home now, I would be leaving my dog behind and walking home with my tail between my legs like a failure. I couldn't bear ending things this way and doing that to my conscience. I don't have the funds to get Chi back to the States with me, but I am determined to find a way. I'm not leaving this country without him. I feel it in my heart that things will work out eventually. I would have never thought it was going to be this challenging, though. My mind is blown away with how hard it is to make a decent living over here.

To be honest, prostitution is legal here. Every day that I go walking around on the streets in the city, I get asked by at least two to five guys if they could pay to have time with me. "Is this really the only way that I can make money here?" I have used my wits to turn them down every time so far, but it's at a point where it has me questioning. I mean, I was at the point where I was struggling to feed myself. I could do it, but would I be proud of myself? Would I be able to look at myself in the mirror the next morning? I have awkwardly turned down the offers that have come already because I wasn't able to answer the questions above just yet. This gave me a whole new perspective on American men. Now I know firsthand, as I am witnessing this other side of our culture that is hidden from the perfect white-picket-fence marriage. I never even knew this existed, yet I was completely perplexed by its perpetual presence. I can kind of get it because I used to work at a strip club, but this was a whole new level of not being able to trust men. Most of these men were married or have fiancées, wives, or girlfriends back home, and they weren't even thinking twice about paying for sex with another person. They believe that because they are in another country it doesn't matter and no one will find out.

In Jaco, there is even a place where you can pose to take pictures to make it look like you're out fishing with your friends, but in reality, they are right outside the casino where all the prostitutes hang out. There is a green screen behind the people to make it look different every time. It's insane what I have seen since I arrived here. It's been hard to get used to this way of life, but this is how it is here. This is how the women feed their babies and pay their rent. It's a reality that I am not sure I'm ready for. There are so many opportunities to fail and fall on your face here. I call this town "Temptation Station." This place has temptations lurking around every corner. Every day here is a challenge to turn down good coke, a wild party, an exotic gorgeous lady, alcohol, and a new experience. It's crazy how I didn't choose Jaco, Costa Rica; this town chose me. I have had to deal with some real demons of my own since I've been here. I've found myself becoming addicted to cocaine because it is so pure and good here that I can't go a day without it. I wake up and can't stop thinking about it until I find a bump. This was never what I came here for. I guess this is a test from the universe as to what path I'm going to choose for myself.

While I'm here, I might as well do some "research" in the dark. I find myself walking alongside others in the same dark place with their demons when I stay out into the late hours of the night. I like to ask the people I meet passing through here, "How do you find your light?" I mean, I'm here writing a book about it, why not ask people what they think about how to get to theirs? Might as well spark the conversation and plant the seeds in some people's minds. This question is my driving force right now because I feel so far away from mine. I can vaguely see it shining up ahead, but I can't feel its warmth or comfort in the darkness; yet, I know it's there.

Tonight, I labeled myself a runaway. I run when things get tough. As I write this, everything I own is packed and ready to leave Felipe in a moment's notice. Why? I have realized that this is my defense mechanism. I hide when I get depressed, I run when my fight or flight takes over, and I feel more comfortable hiding in a bush by myself rather than dealing with reality. I have found that the trigger that will set me on fire is verbal abuse. Being called names always sends me into a tailspin. It hits me right at the core, and I feel like it all stems from when I was initiated into high school. Since then, I was labeled as the "biggest fucking slut" at Robert E. Lee, and that name haunts me even to this day. Being young, I thought I would at least have fun with it and make the label correct, but in the end, I ended up hurting myself even more with my own careless actions. I found that by adding whiskey and cocaine to the mixture, I only became more reckless and lost all the respect for myself and my body. I can tell that over the years, I have some wires mixed up in my brain and heart when it comes to having a loving and nurturing relationship.

My mantra has been "Love Yourself First," and it's helping me to forgive myself for all the pain I've caused my heart. Trust me, I wish by now I knew how to love myself and find my light. The *only thing I do know is it starts by getting to know yourself and loving **all** of yourself; the good and the bad parts. My mom was the one to tell me after I moved to Costa Rica, "You can never run away from yourself." I ran away anyway, thinking I could, and now all I have is myself, my thoughts, my consequences, my guilt, my fear, my shame, my weaknesses, and my insecurities. I have no backbone of family or friends to help lift my spirits. It's almost as if I went away to hide and purge out the nasty side of me that I didn't even know existed. I have so much time to sit and think about what all I have done with my life. All I have is myself, and I want to stand strong and be fierce right now because no one else is going to help me do it. I need to open my eyes and be the person that I want to become. I guess what I am trying to say is, confront your issues head-on, whatever they might be. Give them the space and attention they need to heal. Know them and own them, even if you don't like them. Find the patterns to your failures and notice what keeps coming up when you try different outcomes. What is blocking me from happiness? Let's start by not running from that! It's too easy to avoid confronting the real issue by sweeping things under the rug. Eventually, these weaknesses will come up to the surface. I can't run away from myself forever.*

The rainy season is nearly over, and then I will be able to move out of Felipe's house and make it on my own with confidence. That is one thing that will bring back some happiness--if I regain my pride and dignity to prove that I can live on my own. I didn't come to paradise to get right back in the kind of abusive relationship that I ran away from in the first place. This pattern will only change if I step up to the plate and change it for myself. Leaving Felipe is the only way that my self-love and respect can come back into my world. The more I sit here and cry, the more anxiety I have, and the more of my light and power disappear from my soul. I want this to work with Felipe, but honestly, it's not possible. There's too much anger and betrayal that has weakened us. There's too much distrust and an unbalanced control that has poisoned any hope for a loving relationship. I do know that the person I choose to be with shouldn't give me this kind of anxiety, verbal abuse, and panic attacks to the point where I can't breathe. (Read that again.) I feel it sucking the life out of me.

Chapter Seventeen

Stepping Out into the Real World

Not long after writing this journal entry, I packed up my things and moved out once and for all from Felipe's house in Hermosa. I needed a fresh start on my own, in Jaco. I had enough of my light being taken away by this relationship. I had my taxi angel help me move out and drive me into the city when Felipe left for work. I found a small efficiency room to share with another surfer girl. It wasn't much, but it was all that I could afford on my own for the time being.

The restaurant that I had been waiting to open was finally doing their training, and it was right down the street from this place. I was happy to have an actual waitress job and start making a steady income again. The owners of the restaurant were American men who had shady attitudes. At this point, you would think I'd get used to seeing this side, but it was hard to cope with sometimes. I, of course, was the only American girl working there. I noticed how they gawked and sexually harassed the other waitresses, and me. They were taking a risk by hiring me without papers, so I stayed silent about their comments. I put up with this because I couldn't lose this job. It was my ticket to freedom.

One night at work would change my life forever. I was approached by a younger man who was a stockbroker from New Jersey. It was his second or third night coming into the restaurant, and I made the mental note that he was a great tipper. He seemed charming enough when he offered me $1,000 to sleep with him. I was offered money by so many men while living in Costa Rica, but never that much. It made turning him down fucking hard. My jaw dropped because I wasn't sure if he was serious or not. He continued to promise me that this would be a night to remember, and I couldn't help but think about how much that money would help me out. I could get my own place and not have to live with this girl (and her boyfriend that stayed over every night) in one room anymore. I thought, *Well, at least I can choose who I sell my body to.* This guy seemed like he would be someone I might hook up with anyway. *What's the harm in making some money and having a little fun while I do it!?* Like I said, it's Temptation City, and you have to be a strong individual to say no multiple times a day. Money was my weakness, and someone had finally put a price on me that I couldn't refuse.

I went to his condo that night and couldn't believe what I was about to do. I was nervous and didn't know what to expect. This was my first time doing something like this. When I arrived, he supplied me with plenty of Jack Daniels and cocaine to loosen me up. He kept boasting about how much money he makes in the stock market and how he keeps up with all of it. He even tried to show me on the computer, but all of this information went in one ear and out the other. I wanted to get this over with so that I could get my money and be on my way. My heart was racing enough as it was without all the cocaine running through my veins; those few lines only made it that much more intense. I felt like running then, but I chose not to. I was committed and was going to see this through so I could be comfortable living on my own for a while. It was sad that this had to be the way to make money here, but at this point, I was desperate, single, and saw this as an opportunity to get ahead for a while.

After about seven shots of whiskey and four lines of blow, it was time to do business, and we moved things into the bedroom. This time, in particular, I was prepared with my own latex-free condoms. I am a sexual person, so I make sure to bring these around with me since I have an allergy to latex. I made sure to secure the condom, then proceeded to start on top to give him his money's worth. At first, it was fun and enjoyable, and everything was going smoothly. Then, in an instant, something switched. He grabbed me and flipped me on my back, and that's when things started to go south. He was holding me down as he ripped the condom off and continued to have sex with me. I was screaming for him to stop and was so outraged at what he had just done. At this point, I was squirming to get him off of me, and I kept repeating for him to stop, but this only irritated him even more. I don't like to have sex with anyone who isn't my boyfriend without a condom (especially after my last scare.) That's my rule. End of story. But, at this point, it wasn't sex. I was being raped. I couldn't move because he was holding my arms down, and the more I struggled, the more his grip tightened. I remember, at one point, I was yelling for him to stop, and to keep me quiet, he punched me in the face. That sparked a whole new level of crazy in him, and he continued to fuck and punch me for another five to ten minutes as he went on raping me. I was crying at this point and had no choice but to keep trying to do everything in my power to get this man off of me. I finally kicked him off of me and gathered my clothes as quickly as I could and ran out of that condo half-dressed, without being paid. I felt like I was running for my life, and I just wanted to get away before he tried to do that to me again.

Ashamed, I was shaking and in shock about what had just happened to me as I walked back out onto the streets of Jaco. *Did I just do this to myself?* I put myself in that vulnerable position, but I didn't realize I was going to be violated like this. I chose to put myself in an unsafe space without anyone knowing what I was doing, and nobody to help me if I needed it. Not only did I agree to sell myself for money, but the danger that goes on when you pass through that door was a whole new shock to the system. At least at strip clubs you have bouncers, but out here, all you have is yourself. Once you pass through that door, you have no one to protect you. *Is this really what the women in this town have to experience?* This is how people get killed and go missing. The seriousness of this never even crossed my mind until I was running for my life. I was oblivious and thought nothing could go wrong. I thought he was a nice guy, but he snapped and went insane.

People can get fucking crazy, and when you add drugs and alcohol to the mix, you're just asking for trouble. Without a bodyguard or a man to protect you, you put yourself at risk. Apparently, there are guys that get a percentage to wait outside the room to make sure nothing like this ever happens. I guess I was too embarrassed to ask anyone for help because I didn't want to be known in town for that. I did have a few guy friends who knew the game and protected certain girls when they asked, though. It's strange to get used to seeing this kind of lifestyle on a daily basis while walking in the streets of Jaco, but this job was a way of life for many people there. This was a business. I couldn't imagine having to worry if I was going to be abused or raped against my will on a daily basis. I learned quickly, that there are some men who pay for sex so they can get a whole different kind of experience, like mine.

I went to work the next day with a black eye that looked eerily similar to my co-worker's. The bartender, a sweet Tico (Costa Rican male), asked me where I got it from, and I told him the story. He ended up telling me that there was another waitress from our restaurant that had the same story from the same guy, but from the night before me. I couldn't believe it. We both experienced this kind of evil from this man. My heart went out to her, and I felt her pain immediately. We never spoke about it, but we both knew and were processing this the same way: With shame, guilt, and disgust written all over our faces. Not only that, but this guy kept showing up to our work, acting as if nothing had happened. I couldn't believe I had the guts to ask him for my payment! I guess with the support of the bartender and my co-workers, I felt safe enough to do so. He told me he had his money back at the condo and to meet him there after work, but there was no way in hell I was doing that. I told him to bring it to me, and he said he would, but he kept coming back the next day empty-handed. This guy had some serious mental issues and enjoyed playing these games with me. Honestly, I wanted him gone and I would prefer to never see him again, even if that meant not getting paid.

My bartender friend said he would call some guys and scare this guy out of town for us. Most of the intimidating and scary street guys in Jaco loved me because I wasn't afraid of them. I would talk to them and show them just as much love as I would any other friend. When they found out what this guy did to me, they made sure to fix the problem. I never got paid, but I never saw this guy again after that. I didn't know what they did to get him to leave, nor did I want to know. The Tico men were super protective over their women because of all the dumbass Americans that get drunk over there and treat women like pieces of shit. Just because some are for sale, they think all of them are. They snap behind closed doors and do fucked up shit with them because they are "paying customers." My viewpoint on men was forever changed. I saw and experienced a side of my culture that makes me sick to my stomach. It's like they come to another country to release the evil that they hide from their family and friends in their real life. After this, I had some hardcore shame that I had to walk around with; I couldn't shake it. I didn't want to feel anything for a while. I was fucking up my life even more by getting more wasted than normal now that I was single, and freshly raped.

CHAPTER EIGHTEEN

HERE COMES THE WILD CHILD

I spent my nights raging it at every ladies' night and party spot I could find. I couldn't sit still and I felt as if I couldn't miss out on anything. One night, I met a boy named Beto, who ended up changing the game for me. Beto came into my life at the perfect time. I was going through some trauma and pain from my last sexual experience and I honestly didn't know if I was ever going to get past it. He helped me in ways that I never knew were possible. Since my rape when I was a teenager, I have a hard time allowing anyone to touch or kiss me downstairs. I don't like it because I have flashbacks of that night when my classmate's dad drugged and raped me, especially if they touched me in a similar way. The combination of my two rapes had me losing hope of being able to open up again. When you first meet someone, the evolution of the relationship requires touching and exploring all parts of the body. This is the natural and normal way foreplay begins. Most times when that happens during foreplay, I have to completely ruin the mood by telling them why I don't want to be touched there. Other times it goes straight to sex and I get to avoid that awkward conversation altogether. No one wants to talk about rape right before sex.

Beto had a different way of going about it. He was sweet and understanding when I told him why I didn't want that, but encouraged me to transmute my trauma so I could get on with living my life. I'm so glad I opened up to him because he knew what he was doing with his hands, which made a huge difference. This kid had some kind of magic up his sleeves, because when he touched me, it was almost as if he was touching me in the exact opposite way of my traumatic experiences. It was like a puzzle he was trying to solve, and he figured me out. It's safe to say, Beto opened up the floodgates! I never had produced that much liquid before during sex, and especially not from someone fingering me. This guy made me do more than just cum. He unlocked this door that had never been opened, and it was amazing! Not only was he able to help me get past my trauma, but I was comfortable enough to relax and let him do his magic. I don't know where he learned how to do this trick of his, but he should really make a video describing to men how to do this. He could make a fortune! Most guys don't know what they are doing down there and I was excited to be with one who did. I became hooked instantly and fell hard, fast. I don't know what kind of spell this guy put on me, but the way he touched me was unlike anything I had ever felt before, and I had to explore this more.

This guy became a new addiction to add to the list! Beto was a tour guide for bachelor parties that passed through town. Part of his job description would be to get party favors and women to entertain the party-goers. There was always a stash of drugs at his house and I made sure to take a mental note of that. Shortly after meeting him, I moved in with him and his roommate/business partner, Juanca. They had a house in the center of town, and it was even set up with my own room. I loved it there because I was able to bring Chi back to stay with me. We were finally in a gated house so he couldn't run away (there was no grass, but I had a way to keep him safe.) I was so happy to have my Chi boy back in my arms! All I needed to do was come up with $300 to pay rent each month, which seemed doable. I was still working at that restaurant as a waitress and also hustled to help find weed or drugs for tourists on the side. It was typical for them to ask me first because I was American and they figured I would be less likely to rip them off, which was true.

I was living with them for about two months and I was having a hard time coming up with rent one month. Beto and Juanca had this one bachelor party they were taking care of and they asked me if I wanted to work it to be able to pay rent that week. I was scared that what happened before was going to happen again, but Juanca reassured me that he was a phone call away, and that he was there if I needed him. At least I would have someone protecting me this time. So, I figured why not try to change my perspective about this profession and give it one more shot, but with protection this time. Beto understood the game and the hustle in that town. With his blessing, we talked about what my going rate would be. Most of the other girls at the party were going for $100, but I was an American and more of a rarity, so I went for $200 instead. Honestly, it wasn't the price that I would have picked, but it was one that worked.

Juanca dropped me off in Hermosa at a private villa for the bachelor party. He told me to call him when I was ready to be picked up, and he would be back to get me. Walking into the party, I could tell instantly that this group of guys were going to be super fun! They knew how to party and they were refreshing to be around. Since I was the only American girl there that spoke fluent English, they were all drawn to talk to me. The other girls were a little thrown off by me being there, and they gave me the cold shoulder while they were sizing me up at first. It became a priority for us to pick the men that we wanted to have sex with. I found one of the guys to be super attractive, and we automatically hit it off. I gravitated towards him and made sure to claim him as mine. *Maybe this was going to be a good experience after all.* I felt like he was a firefighter or a personal trainer of some sort from Chicago. He was extremely sweet and confident in himself, which made him even more attractive to me. Overall, we had great chemistry and were thoroughly enjoying each other's company. I explained to him how I got myself into this situation, and he was understanding and kind about everything. All the party favors were being passed around, and the inhibitions began to fade. It came time for the guys to get locked away in their rooms for some fun time with their girls. My guy and I stayed outside by the pool with the bachelor to keep him company because he was the only one not partaking, which I applauded. This bachelor was faithful and truly one of a kind. I decided that just because he couldn't partake, didn't mean he couldn't watch. My guy agreed, and we decided to have sex outside in front of the bachelor and anyone else who was still outside, or on their balconies.

All the local Ticas couldn't believe the balls I had; nor could I. Maybe I earned some credibility with a few of them. It didn't matter to me; I was getting my rent money and having an enjoyable time doing it. This guy took charge and picked me up, and I loved it. It was wild and fun, and what I needed to make a comeback in this game after my last experience. The bachelor got to watch the whole thing as he was DJing for us. He couldn't join, but we made sure to give him a good show. We ended up having sex three times--but then I ran out of condoms. Little did I know, I could have charged him three times and made $600 instead of $200, but I was new to all of this and I was in the moment. After the third condom was used, I knew I had to get out of there. I was extremely attracted to this guy, but I wasn't going to have sex without a condom.

I tried to call Juanca, but of course he didn't answer. I called him until my phone died, then I did the only thing I had control of to get out of there. I didn't even give myself time to think. I gathered my things as fast as I could, ran out of that house, and took off down the beach with my heels in hand. The only thing I forgot were my favorite panties because I couldn't find them in time. I ran about two miles down to the nearest neighborhood and ran to the security desk at the front entrance. I knew they had a phone I could use. Since I didn't have Juanca's number memorized, I ended up calling a taxi to come to pick me up. I was extremely drunk at this point, and the reality of what I did began to sink into my heart. I needed to get home safely and curl up in a ball for a day or two. The taxi came to pick me up and I began my taxi cab confessional. I explained what I had just done and how lost I was living over there without my family. I was doing one of those drunk cries where I was realizing my world was crashing down on me. I couldn't believe that this was my life and how I was paying rent. *Who am I? What is going on? Is this what I want to wake up with on my conscience?* I started to have doubts about my actions and what my mother would think of me if she knew. I was trying to make it on my own, yet this was no way to do it. I had to keep telling myself that I did this to survive. I tried to avoid breaking down in front of the taxi driver, but I did anyway. It was about 20 minutes to get back home, but I talked with the taxi driver for a good hour after we arrived at 4 a.m. I cried to this stranger about how badly I missed my family and how I wished I could hug them to get grounded again. I was beginning to go down the rabbit hole, thinking that I might not ever get to see them again. I felt so lost and like I had gotten myself stuck in another country with no way out. I had no WiFi or any way to connect with them. When I didn't talk with my family, it felt like it pulled me farther away from who I was at the core. I was filling my life with darkness and shame, which began to weigh on my shoulders. I had nobody but myself to bring me back to my light. I wasn't strong enough to do that for myself. I was becoming a lost soul that was slowly being eaten alive by this town and its harsh reality. I ended up giving the taxi driver $40 out of my $200 for listening to me and letting me cry to him. By the time I got out of the car, the words he had told me in broken English were to, "Call your mother in the morning, okay?" I had so much shame about my life that I didn't even know if I could speak to her. She would be able to feel it right away. By being in another country with no real connection back home, I was hiding away in my pain, and no one even knew.

I was too drunk to even open the door to the house that night. I swear, though, most doors there were like a puzzle. I ended up finding a mattress on a pool table in the car-port and passed out there for the rest of the morning. This house was in the center of town, so when the sun rose, everyone walked past our place to get to the beach. Juanca tried to pick me up to take me inside, but Chi was growling at him while he stood strong by my side. He was growling and warning Juanca not to touch me. He left me there until I finally awoke around 2 p.m. When I woke up, I realized that I was basically on display for everyone to see me without my panties on. I had super short cutoffs on, but everything was hanging out when my legs were apart. *Way to keep it classy, Allison.*

Soon enough, Beto and Juanca went back out to the bachelor party to check on the group, only to discover the wildness that happened the night before. Apparently, I was the talk of the weekend because everyone kept raving about how great of a treat I was for all of them. I felt bad that Beto had to hear about the experience with this group, but at the same time, he did give me the go-ahead to do it. You could tell he hated it when he came home and threw my panties back at me. I guess the rule should've been *you can do it as long as I don't have to hear about it.*

After that experience, Beto became extremely distant. He never looked at me the same after that night, which only brought on more shame and depression into my life. Once more, I had this heavy guilt that filled my heart like drying concrete. I had just lost the one man who was able to open me up and make me cum with his hands. I lost him because I felt like I needed to do this to survive and keep a roof over my head. I couldn't believe how fast he turned cold towards me. To nobody's surprise, it didn't take Beto long to find another love interest while I was still living there. It soon got so awkward that I ended up having to move out. This was a good thing though, because I finally had my own space for me and the Chi boy.

I knew it was time to leave that house when Chi started acting up there. He was always good at telling me when it was time for things to change. He kept finding ways to escape from that house and run away to the beach. Most of the time, it was because Juanca was too intoxicated to remember to close the gate. Juanca was scared of Chi and had a hard time chasing after him once he was out. One day, my friend found Chi at the police station, and pulled over to see what was happening. They were about to sell him to the veterinary clinic in San Jose to make some money. Thankfully, my friend Josemar claimed Chi as his, and demanded that they give him back. The police knew that Chi was mine, but Josemar was a well-known surfer in that town and that helped out a lot. They didn't want to be exposed for their dirty dealings, so they agreed to give Chi to Josemar. Apparently, someone was walking home with takeout food and Chi was following them down the street, hoping he could eat some. That's when the person walking called the police. Roaming free on the beach in Hermosa got him poisoned, and Chi running free in the city of Jaco got him arrested (sounds like me.) That day he brought Chi back to me and told me that I needed to step up and be a better mother. He didn't want to be friends with me after that because he didn't care for my life choices. I needed a friend like this to step up and be so straightforward. This was a huge wake-up call for me, and I'm grateful for his sternness. I did need to be a better mother and be more responsible for my dog. From that day forward, Chi remained on a leash with me at all times if he was out walking the streets. It seemed as if we both needed to shape up our lives and find a stable home for us both. It was time we both stepped out of our rebellious roles and started taking care of each other instead.

It took me 13 months living over there to be able to do this, but I finally found a sweet, humble home. Finally, I had something to call my own. This home was a tiny one-room efficiency without AC or even windows, but it was mine. The owner was a sweet woman that I ended up calling Mama. It was a fourplex that was on the corner of a busy street. She helped me build a little fence to keep Chi from roaming into the neighbor's side of the porch, and she welcomed me with open arms. I paid $300 a month to her, and I was barely able to do it. Sometimes I was late on rent, but she was lenient about it. She understood and didn't want to see me have to take alternative routes to pay rent, like I had in the past.

I found this gem of a place to work at called The Green Room. At first, this was my hang out spot and I didn't want to mess it up by working there, but they finally convinced me to join their team. Everything finally felt like it was going in the right direction. I always felt like this place had a similar feel to Austin, Texas. This restaurant and bar was open for breakfast, lunch, and dinner, then turned into a bar/live music venue until 2 a.m. There was local artisan beer and food from local farmers. The Green Room also had amazing local bands, burgers, soup, typical Costa Rican dishes, and it was Americanized to draw in the tourists. It had local artwork for sale and a friendly vibe that was welcoming. This place was the spot where I felt safe. I loved this place and this job the most out of all of the shitty working situations I went through in Costa Rica. The owner, Rachelle, was a local Tica. She was an angel to me. She put up with my craziness and still loved me for who I was and accepted me. I had days that I would show up to work without sleeping from raging the night before. While everyone else was having breakfast, I was calling my drug dealer to bring me a bag so I could make it through my shift. I'm sure people could tell I was on drugs, but everyone accepted it as the way of life there.

I met tons of tourists in town looking for the right places to go and the right people to meet. I was "the connector," so to speak. Sounds better than a drug dealer or a madam. The Green Room was the perfect fishing hole for them to find me because they felt comfortable there, and it reminded them of the States. One time, there was a bachelor party that came through and they asked me to help them out. I always enjoyed this because I ate well, partied well, and had inspirational conversations about life with them when they were really fucked up. At times, they would tip me extra for showing them around town, and most of the time, they would leave me with all of their extra alcohol, drugs, and food when they left town. I saw these groups as jackpots, as I'm sure many local Costa Ricans did, too. I was beginning to understand the way of life in a third world country.

One group in particular that stood out to me the most was a doozie. They asked me to help find them drugs and then to hang out with them for the night. I showed them my favorite bar that night and got them bottle service there. If I set it up and arranged it, then I would get a cut of the tab from the bar. All the while, they had a couple of girls that they had paid for with them from the previous two nights. Some of the men were curious about getting new girls to have fun with and wanted to know what options were out there. We were at the bar, and I showed the boys a few of my "friends" that were available for purchase for the night. Little did I know, the girls they had before were watching what I was doing, and they were not happy about it. When it came time for the group to go back to their house, the guys chose the new girls I had introduced to them. As we were getting into the taxi, I had my phone in my armpit and was about to sit in the backseat. All of a sudden, one of the girls that didn't get chosen by the group came up to me and grabbed me by the hair, pulling me back out of the car. She began to take swings at my face, and I went into protective mode hunching over. I opened my arms to defend myself, and my phone fell to the ground. A giant group formed around us, and we began to battle it out as we both had each other's hair. All during this time, these little street kids snatched up my phone and ran down the street to hide. The bouncers finally pulled us apart, but by that time the bachelor party taxi had sped off without me. I was left at the bar with the bouncer, without my phone, tip, or any way to reach my group. There was a guy outside the bar that told me he could help me get my phone back if I gave him $200 in cash, right then. I only had $12 to my name; there's no way I could come up with that. I basically had to say goodbye to that phone.

That phone was the only way I could talk to my parents. My dad got me my first iPhone 4 so that we could Facetime together and see one another. My heart was completely broken, and once more, this town had gotten the best of me. I was also terrified to leave that bar, thinking that I was going to be followed home. The other girls had to leave the bar since they were the ones who started the fight. I sat with the bouncer for a bit to get my bearings back before finding a cab to get home with my $12. At least that girl was from San Jose and not from Jaco because that would mean I would have a target on my back in my small town (probably seeing her everyday.) I'm glad I didn't have to constantly worry about it. This is how people get killed. I never realized that what I was doing was putting myself in danger. In the other girls' eyes, I was taking away from their business and their livelihood. Shit gets real in this town, really fast. Never in my life did I expect to have my iPhone stolen and get beaten up by a hooker while playing the madam role. Guess I can add another wowza to the list of things I thought I'd never experience.

CHAPTER NINETEEN

LOST AND ALONE

I found myself living on my own, being more depressed than I ever could've expected. I felt more alone than I ever had before. I had no one to tell me what to do or when it was time to come home, except for Chi. I would take him out with me when I would go out for the night. Most bars were in an open space and had a patio, so I could pretty much bring him with me everywhere. I would use his body language and anxiety levels to tell me when it was time to leave. I have to say, his energy was spot on most of the time. We were now beginning to create this bond together by becoming one another's emotional support. This wolf has been the best partner in crime and bodyguard in all my endeavours. My home didn't have any windows or much air flow at all, so I found myself always wanting to be outside with him when I wasn't working. I would only go home to sleep and fuck. Chi was safe there and would hang out on the porch when I would have to leave for work. At times, I left the front door open with the gated screened door locked, and had fans always going, but it still didn't get enough circulation. If I left my front door open (which was my only air flow source) then people walking by were free to look inside. No one ever dared set foot in there without me though, because they knew about Chi. Talk about a beast of a guard dog.

I still had Gustavo in my life and would always get excited when he passed through town. It was sweet that he would stop and check in on me to see how I was doing. He was what kept me grounded when it came to protecting myself with all the men I slept with. He would always encourage me to wear condoms so we could continue to have unprotected sex without having to worry about it. Honestly, I'm glad I kept myself good for this one, but more importantly, I'm glad I did this for myself. When you're mischievous, you should at least protect yourself. It was sweet how much he continued to care for me over the two years I was there. He could see my health starting to decline as I was getting thinner each time he saw me and growing more depressed as the months went by.

Normally after he would leave, I would try to clean up my act for a while. That boy really knows how to party hard, which is probably why I liked him. But afterwards, I would be sick and exhausted from the constant party. I could feel it starting to affect my health and sanity. I would have my friends begging me not to go out every night and telling me that I needed to make myself more of a mystery and take some days off. I tried my hardest, but it was hard to stay inside that hot house for long periods of time. I had a cure for this though. On these days, I would get off of work and immediately put this pill called Sirdalud or Tizanidine in my mouth to stop me from going out. It felt like a quaalude and would put me to sleep within 20 minutes. This drug made my body feel heavy and it was impossible to stay awake after taking it. Over in Costa Rica, they have pharmacies where you go and tell someone your problems and they give you a pill to fix it. So much easier in a lot of ways than going through a doctor, but also it can be a lot more reckless if you have a drug addiction, like I did. I would take one of these pills and by the time I would bike home, I would be passing out as I reached my door. I would use these pills to help me not have anxiety about staying in for the night. I was scared to be alone. I didn't like myself and that's why I was afraid of being in my own presence.

I was finding myself in this vicious cycle of barely making it, always looking for my next score, wondering how I am going to eat, and going into work hungover. I had created this life that I was slowly losing myself in. I hated being alone because I had my own thoughts and shame to deal with, so I chose to always be numb. I lost so much weight living like this. I was killing myself slowly and was surprised I was still alive after a few close calls with overdosing. I lost myself and my sense of direction. I found myself stumbling in the dark, trying to figure out how the heck I was going to get myself back home. I became so homesick and would basically cry to every group I met about how badly I wanted to go home. I couldn't see a way out. A part of me was hoping someone would offer to pay for us to get back home, but all I could do was wait and have faith that something would work out. I was here for a reason; I was here to figure out how to find my light. I was so blinded by the dark side of this town that my light was nowhere to be seen. I even spray painted my walls one night when I was fucked up with the mantra, "Live the life you love, and love the life you live." It helped me put things into perspective and have a visual of what my purpose was. I knew I wanted to begin to live the kind of life I could love, and not the kind I was ashamed of.

The kind of life I could be proud of was waiting for me back home with my family and friends. I had messed it up for myself here when it came to walking with my head held high. I knew I would make my way back home one day, one way or another. I had to learn to enjoy the process and get to know myself, even when I didn't like myself. I was realizing what was important to me for my own happiness to grow. Putting graffiti in my home wasn't enough for me, so I seized the opportunity to engrave my motto in that town on the front steps of the Green Room when it was being repaved. I need mantras in my face for me to remember what's important. This step was on the main street next to the casino and next to a bar where men could pick up a working girl for the night. So many people would be looking down at the ground in shame and guilt for many reasons. I knew this was prime real estate to make my mark on this town. I chose to engrave the phrase "Follow Your Heart" so I could be reminded to do so every time I'd walk into work. This was my reminder to get my ass home, and I desperately needed to find a way to do that.

I made these signs line up to be in my face daily so it could help light the pathway for me. Saying these mantras on a daily basis helped to keep the hope alive in me that I would find a way home. Not only that, but I hoped that these signs could help to inspire others to make the right decisions as well. It was right next to the main bar where people had a choice between following their heart or fucking up their lives. I hoped that this sign would help others find strength. So many people walk with their heads down in that town, not only because the sun is bright as shit, but because they would be hungover or have so much shame from what they did the night before. I'm so grateful the owner of the Green Room allowed me to do that. We all need reminders to be in our view sometimes, especially when the world can seem so dark.

Here are a couple of journal entries from that time period to give you an idea of where my mind was. I started to figure things out and hear my inner voice louder when I was alone with my thoughts, even though I didn't always like what I was hearing. I spent many nights wired on cocaine and alcohol, even acid, writing these pages. When I was lost, I would write, and somehow see the answers. When I had a boy in my bed and I couldn't sleep, I would write. When I needed to hear and see my inner voice, I would turn to my book and write. I found comfort in knowing that deep down inside I knew what I needed to do. I might not have known how to implement this advice into my life just yet, but I felt like I was on the right track. I was writing advice to myself on how to get me through this process to find my own beaming light from within, giving myself some kind of hope.

April 5th, 2015

Learn to love yourself and love being alone

I see a pattern in my life, yes another one. I never actually learned how to love myself, support myself, and search within my heart for my own guidance. I never understood how to stand on my own two feet with my head held high without a backup plan to catch my fall. I find myself not pleased with what I see in the mirror when I wake up in the morning. I need to finally step up and help myself if I ever want to love myself. The way I am treating my body with drugs and sex is not doing anything good for my true self who needs to come out and shine. If anything, it's keeping that stardust locked away out of reach. All I know is, I can do this! I know I can. I have to learn how to enjoy being around myself, without distractions or drugs.

I've decided to make a promise to myself. I am going to try to go one month without going out to bars or doing any cocaine. I would shine so much more if I didn't, and I know that. I just have to do that. It's at a point right now where it isn't even fun anymore. It's a chore to keep up with, if anything. I was out and about tonight on the full moon, feeling weird, lost and alone once more on the streets of Jaco. I have gotten to a point where I am too coked up all the time to even have good people respecting me anymore. I've lost most of my friends because they don't want to be associated with that, and I don't blame them. I got myself into this mess and I didn't want to drag anyone else down or be an annoying druggie hanging around them. I am now the most alone that I have ever been. I walked around at night hoping someone interesting would be around to talk to, but it's as if it's a record player on repeat. It was like I was out there searching for something, I'm not even sure what for, but ended up more alone and down than ever.

I have this crazy friend that I love and admire dearly, named Jaime. At the beginning of the night, I was with her on an adventure out to the rich neighborhood. We ate some acid before going out to explore. She had a super rich and powerful friend who owned a yacht out at Los Sueños, so we met him there. He fed us the most amazing pasta dish! I enjoyed it so much that I felt like I didn't speak a word for the whole time food was in front of me. Maybe it was due to the acid, or the fact that I hadn't eaten anything in two days, but that food was the best thing about my night. Then we went downtown in Jaco and explored the craziness of Semana Santa, which is like Easter in Costa Rica, but everyone in that country went buck wild. It was an extremely dangerous time to be walking around, due to the fact that most people were too out of their minds, like myself. My acid started to kick in and I didn't feel comfortable anywhere I went. I ended up leaving the bar that Jaime and her friend were at because I got super claustrophobic and had to get out of the loud and overcrowded bar. I hurried over to my comfort bar, Swell, thinking I would be able to breathe again once I was there. The first thing I saw when I walked up was Felipe with his new girlfriend. I ran to the back VIP space, hoping to avoid any eye contact or engagement. I felt uncomfortable everywhere I went, even once I got to the back VIP space. Everyone around me was doing bumps and smoking cigarettes, and I was trying so hard not to do any of that. This acid opened up some truths about myself. All I could think about was cocaine. This was my new comfort zone. This was my new best friend, not a human. I was antsy and inpatient while I was awkwardly looking around for who could help me out. The only thing I cared about was how to score a *bag. Even though I had no money for it, I still found a way to scrounge up $20 for a bag. This shit is keeping me stuck in a hole, going in circles. Seriously, though, this town will eat you alive if you let it. I don't even recognize myself anymore.*

I am so skinny that I have now become embarrassed to be seen on the streets. Tonight, I was so uncomfortable out there that I finally had to run home, even though I didn't want to go there either. I just wanted to hide, but I didn't know where to go. Nothing felt comfortable. This trip of mine was going way south with all of these feelings bubbling inside of me. I was feeling like I had these insecurities written all over my face. It was showing in my body and how awkward I've become in my own skin. I barely recognize myself. I need to wake up and set higher standards for myself and love myself. I need to find a way to get out of the grasp of these drugs and this town.

Addiction is a real thing; I always thought I would be strong enough to have control and never let things get out of hand. But, with no one here to care about me or tell me when to stop, I find I don't know how to moderate on my own. I need to love myself enough to try to fix this. I wish I was strong enough to say no ten times a night. There is coke being sold on almost every corner in this town and it makes it so hard when I'm so weak. I need to learn to love being alone and be the one to take care of my own health and sanity. In the end, I'm alone out here anyway. I'm learning and growing, failing and falling, living and experiencing life. I am way too strong, powerful, and beautiful to let this drug or this town eat me alive. I know I can do this! I just need clarity and an outlet for my creativity. I also need to be around people who actually care about me. I want to be strong and prove to myself that I can make it on my own without a man by my side. I want my light to shine bright on my own, from within, without anything stopping me from feeling this. The only way I can reach that is if I get myself out of this mess. It's okay to admit that I have a problem. I am an alcoholic and an addict. Other people have told me, but it's time I believe it for myself. I have to be okay saying this.

May 22nd, 2015

At this moment, I am so proud of myself. On the 15th (my birthday,) I hosted the first pub crawl ever created in Jaco. I don't know why I had to do this on my birthday, but it was like a gift to myself to prove I could do it, if I wanted to. I came here to plan events and I was at least going to plan one on my own while living here. It was the perfect kind of event for this town. There are so many tourists that come here trying to find cool places to check out. I basically gave them a tour and a taste of all my favorite bars, restaurants, and dance clubs in town. I was working with the owners of these places, helping to bring in business, and it was clear that they were intrigued by this tour of mine. I found myself feeling useful again and like I was starting to gain credibility by having a purpose. I had about ten people on my tour and made about $300 from it. Though, at the end of the night, that money got stolen from me because I was a dumbass and left my things in the storage room for the bar. (Never leave your belongings behind in Costa Rica.) I was at my comfort bar hosting an event and thought my things would be safe back there in a locked room. I thought these people were my friends, but I was obviously wrong. I was upset over losing all of my earnings, but I was still proud of myself for accomplishing my goal. I regained confidence from within that I had forgotten about. People saw me shining and in my element. I walked down the streets afterwards feeling proud, like people were extra accepting of me. Maybe it was all in my mind and the way I was carrying myself.

May 24th, 2015

I talk with so many people lost in their own lives that pass through this town. They've forgotten their passions and are searching for a sense of direction. I know deep down that I have a gift to help others, and right now that is sparking that question within them. I know it and believe it is one of my purposes on this planet to help guide the lost souls towards their own inner light. I believe people pass into our lives at a certain time for a reason. Whether it's for a conversation, a long term relationship, or a one-night stand. There is a plan and a purpose behind every interaction we encounter. I love searching for those synchronicities that put it all together in place. If we could only open our eyes and see the signs, the universe will direct us in the right place with the right people. Allow these signs to be a way to help you learn how to follow your heart. When we begin to make decisions from our hearts, we'll see the signs more clearly. This is when you will feel closer to the right place. Follow those nudges.

I'm writing all of this at 5:20 a.m., as I'm alone questioning these things and hearing my answers. I know I'm in this world to change lives. I heard this calling a long time ago when I started this book. I'm here to find the answers to all the questions that are holding us back in life. I lived through these experiences so I can be living proof that there is a way to find your light. This pub crawl event was the first spark that I had in a while that made me feel like I was shining and on the right path. Maybe I felt this way because I was in my element planning events, but everything felt so right. I loved that feeling of people looking up to me. Maybe because I have so little of that in my recent past, but I'm opening my mind to wanting to feel this more often. Even though I am living in a shack with no AC, windows, or any ventilation; even though I use my refrigerator to cool my body temperature down--I am learning how to be humble. What is this teaching me? That this, too, is temporary. Be happy here with where you are in the moment and then you can pass onto the next chapter of your life.

"It is up to you to open the portals in your life that give you conscious access to the unmanifested. Get in touch with the energy field of the inner body, be intensely present, disidentify from the mind and surrender to what is. These are all portals you can use, but you only need to use one. Surely love is one of these portals? No, it isn't. As soon as one of these portals opens, love is present in all of oneness. Love isn't a portal, it's what

comes through the portal into this world. As long as you are completely trapped in your identity, there is no love. Your task is not to search for love, but to find a portal from which love can enter." Excerpt from The Power of Now, by Eckhart Tolle.

It's funny how right now in my life I am pushing away anything that could love me. It isn't right for me right now and it shows with my actions, and my own personal agenda. Anything that I do try to love, I end up pushing away or doing something so harsh to sabotage the relationship so they wouldn't like me anymore. The only love I want is the love from myself. I'm learning how to love being alone. I'm learning how to understand myself as I am, fully in this moment. I can feel myself regaining my trust back inside and hearing my instincts kick in. I'm learning the process of how to follow my heart to what is right for my life.

*Side Note: Learn to love being on your own. Learn to be your own best friend. Learn to hear your thoughts over others'. It is not until you can love being with yourself that another person can love you like that. It's not easy to be alone, especially when you don't like your own company, but it is important to get comfortable with all aspects of yourself, especially the side of you that you dislike.

CHAPTER TWENTY

GET ME OUTTA HERE!

My dreams to break free from this town eventually became a reality when Gustavo came to town for a visit. He saw what was happening to me and how I was falling apart. He loved me, but also wanted to make sure I stayed alive, and happy. Each time he would visit, towards the end, I would always break down in tears to him about how badly I missed my family. I was a walking depressed skeleton that was homesick and dying a slow and painful death from addiction. He will always have a special place in my heart for being the one to see this and help me figure out how I could break away from this town and get back to normalcy. He was in charge of gathering a group of Costa Ricans to be trimigrants at a marijuana farm in Humboldt County, California. He ended up spotting me the money to pay for my plane ticket there, and I would pay him back after I made some money from trimming. Since I didn't own any debit or credit cards, I needed him to do that to help make it possible. Not only was I excited about finally being able to make some money to get Chi and myself home, but I was also looking forward to spending a couple months with my sweet love on a mountain, surrounded by hemp plants.

I had only gotten small doses of Gustavo whenever he came through town, but I thought this would be paradise to get away on vacation for two months with him. I knew it was going to be challenging because I was going to be detoxing off of cocaine on that mountain. There were going to be other people I didn't know out there, but it sounded like an adventure to me. I felt like this was where my heart was leading me and it was my time to say goodbye to this country. *Honestly, take me anywhere but here.* I was so done with that town and so ready to step into a new phase of my life. I knew it was best for me and this was going to be the only way I could raise that much money in such a short amount of time to get myself home.

It came time for me to leave, but I had to make sure Chi was good and set up to be okay without me for a few months. I ended up dropping Chi off with a stranger, who turned out to be the best dog trainer in town. He was a friend of a friend, and was great with dogs. That was all I knew about Eddy before meeting him to drop-off Chi. He was a super kind and gentle soul that lived right on the beach with his girlfriend and his dog, Cookie. I knew Chi would have fun there and hopefully he might learn a few things from Eddy and his dog. That was probably the moment when I practiced my faith to the extreme. He can't be left with just anyone, but something in my heart comforted me and told me this would be okay. I paid Eddy $300 each month to take care of my bodyguard while I was trimming weed in California.

I flew out separately and met up with Gustavo and the group in San Francisco. I knew a few of the people in our trimming group from Costa Rica, but not very well. Gustavo had brought his two best friends who I knew, and then there was one girl from Jaco who was a sweet local but I hadn't ever talked with her before. The first night, we stayed in the city at his friend's house and we partied our asses off! The next day, we took a bus out to the mountains in Humboldt County, the notorious mountains of marijuana. This is an area of California where there aren't many cops. People go missing on these trimming farms, things get stolen, girls get molested, and people get high as fuck. The people growing weed on the mountains are the ones who regulate and protect the land. The farmers had guns and patrolled the mountains to make sure their crops stayed safe. I didn't think too much of it at the time because anywhere was better than where I was; I was honestly just happy to be out of Jaco. I felt like I could breathe fresh air again.

We got out on the mountain and it was absolutely beautiful! The redwood trees grow so tall out there and it was so peaceful to be immersed in nature. Our camp had one main house where the farmers stayed, with one bathroom and one giant room upstairs. Since it wasn't super cold yet, Gustavo and I set up our tent underneath a tree. I didn't have my own tent, but Gustavo happily knew that we would be sharing one during our time there. We made our cozy little space together and settled in for the stay. I was so stoked to have so much time to spend with Gustavo, and to get to know him on a deeper level other than drugs and sex. I think he wanted that too, otherwise I don't feel like he would've invited me. Once we were out on that mountain, we were stuck. We had no way to get back into town without a car, and we didn't have any cell reception, except for at the top on the mountain, which you could only get to with a four wheeler.

As we started to do our jobs trimming weed, I began to feel this anxiety while working. I thought it would be a simple and easy job to do, but I suppose that depends on if you're okay with the thoughts in your head because it gives you a lot of time to ponder. All I could think about was how much better I would be doing if I had cocaine. It was the hardest thing for me to focus on anything else. I guess this was part of the detox. There wasn't any cocaine out there, so I had to find other ways to get over it. I would take lots of breaks and walk away from sitting in the uncomfortable camping chairs. At least there was always alcohol out there, so I used this vise to calm my nerves. I didn't get it. Everyone else was trimming away like it was the best thing in the world, *and I'm over here having anxiety attacks because it's hard for me to focus on the one small task I came out here to do.*

It takes discipline and patience to do this kind of job and I was running low on both of those qualities. I was sitting for eight to 18 hours a day doing the same task: trying to fill up my bag of production. It took me a full day to trim a pound of weed, where others would get two in a day. I didn't like the thoughts in my head that were coming up for me. Most of the time, the others in the group would be speaking fast in Spanish and I wouldn't be a part of their conversation because I couldn't keep up; so I gave up trying to understand after a while. Funny how I was in the States, but no one was speaking English around me. It was frustrating to say the least.

At night when everyone was done, we would normally sit around a fire and get super drunk together. There were about 22 horny guys out there on the farm and only seven girls. The women were outnumbered and it was practically a frenzy of who was going to be hooking up with whom. I had Gustavo, so I wasn't on the hunt. I was, however, more friendly with all the guys because they were easier to get along with than the girls. The girls formed this small group and made sure to let me know I wasn't welcome. I guess they knew of me and my bad habits and stories I made in Jaco, which made them prejudge me.

I was becoming friends with the boys because the girls wouldn't talk to me. Gustavo was becoming friends with the girls because he was getting interesting stories from them. I didn't think anything of it because we were sharing a tent and everyone knew we were together. I tried not to be the jealous type, but over time, that came to bite me in the ass. Little did I know the girls were spreading rumors in front of me and tainting Gustavo's opinion of me. The girls told him I was hooking up with the other boys on the mountain, based on what they already knew about me, when I wasn't. The one girl from Jaco was telling all the girls all of my crazy stories of how wild I was. They were speaking so fast and in slang that I couldn't understand them and had no idea what was going on. After a while, this became so isolating and annoying that I kept to myself. I tried not to think about it and did my best to focus on the job and what I came here to do. I was trying to make my way home so I could get away from this life. My past was haunting me once more, and the thought of starting fresh again was the one thing pulling me through. I never wanted to feel so judged and labeled like this again. I was growing distant from the heart of my Venezulan lover. I could tell by his demeanor. He stopped talking to me for a while, which opened up the opportunity for me to talk to the guys. I felt like I had to talk to someone. *I mean, what else am I going to do? Go mute?* All of them were trying to step in and make a move, but that was the farthest thing from my mind. I didn't want the "rumors" to become true this time, plus, I was going through withdrawals and was easily irritated by everyone. Eventually, I found my comfort by going inward. I wasn't liking what I was processing, but I needed to feel it to learn from it.

When it got too cold to camp outside, we all gathered in this one tiny cabin. This small home had a downstairs for the growers, and an upstairs that was one giant room for all of us trimmers to sleep in. This made things even worse for me, because we were always all around each other, whether we liked each other or not. There's no running away when it's 30 degrees outside. Eventually, I did become mute because it wasn't worth my energy to speak to anyone after a while. I didn't have anything to say, and they were all chirping away in another language anyway. I became a loner and kept to myself towards the end. Gustavo was still sharing a bed with me because he didn't have a choice. I knew he still liked me, but I could tell there was a shift happening in him. We were never meant to be boyfriend/girlfriend or be around each other this long. It had worked with us before this because we would only be together for a few days and then we'd go back to our regular lives.

It wasn't too long before Gustavo began to develop feelings for another girl out there. (Maybe that's why he was so interested in always talking with the girls.) My heart was breaking in front of me and I had no choice but to continue sharing a bed with this guy. Everyone out there felt bad for me because they would see their flirtatiousness, too. I tried to be the one to play it cool when in reality, I wanted to run. I knew Gustavo wasn't a forever boy and to be honest, I was pretty annoyed with him after spending every waking hour together for two months. After all, I was trying to get back to the States, somewhere he wouldn't be, so I did my best to practice non-attachment. There were times when he still wanted to make love to me, and when he tried, I didn't stop him. I still felt his love for me, and maybe it was his way of practicing not getting too attached to me as well. I knew he had other girls when in Costa Rica, so I was somewhat used to sharing him. It was hard to watch and feel him stabbing me in the heart though. We all do stupid things when our reality is morphed by outside influences and animalistic drives. After a while, I started taking allergy medicine so I could ignore them and sleep amongst all their chatting. They would always talk and laugh so late at night; this was the only way I could tune them out to fall asleep.

When it came time to leave and go to the second spot that paid double per pound, Gustavo pulled me to the side. He told me he wasn't going to take me with him because there wasn't enough space for me there. He waited until the day of to tell me this so he didn't have to be around for my heartbreak. He took the new girl he was interested in, instead of me. I was utterly shocked that he would leave me stranded on the side of the mountain with these horny and disgusting guys. I didn't know how to get off that mountain without him. We hadn't been paid yet, so I was stranded without money or a credit card. He assured me he was leaving behind one of his best friends and he was going to look out for me, but I didn't want that. I wanted him to be there. His friend was young and skinny, and couldn't protect me if he wanted to. He tried to give me all these excuses as to why he wasn't taking me, but he would never admit he was taking her over me. I gave up fighting with him about it and accepted that this was how it was going to end with us. After two years of being in each other's lives, this was our grand finale. As he drove off, he knew he was leaving me with a bunch of horny dudes that were hungry to get in my pants, but he didn't care. It wasn't even safe to go walking around on the mountain alone, so there was no escaping this situation. There have been so many stories of girls getting raped and even killed in these parts. I needed to make sure that wasn't going to be me. It's not like I could call the cops if I was in trouble; I couldn't even use my phone without reception. The growers are the law enforcement in that town, and they were the ones patrolling the area and "keeping it safe." I no longer felt safe or protected once Gustavo left.

We spent about two more weeks on the mountain trimming all the tiny plants that no one wanted to deal with. I felt like that weed. I was the leftover that no one wanted. It was the most depressing thing ever to be left like that. I kind of gave up on trimming for a few days after he left. All I wanted was to hide and not be bothered. There was only so much slack time that they would give me, though. Things still needed to happen for the compound to be able to shut down for the season. We went there to do a job and we had to finish this site so we could go on to the next. The boys became more comfortable making vulgar jokes about how they were going to have sex with me, or about me sucking their dicks. It was as if I was stuck in middle school with a bunch of testosterone-driven little boys. I tried my best to ignore what they were saying, laugh it off and not make a big deal. I didn't have the energy to fight back about it ten to 20 times a day, so I stopped fighting it and let the boys be boys.

We moved to the next spot which turned out to be even worse. It was a tiny run-down shack in the suburbs that had trash everywhere. At least the weed was better to trim and we started to get back to work immediately. I was able to get into my groove with trimming when I didn't have such painful distractions around me. I had gone through heartbreak, detoxing, and now I was finally feeling normal again. We stayed at this location for about a month until the people started to dwindle down and the group became thinner and thinner. At this point, I was wondering when I would be getting out of there. I tried to make calls out to Gustavo, but once more, there wasn't phone reception. Only the main grower's phone worked out there. The weed became harder to trim because the pieces were getting smaller again, and all I wanted to do at this point was to go home. I was ready to get paid and leave with what I had made. One of the main guys finally got a hold of Gustavo on the phone and I was finally able to tell him I wanted to go home. I begged him to get me out of there! I found out later on that the girl he took instead of me ended up hooking up with Gustavo's boss at the new location immediately, so the karmic circle was passed all the way back. He felt horrible for leaving me after that happened. I told him how unwanted all this sexual harassment was from his friends, and he finally realized that I never hooked up with any of them. I'm proud that I never made those rumors come true. It was empowering to still stand in my truth. Setting his guilt aside, the one thing he could do to make it up to me was help me get out of here. He still needed to get paid too, so he had to come back anyway to retrieve that.

The night he picked me up was the last night I ever saw Gustavo. He took me to a hotel in the city and we made love for the last time, but it was incredibly awkward. It was a sweet effort to end on a good note, but the passion was gone. It didn't feel right anymore and the connection was lost. That love had served its purpose, and now we only cared for one another as human beings. He helped me get a plane ticket back to Tyler so I could see my family for Christmas, and then took me to the airport. It was the saddest and sweetest goodbye, knowing it was going to be the last time I ever saw him. This man was a turning point in my path and I am so grateful for everything, good and bad, that this relationship taught me.

I made it back home for Christmas and my family was overflowing with joy! It felt so nice to go back home and rest after all of those heightened emotions. I couldn't believe how long it had been since I was able to shut off the protective shield. I was on guard, always feeling on edge or unsafe in my surroundings, for about three months. I had forgotten what it was like to feel safe, protected, and at ease. I could finally settle down and relax. Being home for Christmas was the best present I could've given my family and myself. My mom was finally able to get a good night of sleep after two years of also being on high alert. After Christmas was over, I went back to Costa Rica so I could get Chi and the rest of my things. It was time for me to make my way back home, once and for all.

I was over the moon excited to pick up my Chi boy once I got back into town! I picked up Chi, and to my surprise, he was like a brand new dog! His skin and fur was the healthiest I had seen in the past year, and he gained some much-needed weight. He was not only healthier, but he was also so well behaved. I didn't realize that Eddy was such a dog whisperer! I couldn't have gotten luckier leaving Chi with this angel. I felt like my life was getting back on track, and it was for

Chi as well. I guess me going kind of crazy here made Chi go a little wild, too. We both needed the discipline that we endured over the last three months. My heart flooded with love having Chi back in my arms.

Eddy was excited to show me how well Chi behaved now, so as soon as I got there, we went out to the beach and began a leash-free walk. Before, Chi would run wherever he wanted and was a wild little wolf that liked the "catch me if you can" game. Now, Chi didn't even think twice about running off without a leash on; he would walk right next to my side or behind me, but never in front. Any time he would get slightly off or too far in front, Eddy would correct him and it worked like a charm every time. I couldn't believe it! He worked wonders with my wild beast while I was gone. The only thing was, Chi was getting trained with all the commands being in Spanish. I guess the tone of Spanish commands can be a little more demanding, forcing a response more so than English. I knew Chi was in good hands and Eddy made sure to keep me posted while I was away. The universe will always find a way to show you that there is hope and wonder still left in this world. The trick is, having blind faith in the universe. This was one of those moments when I will always have so much gratitude for this type of human being. Eddy poured his heart into Chi and made sure he was loved plenty while I was away, and it showed.

I couldn't believe that my dream to leave this town was actually happening. I had cried for this day to come for the past year when I knew in my heart that I needed to leave. I raised enough money from trimming weed to get a plane ticket home and get back to normalcy. My list that I still needed to do was packing the rest of my things, cleaning up my mess of a home, and getting Chi his "emotional support" papers from my doctor friend so he could fly next to me on the plane. I could've done this a long time ago if I knew it was an option. For some reason, I was just now finding out how easy it was to get Chi home. Just like getting a prescription was easy, so was getting papers for Chi to be my emotional support dog for the airlines.

I only had a couple more days in Jaco, and it was about time to say all of my goodbyes. I was regretting how I had spent my time here. As I wandered around on the beach, watching one of my favorite pink sunsets, I realized that this wasn't the last time I would be here. This was only the beginning of something bigger than what I knew in that exact moment. I had an aching in my heart that I should have done these past two years differently. If I didn't spend my time partying, I would've been a pro at surfing by now. I wasn't able to travel around and explore more because I spent all of my money on drugs. I slept in the mornings and partied all night, missing out on the sunrises and morning walks on the beach. All these should've, could've, would've scenarios kept playing in my mind. Yet, I knew I could do nothing but put one foot in front of the other and take my ass home before I lost myself entirely. I made some great friends who I would love to come back and visit one day, but they can only be listed on one hand. This country is beautiful to visit and a whole different beast to tackle when trying to live here. I think about the future and see myself back here one day leading a yoga and healing retreat and doing things the right way.

The night before I left, I had one last thing to do, and it happened to be the most important thing. I still needed to get Chi's papers to be my emotional support dog so he could ride on the plane with me at my feet instead of paying $2,000 to fly him in the cargo space. Lucky for me, he was well groomed and trained well, thanks to Eddy. I felt confident in his ability to stay cool throughout the flight in the cabin with all the other humans. No big deal, just flying with a wolf on a plane.

The man who was the key player in helping me with this situation was my friend who I met at the very beginning of my stay in Costa Rica. I met him on the beach one day, and we instantly connected as friends over coffee and a joint. He was a surfer and a doctor who always had a joint in his back pocket. He was a little quiet and reserved for my taste, but I knew I wanted to keep this guy around as a friend. I made sure never to sleep with him because most of the time I would never talk to those boys again. Of course he tried multiple times, but I had a weird feeling about this guy. It was like he had an invisible *do not go there* sign on him. I couldn't put my finger on it, but I never fell for him like that. He was my friend and one of the only guys that I kept in the friend zone, *and* he was still there. There was something to be said about this method of thinking.

He came over on my last night and fed me some takeout sushi from my favorite spot in town. I typically don't eat that much seafood, but since it was my last night right by the sea, I decided to eat every bite without thinking twice. Plus, I was starving. I didn't take the best care of myself there because there wasn't even a real kitchen in my place. It was difficult to cook or even store food so I chose either not to eat, or to eat out. While my friend was there, he had his notepad to write prescriptions and I persuaded him to write me a script for Valium as well. In exchange for the Valium, I had a bottle of wine that I had gotten from the duty-free at the airport. I now had everything I needed to get my happy ass back home with Chi! I had to have something to numb away the pain of being ripped away from paradise. Numbing out the world wasn't the best way to cope, but I was also looking to escape my reality in all shapes and forms until the dust settled from this transition.

That next morning, I went to the pharmacy and got my prescription for Valium filled. I found ways to hide all of it in my carry on, in my wallet, and my purse. Crazy stubborn girl that I am, I still crossed the borders with illegal drugs on hand. I guess going to Nicaraguan jail didn't set me straight. Nonetheless, I got in my friend's taxi and he took me and Chi, and everything I could pack in my two remaining intact suitcases, to the airport. It was time to say goodbye to the life I had created for myself in Costa Rica and step into my new reality. I left behind a lot of clothes that I didn't have space for, and unfortunately, a lot of trash that I didn't have time to pick up. I felt bad, but I had no choice. I don't even think I slept that night. I had my one last night of partying in paradise as I stayed at home packing all my things. I knew I couldn't live like this forever, *but while I'm still here, I'm still too weak to turn it down.* I hated that cocaine was so good there. I never would wish this addiction, or any addiction at that, on anyone. It literally strips you of your common sense and respect for yourself. It strips you of your choice. It floods your thoughts, being the only thing your brain can think about. I felt like I needed this drug in order to function. It tore me away from myself and kept me trapped in this dark hole of vicious cycles. I was so glad to be getting away from that country so I could get closer to my light. At least I had enough of myself still inside of me to make the decision to keep myself alive and come home. For being such a beautiful country, it had created one of the darkest clouds of secrets that would burden my conscience. I knew I was going to have culture shock and mad withdrawals when I got back home, but I was ready to face them.

Once we got to the airport, we unloaded the car and I began to walk into the check-in area. All of a sudden, Chi started freaking out. I wasn't sure if it was because I was high strung from my cocaine binge, or if he knew he was about to get on a plane again. I showed the attendee his paperwork for being an emotional support dog, and the lady kind of looked at me like I was crazy. I grabbed the paper out of her hand and excused myself, and told her I would be right back. I took him outside to calm him down and fed him two Benadryl, and I took a Valium so we could have a more chill vibe. *Time to set the breaks on the emotions and ride the wave, Chi.* I waited a good 15 minutes for the medicine to kick in, and then we walked back in and tried it all over again, but with a different attendant. This time it went way smoother and we went through security with no problems. We were waiting for a good hour and a half outside the gates and both Chi and I fell asleep while we waited. I guess we both took a little too much medicine. I awoke to this sweet young girl who poked me and said, "Ma'am, are you supposed to be on this flight?" and as I woke up, the girl was gone. I didn't know if I had dreamt that or if the girl ran off before I fully woke up. I rushed to the gate and I was the last one to board the plane. I almost missed the flight! Fate had its way though, and I made it just in time. As luck would have it, we were seated right next to a super sweet and understanding lady. Since I had anxiety and an emotional support dog, we had the seats in the front of the plane that had extra leg room. Chi and I were both groggy and ended up falling asleep again immediately once the plane took off. Chi slept with his head on the lady's feet next to me. She reassured me that it was fine and he was keeping her warm. Once we landed in Dallas, we grabbed our bags and slowly made our way out, still in a fog. As soon as Chi saw my mom and dad, he started to freak out again! He was so happy to see them and pulled me intensely towards them. It was like he knew he was safe again and everything was going to be okay. (Kind of an exact representation of how I was feeling at the time.) I could finally breathe, knowing that I could hug my family again and call them whenever I wanted to. *Ah, it feels so good to finally be home.*

CHAPTER TWENTY-ONE

WELCOME HOME

Coming back to reality in the States was hard for me to grasp. I was still stuck in the dark mindset that life had to always be a struggle. I thought I had hit rock bottom, but I hadn't even the slightest idea as to what was in store for me next. I may have been back home, but I wasn't home at all in my body. I had no respect for myself, nor did I know how to honor my body. My addiction to cocaine wasn't over yet. I found myself in a new circle of people who did that drug here in Austin. It wasn't near as good, and sometimes it would actually make me sick to my stomach. I came home and found myself struggling to get a job. I was living in my best friend Katelyn's garage, which happened to be at the house I had shared with my ex-husband. He was renting it out to her while he was out on tours and living in Colorado. The thought of working at the strip club came back to my mind again. I could make way more money in one night than I could working for three weeks at a regular job. That temptation for easy money came back over me like the plague, and it came with a price. It was hard to turn down $1,000 a night. There was one older gentleman that was actually pretty cool who soon became my regular private client. He was into construction and built high-rises around town. He would give me that much money just to talk with him and give him dances for the night. It wasn't that bad, except for the fact that he liked cocaine, and he did a lot of it. I fell right back into what I had ran away from in Costa Rica. I became hooked again, instantly.

On my days off, I would find myself spending everything I was making to feed this habit. My vibration was so low that I couldn't even consider writing in my book at this time; if I did write, it didn't make any sense. I found myself hanging around with others who had similar dark vibes that hovered over them as well. We were like vampires gathering together, only heading outside when darkness fell. We would stay out until the sun rose; our eyes were covered with a red glaze and our pupils were dilated, making it hard to hide our addictions. The spirits of alcohol would constantly haunt me, more so than any other time in my life. I became the weakest and most vulnerable when I was this intoxicated. I could feel other spirits drawn to me when I was in this state of mind, but had no way to stop them from getting too close.

I made enough to get my own place off Riverside and shared a two bedroom apartment with this sweet girl that I met on Craigslist. It wasn't until I moved in there that things began to get out of control with these spirits lurking around me. It became so dark for me that I didn't want to live anymore. I would have these horrible visions of distorted humans walking upside down and backwards, playing over and over again in my head. Evil played like a record player repeating itself some nights, sending chills all over me. I found myself trying to ignore all of this as I finished my bottle of tequila next to my bed. I couldn't sleep or eat hardly anything. It was even difficult for me to get the energy to go out and work anymore. My body was in shock as well because I was having my period and some weird spotting for the first three months I was back in the States. I would muster up everything I had to get my supply of coke so I could go put on a show for work, even though I was being tortured inside.

One night, even my dog was so freaked out that I had to investigate this darkness that was following me. It felt like it had claws in my upper neck, holding onto my spine. It was cold in the room and getting harder to breathe. Chi was running back and forth freaking out, jumping on my bed facing the door, but with his head completely turned around to look at the corner. I was so curious about what was behind me that he refused to look at it; so I pulled his head around to face mine, hoping I could look in the reflections of his eyes to see what he was so scared of. Unfortunately, I saw it and couldn't believe what I was looking at! I saw this black shape, like a Grim Reaper in the reflections in Chi's eyes. This thing was as big as my doorway, blocking the way out. As soon as I saw him, I let go of Chi's head and we both ran out of that room, and out of that house as fast as we could! I was walking on the brink of death, and death was following me. I'm now seeing the signs as well as feeling death lurking around the corner. I could feel it haunting me and pulling me down, telling me my time was close. It didn't feel right to me. Nothing in my life at that time felt right. I was so far off course, and was so lost in the dark, that I literally wanted to die. I knew those weren't my thoughts, but that was all I could think about.

Not only was I the most haunted I have ever been in my life, but I was also becoming extremely sick. Those painful, weird periods, and random sightings of blood were giving me debilitating pains in my left abdomen. I went to the doctor and they prescribed me an antibiotic. After that week of being on the medication they gave me, I was still having my symptoms. They told me that they misread my charts and to take this other medication instead. I was in the middle of the second medication when I felt good enough to go to work. This whole story felt very similar to my grandmother Buzzy's story of how she died. She had ovarian cancer, but the doctors misread her chart, and she ended up dying from it. Like I've mentioned before, I never met my grandmother Buzzy, but I feel as if I am reincarnated as her, or living with her karma. Technically, trauma is stored in our DNA, and can be passed down and repeated until the lesson is finally conquered and the karmic path is changed in the lineage.

On one of my good days, I worked. Towards the end of my shift, there were these two men that came in that looked different than all the other customers. I gave them some dances and began to talk with them a bit more. They were sweet and had a healing vibe compared to the other darkness in the room. I was destined to meet them. The older one was named Frank and he looked at me and explained to me, "You are the reason why I was pulled in here tonight. I was sent here by my guides to find you and help you." I was intrigued by that statement, and had to investigate this further. He told me, "You are a healer. You don't know it yet, but you are. You are also very sick and you will die if you don't go get help." *Okay, so now it's getting surreal. I mean, what? How do I trust this guy that I just met at a strip club?* On the other hand, he was spot on about me being sick, and I did feel like I was dying. It was worth hearing this guy out, so I continued to listen. He said, "I have a healer friend in Monterrey, Mexico, and I have another friend who can put your name on the list to get you healed by this woman. I trust my guides and they have sent me into this dark place to find you and help heal you."

It was as if my angels had taken human form to make sure that I didn't miss this sign that I needed help. I couldn't trust the doctors; if I did, I could end up like my grandma. I took a day to deliberate over what this man had offered me, and I made sure to consult with my mother about this. I made sure to let her know this time that I was going to another country with a man I just met. (Learned my lesson to always tell somewhere where you are going, especially if it is another country; even more so if you don't know the person.) I gave her his name and information, in case something were to happen to me. After telling her about this, it all became more official. I decided once more to trust the universe and know that there is a plan behind it all. I knew I needed help; I was desperate at this point and willing to try anything. What I saw and felt wasn't normal. There wasn't going to be a "normal" way to get rid of what's haunting me and my feelings of wanting to die.

The night before, I had such vivid dreams of running to a group of friends and then each group would all get murdered. I would run to another group and they would also get murdered, and so on. It was on repeat until I ran into the arms of a man in white with long blonde hair. That was when the killing stopped and the murderer disappeared. I wasn't sure what to make of that dream at the time, but it was so vivid and I could feel everything so intensely. It was burned into my brain for some reason.

I had so much anxiety the morning before leaving to drive to Mexico. I was wearing all black with a hood pulled over my head, looking out the window with a heart full of fear of what was about to happen. I was hunched over in a ball, from the pain in my stomach; it felt better for some reason when I was closed up like that. I called my mom on the phone that morning as I waited for Frank to pick me up. He was running late due to crazy Austin traffic, and it gave me plenty of time to freak out and almost back out of this whole adventure. It felt like I had hands pulling me back and trying to keep me from going. I came up with all the possible worst case scenarios in my head. My mom also had her reservations about me going. Her words exactly, "This sounds like snake scum. I don't know if you should do this, Allison." The fact that he was so late made me even more nervous, as I paced around my house.

He finally arrived, and I told him I didn't want to go. I mean, I had just met this guy at a strip club, and he would be driving me through the borders of Mexico. I tried my best to say I wasn't going, but he basically told me that I didn't have a choice. Whatever this thing was, it had a grasp on me. The dark energy was doing everything in its power to try to convince me to stay so *it* could stay. He told me we had to get moving because it was only going to get worse if we stayed longer. He was calm and convincing and could feel what I was feeling, which comforted me in a weird way. All of this was new, but I felt like someone finally understood me. I let my faith in the universe guide me from this point on, and we began our seven-hour drive across the border to Mexico. He had done this a time or two, so he knew the routes and what to do. The whole drive there, he explained to me what was happening with me and what I was processing. He was able to make sense and interpret these energies a lot better than I could. As I sat and listened, he told me that there isn't only one dark thing attached to me. He said I had legions of entities around me, not just one. It was similar to an army of darkness that I carried on my shoulders that I had acquired over the years of recklessness. He informed me that when you are intoxicated, whether it be alcohol or some kind of drug, you open up your crown chakra, making yourself vulnerable. This opening of your crown allows whatever entities are around to seep in and find a cozy new home that they can take over. It appeared that I was a magnet for them.

Frank continued to keep me calm and tried to explain what was going to happen with my healing session. I was in the biggest fear hole of my life and had no idea what to expect. What he was telling me didn't sound like it was real life! This healing technique is more of a spiritual surgery and is performed by a shaman named Betty. She performed a kind of healing ritual where she would transform the negative energy or sickness in your body into the form of an animal. Her modality is called Cunendara healing, popular in the

Mexican culture. The negative energy can either be an illness, a fear, poverty, a haunting, or anything that is holding you back in life. She takes this energy out by light scrapes from a knife against the skin. He explained that she wouldn't cut me, but would only lightly scrape me enough to spark energy and bring it to the surface. Then, it forms into the shape of a dead animal. Whatever animal that is, there is a symbol attached to help make sense of what it is that you need to learn.

It sounded too unrealistic to be true, but Frank swore by Miss Betty. It was hard for me to wrap my head around it all, and to think about what was going to come out of me. Honestly, I was scared to see it. I could feel it and that was enough to make me want to run. Frank had done it several times and had been there to assist others as well, so he felt confident and like he was fullining a mission. He was so sure because his guides were telling him so loudly to help me with this. I would have never sought this out on my own, or even known where to look. I was following his lead and looked up to him for wanting to help a stranger in this way.

I couldn't help but think about what was going to come out of me. *Was it going to be painful? Will my skin be opened up for this animal to come out?* I was filled with so many questions and so much anxiety as we drove those seven hours. It was like a weight was laying on my chest and it became harder to breathe. When we finally got to Mexico, Frank exchanged his Land Rover for a rental car to look more discrete. We headed up into the mountainous roads of Monterrey, through run-down neighborhoods in search of this small building. We were running late, but they said they would still see us that day if we made it there. When we arrived, the lady who had put my name on the list was waiting for us at the front entrance. I couldn't believe I had a team of angels helping me like this! They were helping me without a doubt in their mind that they needed to. I couldn't understand their generosity, but they insisted that I was a healer, meant to change and inspire many lives in this world. I couldn't see it yet, but they were so sure of it.

The lady who put my name on the list was named, Marcel. She began to interpret my situation and what was going on with me as soon as I met her. She told me that I had many souls trapped in me as if I was like a sponge, just as Frank described. I have been absorbing people's energy, and even their intentions, for so many years. She kept mentioning one man that kept coming to her mind. She told me how even intentions can be so powerful, that they can manifest into a curse. Apparently, I had a horrible intention laid upon me. She wasn't sure if it was an actual curse put on me or if this was someone's intent. She did know though, that this was the cause of my pain and sickness.

She was very adamant that this curse was made by a man that was tall, had curly hair, and was a light-skinned black man. She asked if I knew anyone with that description who had also fed me any food recently. I had to think about it for a minute, but I only knew one person with that description. I realized she was describing my doctor friend in Costa Rica. It had been about three months, but that was the only man I knew with those features that had fed me. As I waited with Marcel, we flipped through all the pictures of the guys I had recently been with to see if she could identify a bad vibe. As we looked through all the photos of my exes, she described each one of them and their intentions with great accuracy. It was enough to make me believe that what she was feeling was right. She told me this one doesn't like what you call him, this one was never faithful, this one truly cared for you, etc. We waited for 20 minutes in the waiting room anticipating this procedure. This house was nestled in a neighborhood, with a large, covered waiting room and a long bench for all the patients. She was a popular doctor in Monterrey and had a line of people waiting to be healed by her.

It was finally my time to step into the surgery room to see Miss Betty. As I walked towards the room, I saw a large shrine with Jesus and tons of candles and lights surrounding it. I wasn't religious, but this gave me a sense that I was protected by something more powerful than me. I was being guided to my next steps by these walking angels who were helping me every step of the way. I walked into this windowless little room that had a massage table laid out with clear plastic wrap around it. The room was clean, white, and bare, with only one chair for someone to sit in on the side. Everything was spoken in fast Spanish, so I was taking the cues from the body language and the broken up translations from Frank. Frank told Betty that he felt that I was a healer and needed help to seal my veins so no one else could put a curse on me. This was a whole separate ritual reserved only for the chosen healers, and Miss Betty had to make that decision when she met you. Luckily for me, Betty agreed that I did, in fact, qualify for spiritual protection. *Now another person thinks I'm a healer, too; maybe there is something to this.*

I felt as if I was sitting in a dream with everything that was going on around me. I felt like I was in a daze, being pulled around like a puppet--not quite sure what was going on. They told me to take off my shirt and lay on my back on the massage table. Betty approached me and had a knife in her hands. I was terrified but, at the same time, I felt safe in her presence because of how calm she was. Plus it was helpful that Frank warned me about how the process would go. She assured me to stay calm and breathe. She began to perform the surgery by gently scraping the dull part of the blade in the middle of my chest. As she did this, Marcel had bundles of toilet paper wrapped around her hands, and then created pressure around where Betty was scraping. To complete the ritual, Frank poured holy water on top of where they created the friction. There was an overload of different sensations going through my mind as I stared up at the ceiling, unable to see what was happening. I could feel the scraping, but it wasn't unbearable or breaking the skin to the point where it was hurting. The feelings in that area was like a volcanic eruption that was taking place in my heart. Betty ordered Marcel to cover the area with toilet paper, and then from beneath that toilet paper, an animal formed. For me, I had a lot of black sand that came out, which in their tradition, means that cancer was removed. Then, the animal that came out of me ended up being a snake. This snake's head was chopped off about three inches down. It had fangs and its tongue was still sticking out. Frank picked it up real quick, only to show me what had come out of me so that I would see and believe what I had just experienced.

As I sat up, I began to feel something so wrong happening to my body. The pain in my stomach was so overpowering when I stood up that my limbs started to go numb. This wasn't over yet. Betty and I both knew she had to do this procedure again. The workers in the healing center came in quickly to clean up the space to get rid of all the negative energy that was removed; it's important to clear out the last healing before starting another one. As they did this, I began to lose my focus and feelings in my hands and feet. Then the numbness started moving towards my torso. I started to get cold and weak, and began to hyperventilate because I was freaking out as to what was happening to my stomach. I looked down and could literally see something in my stomach moving from the left side, jumping to the right, and going back and forth. Something was scraping my insides and it was so painful. Whatever they did to me only aggravated the pain I had in my abdomen. Normally, this healing procedure only needs to be performed one time, but I was a different case. Frank, Marcel, and Betty could see this thing moving inside me too. They tried their best to keep me calm while Betty performed a sacred prayer in the corner to protect herself before she began to do the second surgery. I could feel the life being sucked out of me like this thing was trying to kill me. It was one of the most traumatic experiences of my life.

Once the staff cleaned the room and Betty finished her prayer, I was put back on the massage table for the second round. Frank and Marcel were trying to keep me calm by breathing with me and reassuring me between my screams of pain. I probably scared every person that was waiting outside that room. (No one else that went in that room before me had screamed or even made a sound.) This time as I laid down on the bed, Betty came over to me and started yelling in Spanish at my stomach. She was telling whatever was inside to, "Stay down! You stay down!" as she was pointing at it. The procedure began again and everyone was doing their parts once more. This time, the surgery was so painful! I could feel this *thing* inside of me moving around with a mission to damage me before it left me. The process took a bit longer, and Betty scraped harder this time, barely breaking the skin. I could feel something emerge from my stomach, and once it was released, I immediately felt this sense of relief. I took a big gasp of fresh air and was laying in shock for a minute on the table.

Once more, I had more black sand that came out in the process, but I also had a wine cork with a nail stuck in it that was a charcoal black color. That was what was scraping my insides. I couldn't help but think of that bottle of wine that I traded my doctor friend for a prescription of Valium. It was confirmed by Marcel that because that bottle of wine was something of mine that I gave to him, he was able to put a curse on me this way. Same thing with the food. It was something that was his, that he gave to me. Betty told me that because it didn't come out in the form of an animal, that someone had indeed put a curse on me. The curse was to either kill me or stop me from reproducing, which would explain the weird period cramping and spotting. I had no idea that humans were capable of doing this kind of black magic, but just as pure as this white magic was, I came to fully believe in all of it. *There is so much that we don't know about in this world, and now I have a whole new perspective.* My question was, *Why would he put this kind of curse on me?*

After the second surgery was completed, I was weak but I was also filled with tears of joy. I felt as if I could breathe again, and the colors became brighter. I was brittle from the experience because it had taken so much energy out of me. I had to take some time to collect myself before walking back outside of that room. While we waited for me to regain some strength, Betty had confirmed that I was indeed a healer and needed to undergo one more ceremony to seal my veins so no one could ever put another curse on me again. Betty told Frank that I needed to eat some soup and regain my strength for what was about to come. Frank and Marcel were both on each side of my arms, helping to carry me out to the car. As I stumbled out of that house, I could feel all the eyes in the waiting room staring at me, wondering what the hell happened in there. It was like an exorcism had just happened and I was embarrassed, yet so relieved and happy that it was over. Frank and Marcel sat in the front seat of the rental car and I was in the backseat laying down, still in shock. I had a completely eye-opening experience that was so hard to believe, but I could *feel* the difference. This weight of darkness that felt like 10,000 pounds was lifted off my shoulders and everything around me felt new and light. I felt like a baby that was learning how to walk for the first time. This whole experience felt like a dream or another reality that I had never been in before--and there were no drugs involved at all. I couldn't help myself, but I recorded a few videos on my phone of this experience and what happened because I needed to document what had happened.

We ended up at an empty little restaurant so I could recharge my batteries and get ready for the second healing session. I had some chicken soup and deep conversations with Frank and Marcel about what had happened. They were just as relieved as I was because neither of them had seen anything like that before. It was encouraging for Frank to realize his intuitions were right, and that his guides were accurate. As we sat and ate, Frank told me that it wasn't quite over yet. We had to stop at the store and get a bottle of tequila. Not sure why alcohol was a part of the next healing ceremony, but I went with it. He tried to explain that my veins would be sealed, and during the process, I would have to drink a lot of tequila to "purify" my soul. I felt so pure and so fresh in that moment, and the thought of drinking made me gag. For once I didn't even want to drink anything, but if this was what I had to do to protect myself, then that was what I was going to do. We waited about two hours for me to regain my strength before returning to Betty's healing house for round two.

It was after their normal hours of operation at this time, and all of the clients had left. Betty guided us into her home and took us to a different section of the house; I think it was the laundry room. She led me into a small dark corner room and had me stand barefoot in the middle of a circle made from chalk on the ground. She asked Frank for the tequila so she could have it ready. After I stepped inside the circle, Betty lit it on fire. It was far enough away to where I wasn't scared. I could feel a force field beginning to surround me, as if I had the cheering on of all my angels.

The ceremony began and Betty handed me a large cup of tequila, roughly three shots worth, to drink all at once. I had to make sure I did it smoothly, because I couldn't lose a drop of it. The first one barely went down. She set the cup aside and continued to use chalk to mark exes on all of the areas where energy could seep in on my body. She marked all my fingers, my wrists, the insides of my elbows, my neck, third eye, tongue, back of the knees, my feet, and so many more places I couldn't keep track. Then she asked me to drink another three shots straight as she said a prayer. She continued to speak in Spanish while sealing love and light into my body, and Frank was quietly observing what was going on from the side. To finish the ceremony, I had to drink one more glass of tequila. At that point, I was so intoxicated and unsure about what was happening that the ending became a blur. I couldn't understand why alcohol should be involved in a healing ceremony, but my guess is this was a purging of the darkness or "a purifying" as Frank says. I was pretty intoxicated by the time I left Betty's house, unsure of what was going to come next. She gave me a jug of this special tea that I needed to drink three times a day for three days; then once I finished that, I had to pour the rest of the tea over my body in the shower to cleanse my body. (I know, all of this sounds so strange. I guess you had to be there to understand fully.)

Frank and I sat in the rental car for a while after the sealing of the veins and drank the rest of that bottle of tequila as we talked about my experience. Something also began to happen to Frank. He kept asking me questions about why he was feeling a certain way and I was so confused as to why I would know the answer. He was experiencing so much of the same shame, guilt, and addictions that he didn't feel before the ceremony. Something had happened where he took on my energy while I was releasing it. It was like he had turned into me or he was processing what I couldn't. At this point, I was believing anything was possible and I had no idea how to deal with this.

After a couple hours passed by, I had the urge to go out to a bar and let loose. Once you get me going on a few drinks, it's hard to stop me, especially after everything I had just gone through. Frank agreed and took me to a bar around the corner from his friend's house where we were supposed to stay that night. We were at this bar and all of sudden, Frank noticed a change in my demeanor. He told me my face went blank and I had this stare as if I was looking into another world. He was right, but this world wasn't a pretty one. He quickly grabbed me and took me to the car before anything happened. As we got in, I began to squirm and desperately wanted to find coke. I remember feeling like I had a 1,000 hands beating on my chest, wanting to explode with anxiety from withdrawal. I felt like I had claws in the back of my neck again, trying to force me to do something horrible to myself. I started yelling how I didn't want to live and how I wanted to kill myself when I felt the urge to vomit. I had this huge projectile puke exit my body, similar to the movie, *The Exorcist.* It was like a purging was taking place within the depths of my soul. It was a force beyond anything I had experienced. I got half of the puke outside the car and the rest, unfortunately, went inside the rental. Frank took off quickly so he could take me to his friend's house. As he was turning a corner to get on the highway, I opened the car door and literally tried to jump out.

The voices in my head were too much for me at the time. All I wanted was the noise in my brain to stop. He grabbed my arm and held onto me with all his might, swaying the car to the left to force the door closed. He pulled over on the side of the road after I pulled this stunt. As soon as the car stopped, I started running. I don't know where I was running to, I just ran. Frank came running behind me and grabbed me to comfort and control me from running into the street. I was balling my eyes out in a state of panic. I didn't know what was going on, and I had no way to control it, either. Frank described to me that I had those legions of spirits swarming around us like a tornado. They had all these high pitched, bone-chilling laughs coming in close, getting the best of me. They were the evil spirits that had been forcing me to harm myself for all these years, putting in their last and final attempt. They call alcohol a spirit for a reason. I had opened up that door during the ceremony, and I was more vulnerable than ever. I was a clean slate and feeling everything more than ever. He explained that the spirits were there because there was alcohol in the ceremony. This was their finale; the end of their power over me. They were going to do everything in their power to go out with a bang and they were making me feel their presence in my bones. Frank held me until their shrieks started to fade into background noises. He kept repeating the mantra, "I'm sorry--Please forgive me--Thank you--I love you." That seemed to bring some peace to the chaos I was experiencing, and it also helped to clear the energetic field around me. I was glad I had someone else there who could understand what I was going through, because none of this seemed real to me. I don't know if I would've been able to make sense of any of this on my own.

The ceremony wasn't complete until I finished drinking this tea that was blessed for the continual healing and sealing of the veins. That night, after the spirit stopped haunting me, Frank took me back to his friend's house where we all struggled to sleep. His friends asked us to leave because I was being so loud and obnoxious. We ended up finding a hotel that had a vacancy, and we posted up there for the night around 5 a.m. I was finally able to sleep and ended up doing so for about 17 hours. I slept for a full day and a half, only getting up to drink my tea. Frank was also exhausted from what had happened, and I think we were still both in shock from what we went through. Out of all of the healings he has led in Mexico, he said this one was different. I was the most intense and the most extreme case he had ever been a part of.

We spent an extra two days in Mexico to regain our strength after the ceremony was complete. By that time, we finally had the energy to make our way back to the States. Luckily, my roommate was able to watch Chi while we were away. We were on the highway when we realized that I had left the tea behind back in the hotel room! Frank quickly called the hotel to make sure room service didn't throw it away, because if they did, I would've had to do the ceremony all over again. It just so happened that the person who was cleaning the room knew exactly what that tea was, and kept it safe and refrigerated for us. *What are the odds?* We arrived back at the hotel to grab the tea and then once more continued on our way back to Austin.

We decided that it wasn't a good idea that I go back to my old job as a stripper, or that I stay at the same house anymore since we both knew it was haunted. Frank was generous enough to offer me to stay rent-free at his healer's house in Belton, Texas. This was about an hour and a half from Austin, but 15 minutes from Frank's. This would give me a good chance to start over and get myself the help and attention I needed to get clean and stay clean with my newfound sense of purpose. I wouldn't get another opportunity to start over and heal myself like this one. I went back to my apartment with Frank there, only to grab Chi and a few items and then made myself at home in Frank's extra house. I finished the three days with the tea and on the last day, I did as Betty had instructed. I poured the tea over me in the shower. In the jug, it was a light greenish, brown color. I kid you not though, when I poured it over my body, it turned black by the time it touched the tub. It was so wild that I couldn't believe it. I was continually amazed with this healing journey, and the magic that exists that I never knew about.

It felt like this was a real dream that was unfolding all around me. I felt guided and taken care of by Frank because he helped me for no reason, other than believing I was a healer. I was amazed with this experience and didn't want to take this opportunity for granted. This process of healing was unlike anything people could even imagine, and most people I tried to explain this to thought I was crazy. Yet, it worked for me. I didn't need anyone's approval. I felt like I had been reborn, and that was all the proof I needed to be a believer. I was relearning how to understand life from a clear and clean perspective. I was fragile. I was timid and the complete opposite of how I acted before this experience. I saw my reality from a different viewpoint, and didn't feel the weight or heaviness over my shoulders anymore; if anything, I felt light. The pain in my stomach and my abnormal periods cleared up immediately. I was finally able to have a normal cycle after that without any weird spotting or pains. I got off all of my medications, including birth control, alcohol, and any other mind altering drugs. Not many people get the chance to start over, and I felt like this was a gift from my angels and spirit guides.

As I stayed at the Belton house, I had a lot of time to sit in the quietness and listen to what was around me. I could see and feel things that weren't here in this dimension more so than before. Frank was convinced that I was capable of performing healings because the shaman lady had told him that I also had the same gift that she has. She explained to him that if I could move water, then I could do the same energetic work that she does. For hours, Frank and I would sit in the kitchen with a glass of water, staring at it, trying to move it. It seemed silly and like we were wasting time, but then it happened. I created a ripple effect in the water that was sitting two feet away from me on the dining table. He was freaking out with excitement, and I was sitting there shocked. *Could I actually do this?* To be honest, it kind of scared me, but Frank wanted me to keep trying. We tried again and again and I couldn't do it as well as that one time. He became convinced and I became somewhat nervous. This wasn't exactly the kind of work I planned on getting into, nor did I want to. Frank was good at fighting the dark side, but I wasn't sure I was ready to go up against some of the things we can't see with our eyes. I didn't sign up to be this kind of healer.

I made a post on Facebook about my healing journey to Mexico, which I soon deleted after it was released. Many people were in disbelief, and others questioned what kind of drugs I was on. Some people were interested and wanted to try to figure out how they could do it too, and others thought I was crazy. I did have a few people who felt like they needed this kind of spiritual surgery though. One friend of mine in particular knew he was haunted by something; he'd even named this spirit, giving it more power. I dated him for a while in my recent past and I could sense this darkness that he would talk about from time to time when he was around. The moment I agreed to try to figure out how I could help him, whatever darkness he had came swarming into my Belton house. The visions of distorted humans crawling creepily flooded my thoughts. As I sat on the bed, I tried to hide, but you can't hide from something you can't see. It swarms all around you and even gets inside your head. I noticed this black, ghostly figure sliding quickly towards me along the wall. I ran into the other room and it slid along the walls chasing me, filling me with complete terror and fear. I called Frank at one in the morning, begging for his help. I didn't know what to do and I didn't like this thing invading my personal space. This thing knew exactly how to fill me with fear, giving it more power as the minutes passed. I tried my best to stay calm, but this was some evil spirit that packed a punch with its presence. I kept feeling bugs crawling underneath my skin and visions of dismembered humans. It was wild how much this energy was messing with my thoughts. I was so uncomfortable in my own skin as I waited for Frank to come help me.

Frank came over and started blessing the house with sage, repeating his mantra, "I'm sorry--Please forgive me--Thank you--I love you." He paced all around the house, chasing this thing around trying to get it out of the house. He was chasing this darkness like the darkness was chasing me, without any fear or hesitation. I was definitely out of my league. I'm not trained to be a ghostbuster.

We called that friend of mine that I had agreed to help, and asked him what he was experiencing. He said his ghost finally left and he was feeling okay. He told me he would normally talk with this spirit and invite him into his space, which is definitely not the kind of imaginary friend you should ask to come around. This only makes a spirit more powerful when you give them that kind of acknowledgement. First, we asked him to stop encouraging him to come back around and to quit calling it by a name. We explained to him that he's not feeling his ghost because his ghost came over here.

We all needed to work together on saying that mantra to clear this energy. We spent about thirty minutes repeating these words to hopefully clear it out of our houses. Evil cannot live within the walls of love, and this is the kind of bubble we were trying to create. It slowly felt like the tornado was passing and the house was becoming lighter and less dense. This kind of work is exhausting; it's scary as shit to work with something you can't see, but you can only feel their hate and anger. This Belton house was like a portal that had many active souls in its space. There were so many ghosts that were attracted to the energy here. Not all of them were bad or threatening like this last one. Maybe it was my newfound sensitivity, but I was alert and more aware than ever before.

Frank also was experiencing his own side effects from the healing. He was still processing all the things that I had held onto for years. He was going through all of the pain I had carried in my heart. He was feeling the grasp of my addiction, my fear, shame, guilt, and self-doubt. Basically, he was processing all the negative emotions that had held me back, and I wasn't feeling the weight of any of them anymore. I didn't know how to help him. The way I coped with it was drowning it out with drugs and alcohol, which is something he didn't normally do. He said this typically happens after a healing session with someone, but he had never felt so much weight until mine. This was the way the energy gets regenerated and transformed back into the universe. In the past, it would take him up to three months to process it all and feel normal again. I wished I could help him, but I didn't even know where to start. All I could do was sit with him, listen, and sympathize. It was a little crazy to think that he was experiencing my emotions that I carried for so long. It was even more crazy that I didn't feel the weight of this anymore.

After about two months, I couldn't take it any longer. I needed to get out and do normal, human things. I stumbled upon a guy on Facebook who had a bunch of smaller looking surfboards in a picture in Austin. I remember seeing that and wishing I could surf again. I went out on a limb and wrote this stranger a message asking where he was surfing with those boards in Austin. He replied, "Behind my boat on Lake Austin. Want to join me sometime?" I answered with a hell yes! It was a long drive from Belton to Austin, but I was going to make this trip regardless of how far away it was.

When I arrived there, I had a flashback of my dream before the healing ceremony. It was the man in white with the long blond hair that protected and shielded me to keep me safe. I walked up to him the same as in the dream and gave him a huge hug hello. I couldn't believe it. I was told that vivid dreams are the universe's way of sending you messages and I felt like I was following mine. This message was so loud and clear that it was impossible to miss. Instantly, we became friends and had an amazing day surfing together. I had found my new outlet--wakesurfing! I only went out surfing with him two times before the question of me being his new roommate came up. I needed a place to stay and he needed a roommate because his ex just moved out and he needed help with rent. *How perfect was this? A new friend, with a room for me to rent, who has a boat, that allows me to surf with him?!* I couldn't pass this up or let this slide through my fingers. Not only that, but I felt safe with him, like I did in my dream. His name was John. We instantly became the best of friends and not even a week later, I was his new roommate. I explained my situation about what had happened, and he agreed to let me stay in his extra room and help me get back on my feet in Austin. I was so grateful that I had this guy in my life. I was even more grateful to have had that dream to show me the next steps on my journey.

I told Frank that I had to leave, and this was my exit strategy. He was worried about me going back to my old lifestyle and emphasized how important it was to keep my channels clean. My soul was never meant to have those chemicals and spirits pass through me. It was even more important because I had just been through a spiritual surgery, and I was still recovering. I thanked him for his concern and his help along the way. I honestly don't know if I would even be alive today without Frank's help and guidance. I told Frank I needed space from being a ghostbuster and I needed to experience being a normal human again. I thought it was best if we didn't talk for a while, just until the dust settled. It was sad to leave him behind, but his kind of work was far from what I was ready for. He wished that I would stay and work on my healing powers, but honestly, I was over it. I felt it was best to separate myself from that and focus on doing me for a while. He understood and agreed that if this is what was meant to be, then so be it.

*Side Note: Sometimes in life, there are people that we meet that are "Walking Angels." They will feel different from the rest and they will most likely have a message for you. They are important key factors into the evolution of your awakening. Pay attention to vivid dreams or when these people come around. Sometimes they will be friends, sometimes strangers. Trust your intuition to follow their guidance or messages when they come around.

CHAPTER TWENTY-TWO

A FRESH START

When I moved back to Austin to live with John, I had my mind set on working at JuiceLand. If you live in Austin, you would know that this is the most hip and delicious smoothie shop around! They hire super cool employees, and have a reputation for being a mindful company with great core values. This company had my attention and my intuition was communicating so loudly to follow down this path. Somehow, I knew I was supposed to work there. It wasn't so easy to get in with this hip company, but I didn't give up and I wouldn't settle for any other job. I knew it would help keep me clean and sober because it's a healthy environment and this company had some amazing people working for them. I was persistent and patient, and luckily, so was John. I wouldn't even apply at other jobs because my intuition kept screaming "JuiceLand!" I had a new sense of confidence in what I was feeling with a clear channel to my intuition. I was beginning to trust that voice inside of me that was directing me on my path. I had never heard it so loudly before my healings, except for in Nicaraguan jail. I knew I was going to get this job; it was only a matter of time. Sure enough, about a month after persistently trying, I realized that my best friend Katelyn knew the owner's brother. I asked Katelyn if she could talk to him about passing my information along for me. It worked like gold and I was in! I had finally connected the dots, and felt so accomplished.

In the meantime, living with John was a whole different ball game. My first week living there was the week of July 4th. Every year, John takes his boat out on the lake and they party over in the cove and tie up to a bunch of other boats. It was my first time back in this environment and I was still too weak to say no to alcohol, especially when it was a holiday and other people were drinking. (This was what Frank was warning me about.) It was the first time John introduced me as his new roommate to all of his friends. When we arrived at the cove, where all the other boats were tied up, everyone got in the water to swim and travel over to other boats to mingle. Another girl and I made it over to another boat; I didn't know the owners, but she did. The guys on that boat were feeding all the girls shots from the end of a Deep Eddy Vodka bottle. I remember taking a big swig or two from that bottle before hopping off to swim back to John's boat.

About 30 minutes after that happened, shit kind of got crazy for me. I had only had one cider and those two swigs off a bottle, but I could tell I was losing control of my body. Being drunk and having the waves mess with my balance was also a bad combination for me. I started to feel like I had been drugged. This was the first time in about two months that I had let alcohol enter my body. I was around new people, not exactly in the safest environment, and I wasn't sure what was going to happen. To be honest, I didn't think it would be a problem. Well, it was. It was bad, too. I didn't know if this was my new reaction to alcohol or if that other boat had drugged me. The other girl that took those shots with me was acting overly intoxicated, too.

I ended up being a huge pain in the ass that night. I bit John and his friend so hard on their chest that they were bleeding. It wasn't a cute sexy nibble; I was more like a monster that wanted to taste blood. They couldn't believe I did that, but they also didn't know me, so they were trying to give me the benefit of the doubt. Later, I was swimming with John and I kept playing the game of "hold him under water," like I was trying to drown him. It was like I had turned into a scary, evil creature that was stuck in a hot lady's body. That was the only reason why they were bypassing my craziness.

I don't remember the rest of that evening, but John made sure to keep tabs on what was going on. Later that night, we returned home and things escalated to another level. The next morning, I woke up in my new room, naked and confused as to what had happened. I walked into the living room and asked John what had happened, and he replied with, "You got wasted." I asked if anything happened between us and he was hesitant to respond. I think he had all the feelings of guilt surrounding him when I asked that because he could tell I didn't remember. He denied that we had sex, but he said we fooled around. John made sure to record part of the evening on his phone so he could have proof about how I was acting. He showed me one recording in particular on his phone of me sitting in his lap, topless, talking about this book and how he wasn't going to get any of the rights to it. *Oh boy, what else did I tell this kid?* The wild child in me came out that night. Luckily, I had some level of intrigue from John, which must be the only reason he still kept me around. I'm an interesting story, even though I was a hot mess.

After that night, John was more distant with me and decided to friend zone me. Before, he had been flirty and made sure to let me know that he liked me, but after the 4th, I was treated like his roommate. I was confused by it because

I knew he was attracted to me. I kept trying to seduce him anyway, thinking he was playing hard to get. After a while of trying to pursue someone and they constantly turned me down, I began to ask myself, "*What's the point of chasing after someone who doesn't want me?*" I guess I ruined my chances with him that night by acting crazy. I honestly think I was drugged, but I also didn't have a good track record with keeping my shit under control when I would drink. Not to mention, I was warned by Frank about getting intoxicated. *Maybe this was the new normal when I drink?*

Over the first three months of me living there, John made sure to observe me before trying to get into a relationship with me. He was the kind of person that liked to have his glass or two (or bottle) of wine at night, along with a margarita from his favorite little Mexican restaurant down the street. He had his routine and alcohol was definitely part of it. I would try to hang and do what he was doing, but I didn't react the same to alcohol anymore. I had this evil little thing, my shadow side, come out to haunt me. Frank was right when he was worried about me drinking again and letting these spirits enter my body when my crown chakra was open. Not only that, but the ghost of John's ex was swarming in the house. Every time I would drink, he would tell me how much I would act like her. It was like I was channeling what had gone on in that house before me, and I would say the exact same phrases that she would say.

After about four months, John's friend Alec came to town. Keep in mind, John still didn't want to call me his girlfriend and would only introduce me as his roommate. This friend was cute and we instantly hit it off. I figured, *what's the harm? John doesn't like me like that.* Apparently, John and I never had sex, so it shouldn't be an issue if I pursue his friend. Things started to progress between me and Alec, and it became obvious to John that we were falling for each other. I liked the fact that his friend was going to be leaving soon, and I was also super horny and couldn't think about anything else.

One night while he was in town, we all went camping in his RV before a surf tournament. When it was time to go to bed, I asked John to make a third bed out of the kitchen table so I didn't have to choose which bed to get into. He refused just so he could see whose bed I would pick. Pissed off from his decision, I gave him a piece of his own medicine and chose to sleep with his friend. Right before we were about to settle into a nice cuddle, John told me not to sleep with Alec because we had already had sex with each other. He had held out this information and lied about this for the past four months; he was just now fessing up to it. I didn't believe him because he had denied it when I asked him after the night of the 4th. Plus, he had been denying it and had pushed me away like he didn't like me anymore. At this point, John stormed off because he was pissed that I chose his friend over him, and I wasn't believing what he was telling me about us already having had sex. My mind was racing. I was pissed that he lied to me and pissed that he had been blowing me off for so long. I was proving my point that if you don't claim me as yours, I can easily become someone else's. I admit, this is not the best way to prove a point, but I followed through and got the sex I needed that night. John had taken his truck and "drove" home, leaving us in the RV for the night, or so we thought. John was forever scarred because, once more he lied to me about leaving. We thought he had driven back home, but he was waiting outside the RV, peeking in through the windows, spying on us. He waited until we had finished having sex to barge in the front door to bust us. When he walked in, the first thing he saw was the condom wrapper on the floor of the entryway. He flipped out on both of us, scaring us into a frozen state of shock to the point where we didn't know what to say or do. After about 15 minutes of that, he finally left the campsite and slept at home. I knew I fucked up the minute he busted through the door. I should've known that this was a trap or a test that he was giving me, but my sex drive was intensified when alcohol was invovled. Plus, a huge part of me was being selfish and didn't give a fuck in the moment.

After his friend left, things weren't the same at that house. I felt like he hated me for a while, but he soon came around to expressing how he truly felt about me. He admitted to not knowing how to tell me that we slept together that night. He didn't realize I wouldn't remember, therefore he didn't want me to think he raped me by taking advantage of me. The video he took that night was his way of being able to show me what happened, even though I didn't get the full story, only a clip. He told me he was waiting to see the kind of person I truly was before making me his girlfriend. He also told me that he never wanted to see me with another person again. He cared for me, and I could tell. He put up with some major bullshit from me, and was still there to support me.

He did tell me that he thought I had a drinking problem and that if we were to be together, I needed to find a way to figure out how to control myself. After this talk, we slowly progressed into a relationship where we didn't see other people. I began to drink less in hopes that I wouldn't scare him away, and I got back into my yoga practice. I felt as if I was walking on eggshells though, trying my best not to upset him. I made sure to mind my P's and Q's and help keep the house in order for him, so he was able to be more clear headed to do his work from home. He eventually persuaded me to move my things into his room. When this happened, he began to slowly let me into his heart, but it was heavily guarded; he knew what kind of person I was capable of being and had a hard time trusting me after what I did with his former friend. I tried my hardest to regain his trust and get back on his good side, but this was just the beginning of another uphill battle. The start of this relationship should've been a huge red flag for both of us to run the other way.

Beginning the relationship with lying, intoxication, jealousy, and without trust was a recipe for disaster. This relationship, as much as I felt like John was a genuine guy, was toxic for me. I found myself once more in this cycle of being dependent on a man to help take care of me. It was his house, his rules, and I royally fucked it up in the beginning. Because it was so toxic, I found myself wanting to drown out my pain and anxiety with Xanax and alcohol. Both of these substances were always present in the house and it was too difficult for me to turn them down. I found my other cycle of not caring about my body and my limits because I was in a toxic relationship. I would drink because he would drink, but I was the one who never knew how or when to stop. It would freak John out when I would get too drunk because I would act in the same way as his ex girlfriend. We would get into these yelling matches and I would end up punching and kicking holes throughout the house, like she did. I would scream at the top of my lungs as I rummaged through the house, trying to find where John hid the rest of the alcohol. There was one time in particular we were at the neighborhood Mexican Restaurant, and I thought I was locked in the bathroom stall. (This, for some reason, was a continuing theme of mine.) I have a fear of being trapped or confined in small spaces, and I freak out. This happened more times than I can remember, when all I needed to do was turn the lock to open the door. Well, this time, I literally kicked a hole through the wooden slabs on the door and crawled out. To say the least, I was banned from the restaurant after that. I officially could not handle my alcohol anymore. It all became too much. It wasn't fun anymore and there was something else inside me that was this crazy person. My painful realizations when I sobered up started to eat at my conscience, and at our relationship.

He had another sit down conversation with me about a year later. He told me that if I didn't stop drinking, he would break up with me and I would have to move out. I needed that kind of conversation because I knew I was going down a dark path again. Then it started to click as to what Frank had told me; my body is not made for these substances to be in it. This wasn't who I wanted to be forever. I knew there was a bigger purpose for myself on this planet. I could feel the pull of its plea, I just didn't know how or what that purpose was yet.

Working over at JuiceLand was probably one of the best things that I could've done for my future. It didn't quite pay the bills all the time, but it was my safe space that had a crew of people who supported my growth and health. I worked there for about seven months when I realized they had a special bi-annual giveaway called the "Fresh for Life Grant." They would give away $2,000 to one of their employees to chase after their dreams! This contest really made me question what my dreams were. I wanted to apply for it but I didn't know exactly what I wanted to do. I knew I was a healer, I just didn't know what kind. I knew I wanted to help people, I just didn't know how. All I knew was that in order to heal myself, I needed to help others heal. I knew that was my life's purpose, but the details were still pretty fuzzy and it was unclear as to how this would all play out. (**Note**: things were fuzzy for me because I was still drinking and taking mind altering drugs. It's hard to hear your true self when you are drowning that voice away.)

Yoga was the one thing that kept me on track besides working at JuiceLand. Being on my mat was my safe space that I would run to when I needed to get away from John, or when I had the urge to drink. I found myself on my mat when I practiced letting go and moving my body. I felt free, like I was growing into the person I was meant to become. I was beginning to shine my best when I was practicing yoga, and I began to make the connections. I thought back to the message that I had been sent from my angels four years prior, when I was released from the Nicaraguan jail for teaching the girls yoga and making them so happy. When I practiced, I could feel my angels sending me messages to help guide me when I was lost. Either my teacher would say something in class, or I would release something stored in my body somewhere. Thinking back on that day in Nicaragua made me realize what a monumental moment that was for my life.

I didn't understand the meaning of it all until now. I was lying in savasana at the end of one of my classes one day, and I heard the words, *You're meant to be a yoga teacher!* I knew that if yoga could get me released from jail, it could also release me from a lot of other things as well.

I was doing a lot of yoga over at Practice Yoga Austin, when I solidified that this was the story I was going to use for my essay for the Fresh for Life Grant. My teacher, Rey, announced in class that there was one spot left for the 200-hour yoga teacher training. I knew that this spot was for me. I had one of those moments when I could see into my future. I saw myself in the training, I saw winning the grant, and I saw myself finally stepping into my light. Everything felt right about this situation. Once again, I could feel and hear my intuition and my angels beaming with excitement in my head. I could see the path that I needed to take, and it all was so obvious now. I have experienced very few of these moments, but when the voice inside of me is this loud, I have to follow through. It's hard to ignore your higher self when you can feel and see your next steps so clearly.

To apply for the grant with JuiceLand, you must write an essay as to why you deserve to have it. My higher self responded with: *write about your Nicaraguan Jail story.* It's too wild of a story not to win this contest! That was the first time I ever taught yoga, and that was what released me from a third world country jail. *This is my mission. This is my purpose in this lifetime.* Four years ago when I was in jail, I never would have thought that I was supposed to be a yoga teacher. I wasn't ready to see it then; it was meant to be seen now, when I needed to save myself. It finally all made sense as to why I went to jail and had that horrible experience. I was blessed with the opportunity to write an epic story as to why I should win the grant! I vowed to myself when I wrote this essay: *if I won this grant, then I was meant to be a yoga teacher.* As I wrote, I could feel the readers' reactions to my story. I knew I was going to win; I just knew it. This story was too wild not to. I felt like I was protected and guided and had the strength of an army of angels behind me when I sent out my essay.

I found myself stepping into my light when everything started to align and I truly began to follow my heart with a selfless mindset. I could feel my next steps in my heart before they were happening. I knew and was predicting my future because I could feel the path that was right for me. It was as if I was gambling with the universe, knowing that I was going to win the jackpot! The winner of the Fresh for Life grant was being announced after the 200-hour training completed their first weekend. I was certainly cutting it close, but sure enough, I WON! I hopped on the second weekend of training and made sure not to miss a day after that.

Without a doubt, I needed a push like this to change my life. I wasn't in a good space mentally or emotionally, and I needed to focus my mind on something else. I had more people than ever questioning me about my drinking problem during this time in my life. I knew I needed some kind of help, but AA wasn't what I felt like I needed. Having a drinking problem had me on my knees, begging for a new beginning. This was the change and the shift I needed to get myself the help I needed. This opportunity that has been gifted to me to become a yoga teacher was going to save me. I could feel it. It was almost as if I could feel the universe's plan for me and I became 100% devoted to seeing this through. *The time has come for me to put my whole heart into something that could help myself heal, and help the world heal in return.*

*Side Note: When life gives you an opportunity like this, do not waste it. This was a sign that I was on the right track and that I needed to continue marching down this path with my whole heart. If and when it is right for you, everything will align.

CHAPTER TWENTY-THREE

THE SHIFT I NEEDED

I was amazed with how everything lined up. I knew I had to get the job at JuiceLand, and this was why! It was a part of my path. I saw the magnitude of following my heart and not understanding the pull, but trusting it regardless. This gift was an opportunity to start over and discover a new path for myself. I decided going into this 200-hour training that I was going to give it my whole heart by making sure to attend every session and give my full attention to each training session. I still owed a little more money for my training, but I ended up doing a work-trade option by helping to keep the space clean, and working the front desk during the holiday season.

All of a sudden, I became a dorky little kid that was too excited to sleep on training weekends. Going to this training was the highlight of my week. We did Friday nights, and all day Saturdays and Sundays for three months. This training was quickly becoming the answer to my questions and cries for a better life! I never realized that this training was going to be so transformative for my life.

Teacher training became my therapy sessions to dive into my fears. It made me question my battles within myself and how I was going to show up each day. My teachers became my mentors and my classmates became friends. I truly needed this kind foundation in my life. This was a place where we could be real and honest with ourselves, and others. We were all there, holding space for all of us to speak our truths and say how we were feeling. I found magic in becoming vulnerable. It felt great to be freed from my lies that I told myself to *feel safe*. I was beginning to break down the walls and reprogram my brain to think with a different perspective. This training taught me way more tools aside from how to teach yoga. I gained knowledge and skills on how to listen to my body, and I learned my limits and boundaries. I learned how our bodies, and the way we do our practice, are like metaphors for how we live our lives. I learned about the psychology behind why movement is like medicine, helping to clear out negativity. This training gave me valuable tools that I can use to help others. I was soaking it all up like a sponge and wanted to keep learning more. I was the one asking questions, sitting front and center. This was the gift I was looking to share! I knew I was going to help people with this book, but now I have another way that I can reach people. Another added bonus, I was finally on my way to having the happy ending for this book that I was looking for.

Kiely Wolters and Rey Cardenas were my teachers for this training. Rey was one of my first yoga teachers who helped me get through my divorce, and he is one of the owners of Practice. I always saw Rey with a giant beam of light around him. He was like a guru in a young adult's body. Seriously though, some people on my journey stand out in my mind, and he is one of those people. Pay attention to these people along your journey, because they stand out for a reason. I had always felt like he was playing an important role in my growth, and then there he was, the one who helped make this dream a reality for me. Kiely has been a true guiding light for me, as well. She is an inspiring yoga teacher who is also sober. She makes being clean and sober seem cool--I wanted to be like her when it came to her attitude about alcohol. She has always been a role model for me to be open, honest, and vulnerable. She made me feel comfortable enough to be honest with the class about my struggles with alcohol, and this was the first time I admitted to other people that I had a problem. Being in this loving and accepting environment allowed me to feel safe enough to speak these words out loud. After I did, it became my strength to not let everyone see my weak side.

Throughout training, we spent our breaks in the parking lot next to the studio. I found so many rocks in the shape of hearts that it was almost impossible to fathom! Hearts have been my synchronicity in life that showed me that I was on the right path. Every time I went on break, I would find about 20 rocks and put them on the window sills of the studio. This studio is right downtown off of 6th street, and people would stop and notice them, or take one. I would replenish them every weekend, still in shock from how many I could still find. This became my thing to do on our breaks, and others would join in and look for them with me. This also became a way for me to share and show my love for this studio. It was silly, but it was a sweet period of time that changed my life. I feel like those heart rocks were hugs from my angels saying *You GO Girl!!*

September 9th, 2017

I cannot express the importance of having faith and not fear. I know the universe has a plan for me. It will show me and speak to me if I'm conscious enough to listen and see the signs. I can't believe this is happening right now. Becoming a yoga teacher is going to save me. I now know the perfect reason as to why I'm not going out to party! I now have a purpose to become disciplined, responsible, devoted, and gain an inner strength made of courage and grace. I was missing this in my life, and this has become my new backbone and reasoning for waking up. This is what will help keep me on the right path so I can be a good leader and an example for others. This is me stepping into my light!

My promise to the world: I vow to honor the wishes of my higher powers. I make it my promise that this light inside of me will shine upon those walking in the dark. I honor the responsibility of sharing this knowledge and using inspirational messages to lift people's spirits. I promise to devote my time and practice towards helping others vibrate on a higher frequency of happiness. I know I am here to make a difference in this wild world. This, I know, is my calling. I will not take it for granted and I will give it my whole heart. I will do everything in my power to be the best version of myself. I want to help the community, share my light, and help others discover theirs.

I couldn't think of a better way for this story to end. I have been searching for so many painful and confusing years to end this book on a good note. You have seen me struggle and make the same mistakes all while being under the influence of some drug, alcohol, or boys. The only way my struggles will disappear is if I do something drastically different. I am the only one who can change myself, and this is the strength I needed to rediscover myself.

October 20th, 2017

I'm having a breakthrough right now! I'm doing my yoga studies, reading the book, The Bhagavad Gita, and I'm taking notes in Sanskrit. It's a whole new language for me, so I'm making flashcards. One word in particular stood out to me: Shraddha, which means faith. It is placed in the heart. "A person is what his Shraddha is." - The Bhagavad Gita, by Eknath Easwaran,

(17:3). This quote is sinking into my heart right now as I think about what my faith is, and what that says about my character.

When I lived in Costa Rica, I graffitied the walls with my own version of the word Shraddha. Mine was, "Live the life you love and love the life you live." This helped me to be a better version of myself. I have truly come full circle, living the life I love right now. I'm realizing the importance of the gift of teaching. I need to cherish the opportunity to respect and love myself in this world, so I can make an impact on this dimension. I am so proud and honored to have gone on this journey with you. If you have gotten this far in my book, then you know my most bare, raw, real life experiences of how I got here. I didn't want to hide anything because I feel like all of it was crucial to show that we are human and all of us make mistakes. I was meant to go down the path that I did so that I could stand with you and truly sympathize with your pain. There is a way out though. I want to be living proof of that for you.

Another cool thing I learned in yoga is that you can change your kharmic reflection by changing your life. You have to be the driving force behind the change that you wish to create for yourself. You can shift the perspective of your life to be the vibration you wish to create. If you can create the vibration of goodness onto others with non-violence and a pure heart, you will be able to find peace amongst the chaos with how you choose to show up. The only thing you do have control over is your own actions and energetic field. The universe will always be there to test you, but whatever your vibrations are at the time will come right back to you like a boomerang. You can fight the resistance or give in to the moment with grace and ease, observing what this situation is teaching you. Peacefully surrender to trust. Shraddha, or having faith and believing that what is in your heart is pure and allowing it to guide you instead of your fear or lower level vibrations. You have the power and the choice to focus on the negative or the positive.

(Kind of reminds me of the meaning Pura Vida.) Every minute you are alive, you have the choice to be conscious and present with what arises. The more comfortable you become with listening to your true self, the more at peace you'll become with the world.

I can't change the world, but I can change the vibration of the world, one soul at a time. The practice of yoga helps us to find self-love and acceptance. It's time we devote ourselves to going inward and listening in to retune our vibration. I'm truly honored that I get to be the one to help guide my students to being good karma creators for the world!

Life couldn't get any better at the moment. I'm so honored and grateful to be hearing these messages loud and clear: This is my path. But I, like any human, am nervous. This is a whole new world for me. I'm going to have to get over my stage fright and my fear of public speaking. I just need to get my jitters out and teach a time or two, then I'll be okay. I can't wait to watch myself evolve and grow as a yoga teacher. I hope I can stay sober. I have to remember that my body is my temple, and what I feed it matters.

Chapter Twenty-Four

Let the Training for Life Soak In

I could feel a shift happening inside of me. I knew I had the universe on my side, helping me on my journey. I finally felt as if I was coming home. I was finding peace with all of the pain from the past. I understood that the only way I will ever get out of my cycles of destruction is if I do something radically different in my life. I had to stay clear-headed. I needed to walk away from alcohol, from partying, from anything that didn't feed my soul with this kind of love that I found in my training at Practice Yoga Austin. This quickly became the center of my world. I started to rearrange my priorities to make the adjustments needed to protect this space in my life.

I was still working at JuiceLand about 20 hours a week, but that was hardly enough money to be able to pay bills on my own. There was no way that I could've done this training and devoted the time and energy to my growth if it wasn't for John. He allowed me to live there, pretty much rent free. I took on the "woman's" role in the house once more. I had to make sure the house stayed clean, I did his laundry, and I had to make sure the groceries were stocked (which was the one thing I paid for with my earnings.) He had to have all his smoothie supplies come Monday mornings, and the one thing that would haunt us, was him always running out of bananas. He would go through them so fast and I would sometimes not have the time or the energy to go to the store for bananas after training weekends. If I didn't fulfill my chores, then all hell would break loose. I did my best to please him and keep him from flipping his shit, but to be honest, everything I did made him so angry. The eggshells were like bombs all over the house, and I always seemed to step on them.

As I went through my training, learning about the Eight Limbs of Yoga, I couldn't help but use John as my subject (most of the time, the people who trigger you can end up being your biggest teachers in life.) He helped me learn that I can handle challenges in a different way, and it all starts from within and how I choose to show up. Fun Fact: I learned that depression is actually a brain injury! *I know right?* It's because the amygdala outgrows the hippocampus, which is where joy lives, due to stress. (Learned this one from one of my teacher, Shanti Kelley) I was able to bring more compassion to this relationship by understanding this, and myself, better. All these years, I have not cared to look into who I am and what's actually happened to me as a result of my traumas. I never fully healed from those experiences and this training was bringing them to light. I never cared to notice my triggers, not to mention, how I could bring balance into my life.

One of my favorite parts about this training was learning about the studies of Ayurveda. This blew my mind and sparked a whole new understanding of what I was born into. You see, we all have a *Prakriti*, which is who we are, and what we were born into this world with. There are three different *Doshas* that make up your Prakriti: *Vata, Pitta,* and *Kapha.*

You basically take an assessment test of different qualities of your physique, eating habits, emotions, how you make decisions, when you wake up, etc. When you understand your Dosha and who you are, you can find ways to create a more balanced and harmonious life. I'm personally very Pitta. I am a fire sign and my anger and temper run high when I'm not balanced. The things that imbalance me are the things that I have been putting in my body this whole time. We are typically drawn to the things that aren't good for our dosha. Alcohol, fried or greasy foods, and spicy foods are my biggest triggers. These things make me more fired up and angry, along with making my stomach upset. This is when I make mistakes, lash out, make harsh comments, or I simply don't feel my best. I learned that in order to be my best, I needed to start eating and living right by my Dosha; I had to at least give it a try and see if that could help. When I did, I immediately felt a difference. I was calmer, more understanding, happier, and healthier overall. My training was not just one of learning yoga, but it was one of gaining a whole new reclaimed life. A life with a fresh viewpoint to see the world through. I noticed my self-confidence began to rise because I was finally not hiding who I was. I was able to show my true self outwardly towards the world, and I loved it.

My teachers were my guiding lights throughout this process. They showed me what it was to hold space for people, and they gave me the understanding of the magnitude of these teachings. Really, we all come to yoga to un-fuck ourselves. I noticed that I was slowly opening up to the fact that we are all one as a collective, and we are all experiencing some sort of pain or trauma from living on this earth in this timeframe. Yoga is a gateway to understanding this life and one's true higher purpose. It starts with the physical practice and seeing physical results. That is the first layer to keep you coming back. Then it goes deeper into the second Kosha layer, the feelings of lightness and a sense of awakening. This is when the spiritual curiosity and higher meanings in life start to make sense. After this Kosha, you start to find yourself: your *Atman*, or higher self. This lives in the center of it all. The awakening to the light that lives inside of you. There, you can find peace and stillness within the walls that contain you in your human form.

I never sat down long enough to meditate before this training. I didn't ever want to get to know my brain and the *chitta*, or noise, of my thoughts. The thoughts I had when I would meditate would always bring me back to the pain of my experiences or the moments of my past where I was blacked out. Meditating took me back to my traumas that I never fully processed. I feared going there because it wasn't always pretty and peaceful for me. I realized that my pain was coming back up because I never gave myself the space I needed to heal from it. In mediation, it's important to allow yourself to feel what you're feeling. Maybe even ask questions as to why you might be feeling this way. I was taught to get curious with my pain and try to understand the root cause of the actions and the emotions that came with it. I learned to use this pain as my fuel and my guiding light. It showed me what I needed to learn in this lifetime. I began to use my pain as my power to help allow myself to shine brighter. *I am meant to learn from my pain; I am meant to recycle it into something better for myself.* My growth wouldn't be the same if I didn't have anything to learn from. This training showed me how to harness this pain, and to use it as a force for good. My pain makes me relatable, it makes me human. It has given me the opportunity to be vulnerable, and to serve as living proof of what the yoga practice, and a higher conscious awakening, can do for you.

When I graduated from the 200-hour training, I knew I wasn't finished learning. I wanted more of this experience before I felt confident in myself to teach others. I had to find a way to get into the 300-hour training that was coming up next. It was two weeks away, and I didn't know how it was going to happen, I just knew I had to be in it. My intuition was, once more, screaming for me to *learn more* and *dive deeper*. I seriously became one of those intense book worms that just wanted to keep growing. I saw this spark inside of me that had been dead since I was a child. I felt so curious about life. I was following my heart with what felt right because it was louder than ever. Ignoring this voice wasn't an option. I was clearer in my head than I had been in many years, even though I still had to put up with John getting drunk every night. I had a backbone as to why I shouldn't drink and I was growing my life's purpose at the same time. I knew what I wanted, and knew I needed to keep growing.

I was so lucky and had some angels looking out for me. I talked with one of my teachers about how badly I wanted to be in this training, and she ended up talking with the other teachers and working out a deal that I couldn't pass up! The gift of knowledge was presented to me as long as I made sure to pass this knowledge and help future students, just as they were doing for me. I also helped out for the training by unlocking the doors in the morning, cleaning the space afterwards, and I helped out at the studio during the busy times. This karmic offering was the catalyst in my life that changed me forever.

I enjoyed working at the front desk to help my teachers and fluff the place with energy between the classes. I was able to learn how the teachers do their thing on the back end and I felt useful that I was able to help relieve some stress before they taught. More than ever, I was eating, breathing, and living in that studio to try to repay them for their generosity and faith in me. They all saw something inside of me when they saw how devoted I was. You could tell they all wanted to help me succeed in life and it felt amazing to have that kind of support. They could see my light wanting to shine, and they all knew that I could help the community for the future generation of yogis. All they asked in return was for me to keep it a secret from the other students so no one got offended. They didn't want anyone to feel left out, or like I was a star-student. To top this off, this wasn't normally an offer they give to the public. I needed to respect their wishes. I'm not the best with secrets, but I agreed to the terms and jumped right into the 300-hour training.

Yoga had become my new addiction and I poured my heart and full attention into it because in reality, it *did* save me. I was the overachiever that always got there early to open the doors and get the best spot, front and center. I would try to help out any way I could. If the owners or my teachers ever needed anything, I would be there to help. I felt so honored and grateful for this opportunity that there was no way I wanted to fuck this up. I went above and beyond to learn as much as possible so I could share it all. This training was seven months long and it was a hugely transformative time in my life. My teachers were like walking angels who guided me and cared for me in such a motherly and nurturing way. Those teachers were Jenn Wooten, Kiely Wolters, Shanti Kelley, Iva Divrit-Hall, Shawn Kent, and Gioconda Parker. These beautiful humans helped to shape me into the teacher I am today, and I am so grateful for their guidance and teachings.

About three months into this training, I got the news that one of my best friends from High School (literally the only one I still talked to, besides Amanda) had passed away. His name was Andrew Harris and if a Grateful Dead bear could be a person, it was him. He was the sweetest soul and I was devastated from losing him. I had spoken with him two weeks prior, trying to get him to go camping with us. I hadn't ever experienced the loss of someone so close to me before. I cried for so many hours, completely hung up on the fact that I would never get to hear his incredible laugh again. It was in this moment of pain that I felt his presence, unlike anything I had ever felt before. I heard his voice as if he was right behind me in the bathroom, plain as day. He kept telling me, "Host a yoga event for my family and friends in memory of me the day before my funeral. Please, they need to remember this side of me, too." Andrew also struggled with addiction, but his was a bit more lethal. Yoga was his safe space and helped him during his recovery process and when he lost his dad two years before. He did the twelve steps, but would always make it back to the studio, either in Tyler or in Louisiana where he lived. He wanted to be remembered this way and I was going to do everything in my power to help make this happen for Andrew. He was by far the loudest angel that I had ever experienced. I strongly feel that he was so loud of an angel because he practiced being a walking angel on this planet. He was such a light in every life that he touched. He impacted the world with kindness and showed it daily with his heart. I was in disbelief with how strong of a presence he carried in the afterlife; but it was comforting to know that he was right there by my side, helping to guide me.

It would be my first ever, public yoga class and I wasn't sure if I was ready to do it or not. His presence reassured me that he would be there with me, holding my hand throughout the whole process. He was so insistent for me to do this that he wouldn't be quiet until I agreed and started to get the wheels turning. I called around to see what studios I could use in Tyler, and sure enough, the owner of the yoga studio where Andrew had practiced agreed to host the event. It went so smoothly and she, along with two other teachers who were all friends with Andrew, wanted to be a part of it also. Once the word got out about what I was planning, everyone was filled with this "spark" of joy. It soon became a group effort and we all came together in such unity to make it happen. This was such a beautiful way to remember this sweet soul.

The day of the event was stormy. We had about 20 family members and friends join in for his memorial yoga class. It was so beautiful to collaborate and see how easily teaching yoga came to me. Helping others through this painful time felt like such a gift. I could feel Andrew's presence in that room with us! His sister sat in the same spot Andrew would practice in and she was surrounded by all of his friends and loved ones. You could tell it was exactly what everyone needed. After the class, we all went outside and witnessed a beautiful double rainbow that we felt Andrew had sent for us! It was perfectly lined up right when we walked out of the studio. It was seriously the most magical first yoga class I could've ever asked for. As all of us were standing outside watching this spectacular rainbow, one of the girls who taught the class with me came up to me and said that I would be a perfect candidate to work at the yoga studio she manages in Austin! This studio was one of the biggest studios in Austin too, High Low Yoga (name was changed to protect their identity). I didn't realize it when I was teaching, but I was doing an audition during my first public yoga class! All of this was such a gift, and I saw the purpose in the push from Andrew to do this event. I'm so grateful for his message and his support while I jumped off the edge of the cliff into a whole new world of finally being a teacher! This was when my identity of "Alli Bee Yoga" entered my life. I had to create a whole new version of myself, along with an Instagram page to market my teachings and share my newfound light with the world.

Things were aligning for me in my life and I couldn't have been happier, except for when I would come home. I was stepping up for myself and showing myself the respect and love that I needed for the first time in my life. Now that I was beginning to respect myself more, I realized that some things must end if I wanted to invite what was right into my life. All of a sudden, everything that had once felt comfortable to me all began to feel wrong. I couldn't ignore how unsettled I felt at home, which showed up in how I would show up for the world. I knew I wasn't supposed to be with John because our relationship was solely based on toxicity.

There was no way I could be a positive yoga teacher if I was constantly depressed at home. My relationship with John began to take a toll on my happiness. I wasn't drinking anymore because of Andrew's passing and what John told me about what would happen if I kept drinking. I am super grateful for him saying this to me, but he wasn't being respectful to me once I made the choice to give it up. He would always have wine at the house and came home every night smelling like alcohol. It was hard to be around alcohol at such an early stage in recovery, but living in the middle of it made it that much worse. Giving up alcohol was a true blessing and a turning point at this time in my life. Little did I know, the struggle would be real for quite some time after making this decision. After I quit and started my yoga training, I found that the real challenge was being able to handle what surfaced within me when I witnessed him drinking heavily. I would make dinner and he would stand me up because he was at the little Mexican restaurant I was banned from, having a margarita. I would wait for hours for him to come home, and when he did, I could smell the tequila on his skin. I'd already be in bed, pretending to sleep when I was really having an anxiety attack. It was extremely emotional and upsetting for me to know that he chose drinking at the bar over having a home cooked dinner with me.

It was a constant battle of always having to stand up for myself. I didn't want to drink anymore, and I didn't want to be around others who were drinking. I would beg him not to drink so much, but he refused to admit that his drinking was problematic. *But, if he loved me, wouldn't he try to make this a little easier for me and less traumatic?* Over time, this can wear on your soul, especially when you know that y'all aren't meant for one another. If you're in a relationship with someone who doesn't care about what you're going through and doesn't want to adjust or compromise to make your path easier, *why keep trying?* I shared my past with him, hoping it would bring us closer together, yet he used my past to throw it in my face as to why he shouldn't trust me. He was calling me the same names that I was called when I got initiated and hazed to trigger me; they were also the same names my ex-husband would call me. I was still experiencing the same problems from the beginning of our relationship after two years of being with him. It was like life was on repeat with the same fights. I was putting his needs before mine. There were so many trust issues, the alcohol abuse, and the fights, and it all became too much for me to process. I was done with this cycle. I was living a lie trying to stay there any longer. I was simply living there out of convenience because it was rent-free. I couldn't bear to *use* someone like that anymore, while wasting my own energy trying to make this relationship right. The only way to stop repeating the same mistakes is to finally take the leap and do something different, *right?* Man, I have this constant reminder of a cure to my problems, yet it's always harder than you think to do it. It's scary. It's uncharted territory that makes no promises of working out in your favor.

This pain that I was experiencing at home soon became my fuel for wanting a better life. I didn't know what it was going to look like or even if I was going to land on my feet, but this was a risk that I was willing to take. With great lessons in growth, there is pain and destruction of what needs to evolve in your life. The trick is to believe we are worthy of something better. If we don't feel like we deserve it, we won't manifest it. It can sometimes take a lifetime to learn your sense of worth, but I was determined to make mine higher than what it was. I needed to learn how not to be dependent on another person to take care of me. I needed to learn how to thrive on my own and make a name for myself. I knew I needed a break from relationships and I needed to use this time to heal from my toxic past. I had never given myself the time to heal, and this was all I could think about. In my mind, I had to make a drastic move to be able to reinvent myself. I wanted to shine without anyone trying to dim my light or affect my true self in the process.

I knew it was my time to leave John. Luckily, my best friend Katelyn offered me a place to stay in her home (again) with her newborn baby until I could get on my feet. Once I had this lined up, it was time to muster the courage to tell him. Saying goodbye was always the hardest part for me in relationships. I woke up one morning and couldn't hide how my heart felt anymore. I knew the minute I said I was leaving I had to make the moves, and pretty much get out of that house the same day.

When I told him, he was shocked as if he didn't see any of it coming. I explained to him that both of us weren't happy and that I couldn't bear to have another day of fighting. I told him that I was going to be moving out while he was away at work, and I should be completely moved out by the time he got home. I had nothing packed because it would have made things terribly awkward with him finding out that way. I knew he would have made it uncomfortable for me once I ended it with him. I didn't have a plan. I just knew I needed to get out. When he left, I started scrambling and stuffing my things into boxes and into my car. I knew it was going to be a long day and I didn't take the time to pack things safely and nicely with wrapping paper. He wasn't happy when he left; he was quite angry, confused, sad, and hungover. I was trying to get everything out of there before he came back home and decided to make this more difficult than it needed to be. I made sure to invite a few girlfriends over to help make this process easier and quicker. They were also my buffer, in case John did decide to come back home, which he did. He didn't make a scene with the girls there, he just came in the house, looked around, and then left again. I was shocked and scared once I told him I was leaving, but I knew I was doing the right thing. *There's no turning back now.* I had to keep marching into the unknown and I had to do this for my own sense of self-worth and self-respect. For those who are stuck in this kind of emotionally abusive relationship, it might seem like there is no way out. Maybe you don't have the strength, the courage, or the funds to get out, but there is always a way. Know that with each ending, there is a beautiful new beginning waiting for you. It takes truly wanting to see the happy ending for yourself and being willing to take that risk. This was my way of practicing having faith in the universe. I was finally beginning to understand and realize that I was worthy of having this kind of happiness. *This is my birthright.*

Once more, my best friend Katelyn was my saving grace in this process and was more than happy to help me get away from John. Katelyn never liked John because of how often I would go over to her place to complain about how unhappy I was. My girlfriend knew what I was going through, and wanted to do everything in her power to help get me out of this mess. I love this girl with every cell in my body--she has shown to be a true friend over the years. I was staying with them and only paying $400 a month, which is hard to beat in Austin, Texas. It was all I could afford. I had a whole house crammed into a tiny room and a small space in the garage. I felt bad for invading their space, especially after Katelyn just had her baby. I did my best to stay out of the way, but Chi was a different story. He didn't like going from roaming free to being cooped up in a smaller house with more people. This was only supposed to be a couple of months of me staying with them, so I never unpacked my things, and I never got too cozy. It was nice to feel loved and supported by my friends. I didn't have many, but I had my team.

Without a relationship or the drama that comes with it, I was finally able to step into my own skin and figure out who I wanted to be. My yoga training brought out this curiosity of living my dharma and what my path was truly supposed to be. I knew I was supposed to be strong, courageous, expressive, and caring with everything that I do. I also became very protective of my energetic field and my surroundings. I didn't want anyone or anything dampening my spirits. I could only do this if I were to walk this path alone, and I was dead set on that decision. I made an oath to myself that I wouldn't jump into another relationship without solidifying my career first. I knew I needed to build this before any other relationship came along to rain on my parade.

Sure enough, as soon as I broke it off with John, High Low Yoga came to watch me teach at one of my donation-based classes I held outside of a JuiceLand. I only had one girl who came to class, but that was all I needed to keep practicing. I was still able to work on my sequencing and cueing. It was almost like the bow and arrow metaphor. John was the arrow, pulling me back in life, but as soon as I let that relationship go, the arrow sprung forward in action. They hired me on the spot and I started working there on August 13th, 2018. By this time, I was about half way through my 300-hour training. Everything was aligning and happening when I was ready to receive it.

There's a lot that can be said about the power behind the practice of letting go. When we release what is no longer serving us, we can make space in our life for the things that are right for us; even if we don't know what those things are. We have to be willing to know when it's time to release and make ourselves available with an open heart to life. It's hard as hell to let go because we create an identity around who we are with that person, or job, or past that defines us. It's this hard because it is sometimes more difficult to start back at the beginning. Sometimes it's easier to stay comfortably uncomfortable because that is what's familiar to us. We all know that isn't living, though. I feel like we're supposed to feel, explore, grow, be happy, and express ourselves however we choose. If someone can't love you for exactly who you are, then they don't deserve you. Even if you want them to be the one, you would be fighting a strong resistance and lowering your vibration in the process. It isn't worth fighting for something that isn't meant to be. You are the owner of your energetic field, and only you can be the person who sets that boundary. *Are you going to allow those people into your life, or not?* Everyday, we have choices. Choices that will shape our environment, and inevitably set the vibration of what we put out into the world, allowing that vibration to come back in your world. The more you focus on those good vibrations, the more good things will keep coming your way.

Once I got stable in the vibration I wanted, I was finally able to reap the rewards of landing a full-time teaching gig. I was amazed at the amount of students this place pulled in. It's donation based, and this studio brings in a lot of new students. It also pulls in students on a budget, making it more accessible for more people. This was my first yoga teaching job at a studio. I was the one to work the early 6 a.m. classes and the 9 p.m. classes, sometimes on the same day. I was picking up as many shifts as possible to try to get the most experience in. I was hooked, and would sometimes work up to 16 shifts in one week. Some people would warn me to not get burned out by taking on too much, but I honestly wanted to work. I love teaching yoga! The more I taught, the better and more comfortable I became. I could see how some teachers could get burned out on teaching. Each time I taught, I was giving away a certain amount of energy. I was new, fresh to the field, and had an excess amount of energy to give. Since I wasn't pouring my energy into a relationship, I poured my energy into my students instead. This became my way of sharing my love with the world. I loved teaching so much, I would teach almost every day of the week. Some days, up to four classes. To be honest, it was nice to make a decent living on my own, and that's what I became addicted to as well. I was so proud that I was becoming independent by doing something that I loved. *Who would've thought that was possible?*

I began to get a following and started to step into this role as a teacher. I never had anything feel more in place than when I would teach. My jitters and all the fear of public speaking I created in my head were forced to go away. Sometimes, up to 80 people would show up for a class. In this case, I had to get over my fears immediately and find a way to go to my happy place to be able to "perform." It's almost as if I have something else take over and channel my words and sequencing when I'm teaching a class. At first I would write down my yoga flow, but soon after, I realized that it didn't feel right to be so rigid and precise. Plus, I didn't like carrying around my notes, or when I would miss a pose on my sequence. The whole "trying to be perfect" about it threw me off. It was easier for me to improv my classes and have my flows come out of me naturally. I could better cater to the students I had in front of me. I enjoyed witnessing myself relax into my intuition, and learning the game of trust. I had the knowledge and tools within me to make a great class, and I used this in an artistic way. I love being able to create my own playlist and used this as my building blocks for how the sequencing would go and feel mood-wise. I was channelling my creative flow to get my students' blood flowing, and it seemed like people were receptive to it. My vinyasa classes are more on the fast-paced side because I noticed I enjoy making the energy move. Moving out that rajistic energy (intense or heated energy) helps my students to feel more calm and at peace when they go back out into the world. I could see my students growing in their practice, and it was such a wonderful feeling to know that I helped them on their journey. I felt like I had a purpose and a reason to wake up in the morning when I had my students depending on me; even if it was at 4:30 a.m.

At the end of the year, it came time to graduate from my 300-hour training with Practice Yoga Austin. I had a disturbing phone call from one of my teachers right before graduation. She questioned me about breaking my promise that I had with her. Nervous about what I had done, I listened to her version of the situation. She told me she had angry students who were calling her, and they were upset because they found out that I got a free ride. *Oh shit.* I had done so good about keeping this a secret, but it slipped my mind that at the beginning of the training I messed up. I was trying to make friends with a group of girls after class; and well, they liked to drink. I was weaker at the beginning of this training before Andrew died, drinking occasionally. One time I was trying to hang, and I had too many. I made a drunken confession to one of them about my fears of being judged by my classmates. She was curious as to what I meant by this, and I explained to her further as to why I didn't want to feel that way. I barely remember speaking it out loud, because it was right after I had thrown up outside of her car. I begged her not to tell anyone and she did a good job, up until the end of the training. Little did I realize when I said this, but I was talking with the one girl who had the hardest time making her payments. She went most of the training without saying anything and pretending to be my friend, but towards the end, things got weird. I wasn't hanging out with them afterwards because I knew they would drink, and I needed to protect my sobriety. So, I stopped hanging out with them as much and they began to slowly cast me out of the circle.

The group of friends I made in training stopped talking to me in class; they gave me the cold shoulder towards the end. I couldn't figure it out and thought it was because I stopped drinking with them. It wasn't until my teacher called me and told me the news: the word was out about my scholarship. This is why my teacher asked me to keep it a secret; so I wouldn't be judged, and also so it wouldn't offend the other students. Drunken Alli-sin had creeped up to haunt me and my growth. I was devastated to know that I had disappointed my teachers. I broke my promise. They have been so kind to me and have believed in me from the beginning; I felt horrible for things ending on this note. This was a lesson in holding true to my word and taking the advice from my teachers. I learned this lesson even more when I felt a few classmates judging me during graduation. Not all of them did, which I'm grateful for. This helped me see the true colors of those that I *thought* were my friends. This vibe that I had created for myself made that day bittersweet. I wanted my training to end on a good note, but it was ending with a cold, harsh lesson of karma. My teachers were all so graceful about it, and I am so grateful for their unconditional love. I felt like

I was putting more pressure on myself than what they gave me, because I felt bad for breaking my promise to them. I looked up and admired them for helping me on my journey and felt this sense of shame for letting alcohol get in the way of my life.

Still, it was monumental for me to go through the most transformational time of my life during my two training courses in a year. My teachers had become the backbone for my practice, and my teachings for others. I was still so grateful and in their debt for the faith they placed in me to help others. Their strength and rawness helped me have major breakthroughs in my life, regarding vulnerability, that I couldn't have found anywhere else. Practice Yoga Austin has been amazing to me and I have learned so much from all of the amazing teachers that teach here. If you're looking to find yourself, or dive deeper into the meaning of life, I highly encourage a yoga teacher training. Even if you do it for yourself and not with the intent to teach, you can learn so much. Eventually, the dust settled from my incident in training and my teachers continued to show up for me with open arms. They are the true pillars of what a teacher should be. I was so grateful for their loving kindness and their forgiveness after I betrayed them and made their lives harder for a minute.

*Side Note: Do what you have to do to protect your energetic field. You are the only one who can control how you feel, therefore you must be cautious of what you surround yourself with. If someone drags you down, they don't deserve you. It is better to be free than to be in a toxic relationship. Yoga training was the best decision I could have made for myself and my growth. I found so much healing and understanding about myself and gained a new, healthy addiction. Learning my dosha with Ayurveda was a game-changer in balancing my life. This helped me create a more mindful approach about how I led my life and what I fed my body.

CHAPTER TWENTY-FIVE

ALLI-SIN

My life revolved around teaching yoga, and I made sure to do a good job about protecting my energetic space. I put up this wall around my heart because I didn't want to be hurt by anyone, or have it affect my teachings. Of course, I still had urges and would go out and try to date. These attempts resulted in me drinking too much, sleeping with them too soon, and never calling them again. I would do fine not drinking on my own, and I came to terms with trying to be a "responsible drinker" after some time. I would have a glass of wine here and there after a long day's work. It was only when I would go out on dates that I fell victim to Alli-sin coming out. I would get so nervous on dates and felt like I needed to loosen up with a few drinks, but it would turn into a shit show every single time. One night, Alli-sin came out to play and tried to wreck my life by accidentally getting me pregnant.

I knew immediately the next morning that something was off because I couldn't remember how I got home. All I could feel were the lingering effects of a shock wave of something that invaded my soul. I never shot up any drugs before, but it felt like a zinger bolt of a drug shooting through my body, warning me of its existence. I knew from that strange moment something was up, and I needed to question the things that had happened the night before. Sure enough, my intuition was right. I did a follow up with this guy to confirm what I had felt. Check out my journal entry from this time.

December 23rd, 2018

This morning, I woke up alone. I'm filled with so many emotions running through my blood. Last night on the full moon in Cancer, I said goodbye to my unborn child by taking the morning-after pill. Two nights prior, I met a man who was sweet, gentle, and actually gave a shit, but maybe too much. We got lost on the dance floor under the influence of one too many Jameson shots and soon it all became a blur. I have been doing this thing lately where I black out when I drink and something else takes over. In all reality, it's not fun for me anymore. I wake up with questions in my head, finding out embarrassing stories when I try to piece everything together the next day. The last thing I remember was showing this guy my dad's dance moves, and now I'm waking up feeling something else inside me. Bringing another life into this world could have changed my life around, and not in the direction I wanted to go. I could feel the moment that soul entered my life. It was like I had a rush of adrenaline, or a drug, and I could feel the charge run through my body and end in my eyes. I felt something other than me when it entered my soul. That same feeling of a drug or adrenaline rushed over me again the minute I awoke, to be a warning for me to get this checked out, and soon. I was replaying that night, wondering what the fuck had happened. I scrambled over to my purse to see if I used my condoms. Nope.

Fuck! Was this a nightmare? I don't understand. I can't put all the pieces together on my own.

So, of course I had to find out. My maternal instincts were kicking in and I am nowhere near ready to have a baby with a man I barely know from a first date! That's not ideal. He came over the night after and explained all of my crazy, wild stories of Alli-sin. I hate her so much. I really do. I feel like she tries to ruin my life every time I give her the opportunity. Apparently, I was begging for him to cum inside of me, like I knew what I was doing. When he did, that's when I had the feeling of a drug or adrenaline or a sperm entering into my egg. He said I sat still on his bed with this look in my eyes like a deer in the headlights after he did it. Then I finally turned around with fear in my eyes, telling him I wasn't on birth control. Why did I do this? I know I want the end-all-family-tribe that I could count on, but not like this! I'm 32-years-old, my maternal clock is ticking, but I'm nowhere ready for anything like this, and especially not with this guy.

Last night was the full moon in Cancer, back in her original home, the night after the Winter Solstice. A time of family and grounding into your roots is what this is supposed to represent. A time to let go and release old patterns, ideas, beliefs, and fears, so you can make room for the new and improved life of abundance. Last night, I took the morning-after pill, alone in my home, unable to go home for Christmas because I was stuck working. I am filled with sadness that I might not ever meet this unborn child of mine during this lifetime. I made sure to have a conversation with it first, wishing and hoping that one day it would be the right time for them to enter into this world. I still feel the weakness and sadness in my body and bones this morning. I still feel the cramping of the medicine reversing my child away. Sadness keeps washing over me as I'm trying to talk myself into the fact that I made the right decision. I know I will feel better when I stop feeling the pain of the cramps from my decision. So, I'm all alone, sad, and grieving this loss by myself. It's painful, yet once more gives me the chance to practice letting go. Releasing old habits that no longer serve me. I mean, think about it. We get drunk and make stupid decisions that can change our lives forever. Is it worth it to have that drink, or six? I don't have the time or the energy to handle any more of these nights.

It's a double-edged sword, though. I want to have a stable, solid man in my life that I love more than anything else. But it is the hardest thing to date in this town without going out for drinks, or having them at dinner. Austin, Texas, I love you, but you are a small music town with a big drinking problem. I'm just as guilty as most for falling victim to it. How do we go out and meet, mingle, and be merry without involving a substance that will chill us out and fuck us up. I don't want anyone to fall in love with ALLI-SIN!!! That's just asking for a repeat of bad choices and boys that won't help me grow.

All of that aside, today my heart feels heavy. I am yearning and wishing for the growth of my roots and the blooms of my flowers to emerge into this world. I will sit for as long as it takes, alone in my head and heart until I can feel the unconditional love of the purest version of myself. Starting from within, seeping through my thoughts, words, and soul. That is truly what I need in order to evolve. I don't need distractions. I don't need the support of others. I need myself right now. I need that undying love for myself to want a better life. I need to nurture my heart and be kind and gentle with it; I need to love myself like I would want to be loved by others. It all starts within. As within, as without.

This shook me up inside. I guess I had been pretty responsible my whole life to be using the Plan B method for the first time at 32, but I never want to do that again. I'm done not having control over myself and my actions. I am over blacking out and abusing my body in this way. That's not the example I want to be for people as a teacher. I took this as a sign that I needed to start focusing on loving myself, even more. Basically, I need to be practicing what I'm preaching in class. This meant not getting distracted. I had so much more I needed to build up in my life to feel stable and secure before I added anyone else to my mix. I had finally come to terms with saying goodbye to the little urges inside of me that craved sex and the attention of others. I turned that craving into the attention I needed for my growth. I was on the right path and I knew it, but there were still some missing links that I needed to complete on my own. I needed to find my own living space that I could be creative in; I needed something I could call mine. I need to stand on my own two feet without a boy *or* my best friend helping me.

I was finally bringing in more money working as a full-time yoga teacher. It was nice to be able to save up some money while living with Katelyn. I could feel that I was beginning to overstay my welcome with her and her family. Heidi, Katelyn's baby, was also getting older and starting to crawl, and Chi isn't the best with babies. It must have been hard for her, too, being a new mother. I tried to help out, but I was beginning to feel more in the way, especially with Chi. She wanted to make sure I went to a good spot once I moved out, so she was patient with me while I searched for a new home. I knew my new focus shouldn't be on boys or drinking right now, it should be on manifesting a new home! I did well with manifesting my job at High Low Yoga, but it was time I focused my energy on manifesting a new home for Chi and myself.

CHAPTER TWENTY-SIX

MANIFESTING MY LIFE

Manifesting seems like a simple enough process. If you've ever watched the movie *The Secret,* you would think that it would be within reach to begin to create the life you wanted. Sometimes though, it takes time. I learned that I must be fully ripe and ready for what I'm trying to manifest. If I'm not ready, my dreams won't be able to reach me. It took me seven months, filled with patience, to manifest a new home. I was pretty particular about this dream, though. I had visions of my own space, with a yard for Chi. I wanted loving roommates that felt like family when I walked in the door. I wanted to live in a space that was peaceful, yet affordable. I made sure to be picky and precise about what I wanted to create for myself.

You see, the universe loves details when you manifest, especially if you write them down with a pen and paper: this solidifies it. It's important to be as clear and descriptive as possible so the vibrations can be picked up, and turned into reality. I started getting into manifesting because at the time, I had nowhere else to draw from. I used manifesting to bring my jobs into my life, so I knew it was possible! I had been searching for homes for months, and nothing was popping up. I never gave up though. I never settled for anything less than what I had in mind. I was grateful that Katelyn was patient with me. She was the one who told me to be picky about the next place I moved to. She didn't want to see me have to pack up my things and move again in another six months. She genuinely only wanted me to be safe and happy in my next home. With patience and persistence, along with a little manifesting, my dreams finally came true.

I'll share with you my little tips and tricks for manifesting. First, it starts with **setting a good intention.** A good intention should consist of three parts: **1)** a feeling, **2)** what you would like to manifest, **3)** an end result. An example would be: I am so relieved and grateful to have a home that I can afford, with people who love me, and where Chi is happy! Make your intention clear and precise because the universe loves details. This also helps the manifestor get clear on what they want as well. When you attach a feeling to what your manifesting, it becomes a part of you and your vibration.

Once you have a powerful intention, then you write that intention down **as many times as you can (over 50), every night for a week.** (Fun trick: Add up the number that you landed on (i.e. 64 times, so add 6+4=10, which equals 1. Once you do this, research the meaning of this number; this will give you the hidden meaning and advice given for this intention.) **The number you finished on during the first night, must be the number of times you write the intention each night, for the rest of the week.** It is important that you do this for one full week because it shows yourself how badly you want it. It also shows you how much you truly believe that it is right for you. If you miss a night, it proves that you probably don't want it or it's not meant to be in your life. If you do miss a day though and want to keep manifesting this intention, you must start all the way back on day one and repeat the process. It's important to number each sentence, and circle the number, so you can easily see it at the beginning of the intention. This way you don't have to keep up with counting, and you can stay in your flow state. It will almost feel like a meditation. It takes about an hour each time to sit down, maybe longer, depending on how long your intention is and how fast of a writer you are. Make sure you are in a space where you won't be disturbed or have to get up. Grab some water or tea and make yourself comfortable. When I do this, I notice that I find myself in a meditative space where I can hear my higher self predicting what I should do next to make sure this intention comes true. If you have a thought or a vision of your next steps to creating your intention, make sure to put a quick note on the side (only one or two words so you remember the thought) and then go back to review your side notes afterwards. Try not to get out of your flow state during this process because this is when the magic is created. Afterwards, make your final notes in more detail so that you can remember and game plan for the future. If you only do it for a night or two, but then forget, then this is a sign that this is not the path for you. You'll begin to notice the resistance of what you're trying to manifest; if you feel this anxiety or unsettledness, don't fight it. It only means that it is not right for you. If you are dreading doing this technique for a week, then this is not something that will spark joy for you and your future. Come to terms with this and find the next route to take. I encourage you not to fight or force anything into your life. Simply use these diversions to change your course of action to what feels better aligned with your vibration.

The trick with manifesting is you must believe that you deserve this. You must *know* in your heart that you're worthy of having this kind of happiness in your life. Set your standard high and never settle for anything less. I found manifesting came easier to me when I created the sense around me, *as if something magical is about to happen to me all the time.* Most of the time, magical things did come my way. It's all in how I choose to perceive the world. It's a vibration and a frequency that is given out to the universe and sent back like a boomerang. When I believed in my heart that what I was trying to manifest was meant for me, I found that this was when my world began to change. Sometimes, that required having faith and not fear. Having faith that it will all work out in the way it is supposed to. Just let the universe decide when our dreams are ready to enter our lives. Don't lack the faith that this dream is possible. If anything, dream bigger than what you expect is possible; this is when the universe will give you exactly what you are able to handle. Understand that we define our lives from years of conditioning and trauma, a lot of which we have no control over. This trauma can be passed down through generations through our DNA (up to seven generations.) We only understand and know what we know, so we have to bring forth a new perspective and be willing to break the generations of karmic actions.

To hone into my skills of manifesting, I had to go back to having this childlike curiosity and wonderment; where the world became bigger, more expansive, and a friendlier place than what I believed. I began to use the stars in retrograde as portals of awakening for myself to tap into manifesting and recreate my life. I also used certain dates (like 11/11), certain stars lining up, or new and full moons to make my manifesting more powerful.

I had been patient and understanding when manifesting my home. I didn't want to rush it. Also, I was practicing the part of manifesting that isn't taught in The Secret, which is letting your dreams go. Once you do this manifesting technique, it's important to put it away and not focus on why it hasn't come into your life yet. When you focus on that, you are creating the energy of resistance and frustration, which is the opposite of having faith. So, I kept to myself and stayed as busy as I could working my ass off as a yoga teacher. I was saving up as much as I could for my move. I barely had time to do anything else in my life besides work and walking the Chi boy. I remained focused and had a vision of what I wanted. I was brewing up that energy for my life for what was next.

One day, I had the intuition to finally make a post about myself on a Facebook group called "Austin Community Housing." I explained here exactly what I wanted in a dream home and what I needed in a roommate situation. I don't know why I was never called to do this before. I got a flood of responses with a lot of different options to choose from. Before this, I only viewed others posts because I still wanted to remain hidden for some reason. It was getting to the point where I needed to make my situation clear and precise to the world. If I wanted to see results, I had to take some steps towards where I wanted to go. When you put it out there for the world, like I did with my post, the universe will then respond somehow. It's important to take action over ways you can bring your dreams closer to reality. They won't come into your life if you only hide in your room. Meaning, you can manifest all you want, but you must also take steps in the right direction of feeding and nurturing this dream. From this post I made, I got an overwhelming amount of responses. I filled up the next two weeks with appointments with possible candidates for a new home to see if it would be a good fit. Of course, I took Chi with me to see how he would react. After all, he is a vital piece to my pack.

The moment I stepped into the home where I currently live, I had a feeling of déjà vu when I walked into what would be my bathroom. I was overwhelmed by a sense of having been there before. I couldn't remember if it was from a party from years ago, when I was wild and couldn't remember, or if I was seeing the future of me waking up here every morning. It felt too strange to ignore because it felt so familiar. A calming sense of *this is where I'm supposed to be,* came over me. I would live in the master bedroom which has vaulted ceilings, my own bathroom, plenty of room for Chi with a yard, and on top of that, my landlord is a 23-year-old photographer, so this would be a creative and encouraging household. Chi got along super well with his dog and he seemed happy to be here, too! It checked off all of the requirements from my list, so I jumped on the opportunity and put down my deposit the next day. It was perfectly divine timing because my new roommate had bought the house two weeks prior to my post. He had moved to Austin when he bought the house and didn't know anyone here yet. He had only just begun his search to fill this spot when he saw my post. He interviewed a few other people who came to look at the space before me; all of whom he didn't like. It was an instant yes from both of us, and I was excited to finally make this move! I love the way the universe works sometimes. I loved how it aligned the right path for me, with all the signs saying, "GO!"

I moved in, and was immediately at peace with where I was in my life. I could finally rest. I never realized the importance of having a stable, safe, and comforting home until I finally was able to experience having it, firsthand. My whole adult life, I have been living with my boyfriends with nowhere to run when it got hard, or barely being able to make it on my own. My home life has always been a struggle because my home was never mine to begin with. I was always in a desperate space of needing someone to save me. I would be living with them out of convenience because it was less expensive. But now, this is a home that I can call mine and have all to myself. This is something that I created for my life. This is what I envisioned a happy home should be like. No one is here to threaten me or mess with my vibe as I replenish myself within the comfort of these walls. Finally, I am able to breathe and grow as a human on my own, without the distractions of other people's worlds affecting mine.

As soon as I moved in, I could feel a difference in my world. My work became easier and I started to bloom in my teaching style. I became more creative and was able to finally finish this book. Completing this book took me longer than I expected, but this was because I felt like the only way I could end it was if I was in a good space. This book, and how it was going to end, was in the forefront of my brain. I needed to be in a good space to be able to write about some of these dark moments in my life without getting depressed, or going for a glass of wine to comfort me while I wrote. I finally was in a position to do so and I felt the need to end this chapter of my life. Of course, in order to keep this place, I needed to work a lot to be able to keep up with the bills. It was an adjustment financially, but I made due by going out less and staying home more. I was truly happy to be there, so it was an enjoyable sacrifice.

I made some great friends during this time. I believe I was having such luck because of my vibrations that I was putting out into the world. I was attracting that kind of energy. Most of the people around me didn't drink and I was able to feel safe, which is crucial in the recovery process. Change was coming into my world and all of it started to roll in with open arms on my end. I had a friend from Costa Rica who kept reaching out to me, asking when I was going to plan a yoga retreat over there. The thought of this became so intriguing that I had to figure out a way to make it happen. I knew this was something I needed to do for myself because it would mean I would have come full circle from the last time I was there. I knew I could be strong enough and lead a beautiful group of people into this magical country! It was nice to know I had a team of people who were cheering me on, encouraging me to do this. I just needed to make a website first so I could sell the spots to my students. The seed was planted. It was only a matter of a day or two before I had another alignment message come through from my angels.

I had one student in particular who came into my life and helped to create a deep shift from within myself. His name is Michael, known on Instagram and YouTube as "Deep Shift." He had attended my classes but I never spoke much to him, or even knew what he did for a living. One night, we talked after class, and he explained that he helps spiritual teachers grow their business by helping them to create an online presence. *Wait, seriously, Universe?* This amazing human came into my life at the perfect time. He was more than happy to help me build my website so I could help the world, without wanting anything in return. He helped me not only gain the confidence to chase my dreams, but also taught me how to build and work my website, www.allibeeyoga.com, on my own. With his help and guidance, I was able to launch my retreat and start making this dream into a reality!

Another great friend that I made during this time was named Alison Tugwell. She was the one who was my catalyst for finishing my book. She became one of my mentors, and life coach for my book. Alison became such an important part of my life by helping to hold me accountable for my dreams. Soon after meeting her, she became my accountability buddy to help me with the moral support to sit down for periods of time and write. I couldn't have asked for a better person to be that presence. She was also finishing her book, so it was nice to have someone there who understood the process and gave me advice with how I should end this book and wrap up my final thoughts. I needed someone to talk to towards the end because I was processing some heavy layers that I had to shed away. I was nervous and scared about what was going to happen once my book was released. Of course, I had my fears and anxiety about what people would think of me. I was also worried about not being able to reverse things once it was published. At times, this fear would basically stop me from writing altogether. I would lock up and have writer's block. I had to get past this freeze mode with the reminder from Alison that this book will also help so many. Not only that, but Alison helped give me valuable tools and insights as to why I was writing in the first place. She helped bring in a different mindset to writing for me. We would basically chat for an hour, and then flow write for an hour. It was time for this book to end, and Alison was there to give me that push and sage advice when I needed it. She helped me to complete the tasks and goals needed for this book to be what it is today.

Since living on my own, my career skyrocketed. My focus was building my career and that was what happened. I still wasn't at a point where I wanted to let love in and add another person to my mix. I was beginning to rock it and finally succeed in life on my own. I began to produce some amazing yoga events which helped bring me more exposure. My favorite event that I did was the Boats and Yoga series. I have a friend who owns a party barge with Premier Party Cruises, and he let us use his boat to host three events with High Low Yoga over the summer. I was so stoked and proud of myself for these events, and so was the community! The first two sold out, and the third one almost did. It was the talk of the town for a little bit and I was feeling the high of accomplishment. No one had ever done a yoga event this way, so it set me apart from the rest. It was such a blast, that I might make it an annual thing for myself!

I was finally stepping into my power and owning being a leader and a teacher. Just when I felt like my whole life was aligning and I was shining my brightest, I got a message one day from my boss. My boss called and said she needed to speak to me about something important. Perplexed by this, I had no idea what I had done.

She wanted to tell me that she was super proud of me and my growth and she was noticing how much I was killing it in the yoga game, but she also wanted to warn me that getting this kind of fame and acknowledgment was a double-edged sword. She said that there were a couple of teachers who had complained about me since my Boats and Yoga success. They had complained that I was rude to them when asking to modify the classroom to what I felt was creating my space to teach. They recommended that I read the book *Nonviolent Communication* so I could better relate to my co-workers. Shocked by the realization that I had haters all of a sudden, I knew I wanted to try to fix this. I did what I could, and bought the book and started to read it to try to change my behavior. I never realized it, but all the time I spent in abusive relationships taught me to speak more aggressively when feeling attacked. I felt the jealousy or the negative vibes from some of the teachers there, and I would put up a wall in return that only backfired against me. I tried to not get too close to those people and just go to work to do my job, but me being more distant only created more friction between my co-workers and myself. They would have no problem calling and tattling to my bosses if they felt I was rude. Most of the time, I didn't even realize I had done something wrong. If I did, I apologized immediately and tried to talk it out with them, but that didn't matter.

I realize I may have come on a little strong in my career. I started teaching and then immediately gained a following and it made the other teachers upset with how fast I grew. There are some teachers who have worked years to build up the courage to host an international retreat or get creative with their events, and I came in here wanting to do all of the things, all at once, all at the beginning. I was a force to be reckoned with, I suppose. I was here to shake things up. I could see why they would be jealous or maybe feel threatened by me. I was going after my goals, and I wasn't going to let anyone stop me from doing the best job that I can do. Fun Fact: When your light begins to shine bright, it will make others around you uncomfortable. **Keep growing anyway!**

It got to a point working at this studio where I felt like I was in high school again and the kids were tattling to the teachers about what he or she said. I figured at this age we would be able to have a conversation face to face and be able to solve any issues, but apparently, I am not the easiest person to confront. I never tried to tattle to the management because that's not my style. This ended up being my downfall because they never heard my side of the story. I started to get overly aware when I went to work and felt like I was walking on eggshells around the other teachers. I didn't know who I had offended because they kept the other teachers' complaints anonymous. It soon became obvious who had tattled on me and it was hard to fake being nice to them at work. Eventually, I saw how they were like spies for the management there.

I guess being a bright light draws in the attention from others; whether it's the kind of attention you want, or not. Some of the teachers had complained to management that I was doing too many events. They thought it wasn't fair that I was getting to do one each month. I was doing an event a month because it was helping me to keep up with my bills. Soon after my Boats and Yoga series, High Low told me I couldn't do any more events for a while so that the other teachers wouldn't complain. I tried to look at it from my co-workers' point of view and decided to chill out on pursuing events with the studio. I decided it was best for me to host my next few events on my own. It was sad that I was getting this response from my studio, but I figured I'd let them do things their way for a while; then it might go back to being normal, eventually.

I was spending a lot of time working and minding my own business. Unfortunately I noticed my own yoga practice fading away. I would practice sometimes with my students when I taught, but it wasn't the same as getting in my zone before I was a teacher. I was exhausted by the end of the day and the last place I wanted to be was back in a yoga studio when I had been in one all day. I found my solace while walking my wolf. He always pushes me to get outside, ground back into nature, and get back to myself. Plus, he is very loud when he wants you to walk him, and it's the hardest thing to say no to him. I know it's important for me to work out this energy, and I know movement is what my body needs. If I can't practice yoga to release this energy, then at least I'll go for a run or get lost in the woods; either way, this energy needs to keep moving through me.

I spent my days teaching, coming up with new events, finishing this book, sleeping, eating, and walking my dog. I had no life outside of this. I worked hard, to the point where there was a huge imbalance in the amount of energy I was giving out to the world, and the energy I was replenishing myself with. I was giving so much of myself to my classes and busting my ass to barely be able to make it. (I was feeling the burnout effects of teaching too much.) I was doing my best, but I wasn't doing the best job replenishing my body and mind during this time. I would rarely go out, and when I did, it had to be a special occasion. This one special evening, August 20th, 2019, will be one for the books that I will remember for the rest of my life.

CHAPTER TWENTY-SEVEN

MY IMPACT WITH THE TRUTH

You would think that by now in the book I would be fully in my light and living my best life. Well, when you think you have the world, the universe will bring on one more challenge to test you. *Far more dangerous than ignorance, is certainty.* I was certain I was on the right track and had finally gotten control of my life. I mentioned earlier that I was now an occasional "responsible drinker." You would think being a yoga teacher, I would know how to be in charge of my body and my limits, but I had to learn things the hard way. I struggled with alcohol and I was at a point in my life where I didn't drink that much anymore. I didn't want to give myself any room or a chance to fuck up. I lived a strict life and I would maybe drink once every three weeks. If I did, it would only be a glass of wine. I haven't been this clear since I was 13, and I think that's why I had so much goodness flowing into my life.

Well, life does call for you to be social at some point, so I eventually had to venture out of my cave. I also started to work at Practice Yoga Austin one night a week, which meant that I got invited to their 6th Year Anniversary Party for all of their teachers. We had dinner at this fancy restaurant called Odd Duck. If you're ever in Austin, I highly recommend this place. Fair warning, though, they have strong margaritas! It was such a lovely night with all of my teachers and co-workers and all the beautiful people who have shed so much light during my journey. I thought I was safe and in control with my actions being in their presence.

At this point in my progress with alcohol, I would be able to have a drink or two, then know when it was time to call it a night. But as we all know, when I drink I lose control of my crown chakra and something else starts to seep in. I had a couple of margaritas and mingled with my friends and teachers before deciding to go outside for a change of scenery. When I walked back in, the food had already been served and picked over. I missed out on dinner, but didn't miss the opportunity to request another margarita. I had to teach the 6 a.m. class the next morning, so I was going to go home after this one. By this time, I was already buzzing pretty hard and should've gone home instead of ordering that last margarita.

Well, that third one did the trick and put me over the edge into the overload zone. Since I missed dinner and wasn't drinking a lot anymore, I became a lightweight; I didn't think two and a half drinks would've gotten me this buzzed. One of my teachers started to notice what was happening to me and kindly told me it was time to go home. She even walked me out to my car, gave me a hug, and then sent me on my way. I don't remember clearly what was going on at this point, but I knew I probably shouldn't have driven home. I probably insisted that I was going to drive though, since I had such an early class the next morning. I am guessing on this right now, but I'm thinking "Alli-sin" didn't like being told that she needed to leave the party. Therefore, she made the decision to go to the bar next door and have "one more drink." When I get too drunk, I start craving my old vice, Jameson. When Jameson is involved, I've learned that nothing good ever comes from it. Apparently, I went to the Gibson Bar next door instead of my car and got myself three more shots of whiskey. I figured this out the next day when I looked at my bank statements while trying to piece together the puzzle of my night.

After my excessive shots, I drove home, even less okay to drive. I'm so thankful I made it home safe and didn't hurt anyone. I got home and my roommate, Zach, was in shock with how drunk I was. I was searching the house, rummaging for more alcohol, when Zach decided it was time to help get me to bed. He held me up with my arm around his shoulder and did his best to guide me into my room. I was almost to the bed when my worst nightmare became a reality. I tripped over my feet and fell face first on my tile floor. I ended up landing on my front tooth, breaking half of the tooth off at impact. Zach didn't know what to do with me screaming and freaking out in my room, so he woke up Nadley, my second roommate, for backup.

I was scrambling on the floor trying to find the broken half so that I could make sense of it all and hopefully be able to glue it back on (not realizing that teeth don't work the same way as an amputated finger.) I looked in the mirror and started to try to break it because I was disgusted with my reflection and what I was seeing. I looked like a demon, or this evil thing that took over my face; it was all distorted and messed up and I felt ruined. I didn't look like me anymore without my perfect smile. One of my best features, my smile, was ruined because of "Alli-sin." *How many more times am I going to let her hurt me?* I hated her so much! I would freak out to my roommates asking, "No, seriously guys, what happened?!" and they would reply with, "You fell" and then I would slam the door, go in my closet, look at my face in the mirror and freak out. Then I would run back out into the living room and ask them the same thing over and over. I must have asked them a total of 20 times.

They figured I hit my head pretty hard, and it could have caused a concussion. I kept repeating myself, and I wasn't making any sense to them. I honestly wasn't able to process this traumatic experience in my mind at the time; I was that drunk. It felt like a nightmare that was replaying in my head. I can remember being so upset, looking at myself and hating who I saw. I remember throwing things and breaking glass in my closet. I turned into a terrified, belligerent, lost soul, and I seriously didn't want to live. *Who was this?* I felt like a monster all of a sudden. Life can change so quickly.

My roommates were pretty freaked out and didn't know what to do. They told me later on that I was begging them to take me to the hospital so they could fix me. It's not like the hospital can do anything to bring my tooth back or make me look normal again, but they took me anyway to make sure I didn't have a concussion. They took me to get an MRI scan of my brain to make sure everything was okay. I sobered up enough and came back to my wits when I was getting my scan in the machine. I thought I had killed someone or had been in an accident when the fog lifted. I was terrified and the nurse explained the same words, "You fell." This took me back to Zach and Nadley telling me these words while I was at home freaking out. *How could I be so clumsy to fall like this?* I could feel the pain of the tooth getting jammed in my nasal passages and I had a screaming headache from it. After the MRI, I was taken back to the hospital room where I tried to get in touch with my bosses for my 6 a.m. class to try to get it covered. Of course, I didn't have my phone and I had no luck getting a hold of anyone from my roommate's Facebook. I came to terms with the fact that I was still going to teach my class no matter what. I didn't want to lose my job. I was worried I might have lost my dream home on top of everything because I scared my roommates so badly.

My life was falling apart and it was 4 a.m. before I got home from the hospital. I normally leave to get to class by five. I had an hour to kill before I went to teach and there was no way I could nap for one hour; I wouldn't wake up if I did that. I used that hour to walk Chi instead and try to sober up. I needed to try to process what had just happened to me. I was also walking off the nerves of what was about to happen when I teach a class with half of a broken tooth. I had no choice but to show up that morning for my class anyway.

I had to set my pride to the side and face my biggest fears. I didn't want to be in public like this. It was like integrating shame all over my soul, unlike anything I could've imagined. Having to teach like this made the experience more surreal, hitting closest to my heart, more than anything I had ever done to myself before. Yet, I had to own the fact that I did this to myself. I remember getting there extra early so I could at least clear the space and try to get my mindset right. I ended up having 26 students come to this class, which was way more than normal. *Why though? This was just my luck.* I had a mixture of my regulars and new students, and I couldn't have been more embarrassed to greet and teach them all. I had my students asking what happened, and my automatic response was that I fell from my dog pulling me on a walk. I couldn't bear the shame to tell them the truth. It was too humiliating to say that I got too drunk and fell on my face, even though they could probably smell the reminisce of the night before. I continued with the class anyway and made sure to apologize beforehand for my slurred speech and lisp due to my broken tooth. I struggled to make it through teaching the class without crying and running into the bathroom to hide. It was the most challenging thing I have ever had to do. It was so hard to look at my students in the eyes and see the concerned looks on their faces. I wanted to hide, and yet I couldn't. I was exposed in my most vulnerable state because I chose to show up for my students, no matter what was happening in my world. I proved a lot to myself this day about my devotion to being a teacher, and exactly what kind of teacher I didn't want to be. It was as if this moment was burned into my memories so that I wouldn't ever forget the humiliation that followed my poor choices. It was finally time for me to learn my lesson with alcohol, once and for all. It had to be this brutal; I had to fall on my face to figure it out.

Later that day, I went to the dentist and they put half of a fake tooth in the place that had gone missing. The second from the front tooth got broken as well, but I couldn't afford to get both of them fixed. Luckily, I had some money set aside from my retreat to Costa Rica, otherwise I would've been stuck with a broken front tooth for a lot longer than just a day. This traumatic experience was *the moment* that truly shaped my future. I apparently needed to have this awakening hit home, so I could remember why alcohol is not meant for me. Having a broken front tooth is more permanent than a tattoo and a constant reminder every time I put something up to my mouth. I'll never be able to forget the trauma that this experience caused me. Now, I feel like I have the strength, and the story, I needed to convince myself that I never want to drink alcohol again. No one will pressure me to drink if I tell them the last time I did, I fell on my face and broke my front tooth. It has a powerful punch and ring to it. August 21st, 2019, was the day I finally gave up alcohol for good. I never made a sober date for myself, so this was a huge step in the right direction. This substance isn't doing anything to bring me closer to my light, and it's time that I stop allowing myself to be weak in its presence. I have to make this shift within myself if I truly want to reach my full potential to shine--for my future, and for the world.

*Side Note: Sometimes you have to fall on your face to wake up and realize that something isn't working for you. I only hope no one has to experience it the way I had to. When life shakes you up like this, don't quit and give up. Use this as your power--use this as your fuel and fire under your ass to make that change needed for your growth. **Turn your pain**

into your power! Let this become the time when you walk hand in hand with your shadow-side and tell him/her, "It's going to be okay. I see you. I hear you. I forgive you."

CHAPTER TWENTY-EIGHT

THE GROWTH FROM THE PAIN

I would never wish my experience upon anyone. Yet, this could easily happen to anybody who has had a few too many drinks. I'm surprised it took me this many years to get such a negative consequence like this from being too intoxicated. I suppose this is what I needed to get the picture. I will never forget about this, though. It's impossible to put this experience to the side and act like nothing happened. Every time I put something up to my mouth, I think about it. Anytime I drink coffee, I'm hoping it doesn't stain my fake tooth. I'm traumatized now, and I was the one that traumatized myself.

I decided that was going to be the last time I ever saw Alli-sin again. I'm going to lock her in the cage and never give her the keys to escape. This is my shadow-side. We all have one and it's important to recognize this part of ourselves so that we can tend to it. It's one thing to forget and ignore that side, like I did for so many years, and it's another thing to do the conscious work to identify, and give that shadow-side some love and much needed attention, by making space for it. To this day, I'm still going strong without alcohol in my life. It's nearly been a year and I feel as if I'm finally able to walk side by side with my shadow. I know she's there in me. I know she did all these things to me in the past to help me wake up to my true self. I know that it doesn't help to hate her, but instead to be grateful that she exists. She exists to be my teacher. I'm blessed to have learned so many lessons from her, but now my whole world has undergone a huge shift, one that has needed to happen for many, many years.

No more dancing with the idea that I can let this poison in my body and everything will be okay; this is crystal clear, and undeniably apparent to me. Good things never happen from it. I have spent most of my life drinking and being social, so this will be a whole new way for me to reprogram my brain. Drinking is what I normally do when I socialize with my family and friends; it's what I do when I go out to concerts, go on dates, or attend most any event. Alcohol is what shapes our society with pervasive advertisements all over every city; their commercials desensitize us and normalize a culture of alcohol use and abuse. I had to learn a whole new way to live and interact with the outside world.

I knew I was going to be swimming against the current by not drinking anymore. These next few months were ones where I stayed at home and nurtured my animal body back into a positive mindset. I needed to help myself feel safe again. I gave myself the alone time I needed to be able to process everything I just went through. I was depressed for a while and was beating myself up about why I had to be so different. It took me a while to be able to speak about this to other people. I had so much shame and humiliation surrounding the trauma I created for myself that night. I took the time I needed to make some necessary repairs. I basically hibernated from the world and focused all of my attention on typing up the end of this book. I was finally able to get clear in my thoughts and piece together the words in a way that felt right. I was also able to find some healing by writing while sober. I could process my past more easily and allow for the feelings to serve their purpose. I never realized how much more energy and productivity could come out of me when I didn't have alcohol weighing me down. This was my life now and I had come to terms with the path that was so loudly spoken for me to go down. Walking Chi three miles, twice a day, became my new hobby. Walking helped me process my thoughts and clear my mind, especially after I typed up my book for hours. I also found myself walking this one particular route every day because of the chance that I might run into this cute neighbor boy. He was usually working outside on his new truck or doing some kind of construction in his garage, and that had me intrigued. I wasn't sure what it was about him, but I enjoyed the moments when I would walk by and we would say a quick hello in passing.

I finally got bored after a couple months of not drinking or socializing and decided to take measures into my own hands. There weren't a lot of sober-friendly events in Austin and I wanted to change that. So, I created some events of my own. The first one that I ended up doing was a speed dating event. I found it difficult to go out on dates without alcohol being involved, and I refused to ever meet anyone from an app. I had a backyard venue in the heart of Austin where I hosted this event, and it was beautiful. We had a total of 11 people who all came together to do this and it seemed like a hot commodity for Austin! I was searching for people who might want to attend this event and when I passed by my cute neighbor again, I asked him if he was interested. Not going to lie, I also wanted to see if he was single in the first place. He told me he was more of an "organic meeting kind of guy," and this is when I realized he was talking about me and our current moment together. I shyly replied by giving him my number and encouraging him that we should hang out sometime soon. I didn't think too much about giving him my number because my brain was swimming in planning events and staying busy by keeping my career growing. I liked him, but I wasn't super sold on a committed relationship yet. I was still healing and freshly sober. It had been about two years since I had a boyfriend and I hadn't endured a sober relationship yet. I didn't want to create any other pressure factors in my life at this time. Although, a distraction could be exactly what I needed to stay in a positive mindset. Each time I walked by his house, I hoped that he would be working outside.

One day while walking with my roommate, Nadley, we ran into Stuart, the cute neighbor. I was in a hurry because I had a private yoga class that I needed to get to, and I still needed to finish walking Chi. Stuart insisted that we come check out something that he thought we would like in his backyard. Curious as to what it could be, we popped back there for a minute to see what this guy was up to. He wanted to show us his aqua-ponic garden and his beautifully speckled chickens. He was so sweet and was trying to make us a care package from his garden to take home with us. He was nervously scrambling to cut some basil and gather some eggs for us. Nadley saw the sparks that he had for me instantly and was encouraging me to act interested. I brushed it off and was hesitant to jump into a relationship with my neighbor, nonetheless. I didn't want my walking routes to be ruined if it didn't work out with him. I also didn't have time to dedicate to a relationship while working full-time and finishing my book. I didn't know what would happen if I added another person into my mix; I didn't want my career or my life to change. I was shaking my head no, no, no, but she knew all along that we were the perfect match. I was trying to come up with any excuse not to let love in.

You could tell how much Stuart was into me, even though he would try to play it off every time he saw me notice. He wasn't pushy about jumping into anything too fast though; he was perfectly patient. He knew he needed to lay low and not blow up my phone, and I think that's why I kept coming back around. He would wait for me to reach out when I was ready, and I appreciated the space to make that decision on my own. He could tell I was guarded and it wasn't going to be a cakewalk to unlock the cage around my heart. I also appreciated that he was sensitive enough to see that this was how I needed to be approached.

I still didn't have the go ahead to produce any more events at High Low, but I needed to come up with a way to pay for my tooth expense. I needed to put that money back into my retreat account. For my next event on my own, I brainstormed and came up with the idea to host Yoga, Tarot, and Full Moon Events out in my friend's lovely backyard. This would be perfect because there was a full moon once a month. I pushed through and made this a reality by selling tickets on EventBrite and had a huge success, even though it was cold outside. I had two tarot readers, a bonfire, some cacao, an hour of yoga practice, and a meditation to settle into the full moon's energy. I needed help to make this event a success. I needed to find some firewood for the bonfire because the temperatures were dropping that evening. I knew of the perfect person who would totally be willing to help me: Stuart. I decided to ask him for help and he eagerly agreed without hesitation. He was such a gem and helped me cut down some firewood faster than I could've imagined. He also helped me deliver the wood to the property and helped me move furniture around so we could set up the yoga space. He was so helpful and understanding, and then when it came time for it, he gave me my space so I could focus on my event. I was shocked with how healthy our interactions were. I mean, I know I was kind of stressed, but he was so calm and helped me figure things out logistically instead of distracting me, or taking offense to me being slightly bossy. I didn't have to explain myself and he didn't make me feel guilty for not spending more time with him after we got everything set up. Maybe this guy could grow on me. I still wasn't sure that

I could even let my walls down enough for him to win my heart over.

November 2, 2019

Break down those walls.

This morning, I find myself feeling like I've created too hard of an armor to let anyone in. I have protected myself with these walls and have built my own castle within the walls where I feel comfortable and safe. I know that in order to grow and understand myself on a deeper level, I have to knock down these walls one by one to allow for someone to see my heart. It's scary, vulnerable, and unfamiliar ground. Since I stopped drinking, I have felt even more guarded with my heart because I'm feeling everything. Feeling life is sometimes overwhelming and hard to handle all the time without numbing yourself with a glass of wine. I find myself more content with being alone and finding my own piece of heaven on Earth, yet I yearn for someone to share this world with. In order to do this, I have to break down these walls to let them in. But how? Slowly. Mindfully. Building an emotional connection before anything physical takes place. It is the only way that I can slowly open up. Yet, I still struggle. With the holidays coming up and my new found sobriety, I know I will have to break down my walls for myself to heal. 95% of this world drinks alcohol and I need to have compassion for that, and for myself, as I choose to be the other 5%. This is my choice and my path and I realize that this is what is best for my highest vibration, no one else's. Maybe it's Mercury retrograde, but I'm feeling all the things of my past and feel like this time around, I need to break down my walls. They have been holding me back and keeping me so heavily guarded for so long. For someone with such an open heart as a yoga teacher, I struggle with opening my heart on a personal level due to my past and everything that has happened to me.

I guess now is the time to feel all of the feels and find a way to tear down the walls, so I can let love in.

To nobody's surprise, all the men that I dated in the past have left a nasty taste in my mouth. I have never had a healthy relationship and, to be real with you, I wasn't sure if it was even possible. I wasn't going to settle for anyone who didn't treat me like a princess. I would've been fine and happy on my own otherwise. I think I'll pass on getting stuck in another abusive relationship. I'd leave the minute I saw the first red flag.

I wasn't ready to meet Stuart until I quit drinking. I never noticed him before that, and he never noticed me. Even though we were neighbors this whole time, and I would walk by his place almost daily. It was the universe's gift, telling me I was ready to find love when I was ready to let go of alcohol. He probably wouldn't have liked the old me anyway. What was important was that he liked the *real* version of me.

The universe has a funny way of bringing what you need in life when you're ready and ripe to receive it. After he helped me with my first Yoga, Tarot, and Full Moon event, he asked me out on our first date to go mountain biking on the trails in our neighborhood. I thought this was a super cute and active way to get to know someone, plus there was no pressure to have anything to drink during the date. It was perfect. I happily said yes and decided to give this guy a shot. Our first date went so well! I made sure to be overly honest with him and tell him most of my wild stories before he fell in love with me. I do this thing with the guys I date to see if I can scare them off before my heart gets involved. I tell them all these stories from this book right off the bat, for a few reasons. The first being, this book will go out to the public and everyone will know this about me. I need to know that the guy who stands next to me is okay with the world knowing, as well. Second, I try to see if they accept me for who I am, or if they are terrified of me and want to run away.

And lastly, I do this to see if they will hold this over my head later in the relationship and judge me, which will show their character. Stuart passed all the tests with flying colors. He wasn't wanting to run away, and he wasn't being judgmental or harsh with his reactions. If anything, all of my stories just made me more appealing to him, and he wanted to know more. The rest of the date was so refreshing and we were able to learn so much about one another. We were honest about what we wanted in a relationship and why our past ones didn't work out. We were asking about each other's ethics and core values. Sure enough, all of them were aligning perfectly with mine.

I couldn't believe this was real. I mean, he's my neighbor! I didn't see him for the first six months I lived in this area and, all of a sudden, when I stopped drinking he magically appeared. Crazy story behind all of this, too; this isn't the first time he's been my neighbor. When I lived with my ex-husband, Stuart was living at the end of my street for three years doing repairs on a house, in exchange for rent. It was the same time frame that I would go for walks to get away from my ex and when I would have been running past his house to hide in a bush. I know for a fact I wasn't ready to meet him then. It was like the universe had been trying to get us to meet, but it wasn't until now that we were finally ready for each other. Realistically, I wouldn't have met him, or any other man, at this time in my life. I happened to be walking my dog, which was the only other thing that I did besides eat, sleep, work on this book, and teach yoga. It's so ironic how the world works sometimes. Trust in the universe and have faith in divine timing, I suppose. Love happened to find me the moment I stopped looking.

It had only been about two weeks since our first date when he asked me to go camping with him and his friends out on the Texas-Oklahoma border. He knew he was asking for a lot since we just met, and we hadn't even kissed yet. I was hesitant because that meant that I would have to sleep next to him and I wasn't sure I was ready for that yet. It would mean I would have to tear down the walls that kept me guarded. I have always had a hard time sleeping over at guys' houses; I can't sleep next to just anyone. I was the girl that would have sex but then want to go back home to my bed afterwards. *How was I going to spend four nights sleeping with someone with no escape route to my bed?* I figured I needed to get out of my comfort zone, and get out of town for a bit to relax. I was craving a break from working so much, and burning my candles at both ends. I needed to replenish myself in nature, bonding with a cute boy. We weren't officially boyfriend and girlfriend yet either, so this was a good test to see how well we got along. I accepted the offer, but stood strong about not having sex with him or drinking while I was there. That part was clear and I was extremely firm on this boundary. I told him I wanted to go slow and build an emotional connection before anything physical happened. If I was going to get myself into something serious, then I needed to do things differently to get myself out of this cycle of toxic relationships. I thought not having sex at the beginning would be a good way for me to avoid running away from him. In the past, I would go straight to the physical, then it would be hard to build on the emotional connection afterwards. I never got to know my partners before sleeping with them. When we would see each other the next time, *if* we saw each other again, it would go straight to physical, skipping over the emotional part. This caused the relationship to be based on sex, and not about truly caring for someone. I knew if I wanted a different, healthier relationship, I needed to do things this way. So we tried this approach and Stuart was the most patient and understanding soul about all of this. He knew I had my own trauma and he was willing to try my approach to make me feel more comfortable. He admitted that it was a first for him to be starting a relationship this way. I guess a huge part of me simply wanted to be courted like a princess. I deserved that much.

This was the cutest courtship I could have ever asked for! As we were camping, he was such a gentleman and never tried to do anything with me sexually. I felt safe enough to sleep like a baby without feeling like he was going to jump me in the middle of the night for sex. We were all sitting around the fire one morning and I could tell he needed something to do with his hands. I asked him if he could make me a dumbbell out of some of the firewood we brought. I knew he was a woodworker, and I wanted to give him a task that could show his skills. He eagerly got his axe and went to work on it without hesitation. He finished the dumbbell within an hour; it was the most amazing Flintstones dumbbell that I will cherish forever! I was so excited to make some yoga and workout videos with it and show off how much this guy is winning my heart. This gesture and his cooking was what really won my heart. I've never seen anyone show off their skills and ruffle their feathers like he did, but he sure was good at it. He made a ten foot bonfire pit for the crew of campers and brought a whole cast iron kitchen collection. Plus, he was the one who had all the tools and skills to keep us alive and comfortable on our adventure. I think he wanted to take me on this trip so he could show me how well he could provide if I did decide I wanted to be with him. It was a smart move on his part for getting himself in his element where he could shine in my eyes. I noticed all the things I was seeing with this guy and I was beginning to fall for him hard. Slowly but surely, he was helping me to tear down the walls so I could open up.

*Side Note: Take your time getting to know someone. If they are right for you, they will wait until you are ready. They will show you patience and understanding, which are both important roles in a relationship. If they can't wait, then it shows you what their real intentions were with you.

CHAPTER TWENTY-NINE

THE ROLLERCOASTER OF LIFE

This trip was exactly what I needed to break away and realize what was important to me. I found myself rejuvenated, refreshed, and falling in love. Maybe it could be possible afterall for someone to win my heart. Maybe I could allow myself the time and freedom to explore other interests rather than work. When I got back home to Austin, I hit the ground running again with work and picking up as many shifts as I could to play catch up from missing four days. I had only been back three days, when my manager abruptly came in after a class of mine. She asked me to get all my things and meet her out back. Instantly, I knew something was wrong by the coldness in her voice.

I finished calculating my money for my class and rushed out back to hear what she was about to tell me. She was standing out back with the general manager and she abruptly said, "We have to let you go today and there is nothing you can say to change this." I was shocked and clueless as to what I had done to cause this. She said she had the last teacher to complain about me, and that this was the last straw. I couldn't wrap my head around it at the time. I wanted to know why and what happened exactly, but they wouldn't give me an answer because they were trying to protect whoever had tattled on me. Flustered and confused, I figured there was no hope even trying to explain my side of the story. In my mind, nothing that I did was overly rude or calling for attention to alert my managers. I didn't even want to fight back to try to keep my job. I thanked them for the opportunity to start my teaching career with them and for the space they gave me to share my practice. I expressed how very sorry I was for disappointing them and walked away with my tail between my legs. I wanted to leave as soon as possible, so I could run to hide. *How would I recover from being fired from teaching yoga at one of the biggest studios in town?* My ego was shot and I knew it was going to be hard for me to make a comeback. I honestly thought I was progressing with the way I spoke to people. I was using the tips from the book they recommended. If anything, I was being more of a pushover when it came to standing up for myself because I didn't want to be noticed or tattled on. I found it easier to keep quiet. There were times when I had to deal with a harsh situation, but I was using the techniques recommended by my manager, or so I thought.

It dawned on me later that night as to what I had done to get myself fired. It was because I asked the teacher a couple days before to please not vacuum next to my student's head. It was ten minutes before my class and the teacher was literally a foot away from my student's head while he was trying to decompress from his day. Surprisingly, this exact situation had happened a few weeks prior. I kindly asked her to move closer to the door to vacuum, or I could do this side work after class. Meanwhile, I had a line of people trying to check in and I could have used her help up front. There are

30 minutes to do side work and switch over shifts between the classes at this studio. The first 15 minutes are the previous teacher's time to do side work, and the last 15 minutes are the next teacher's time to set up the space in a way that makes them feel most comfortable. I talked with my manager after this happened the first time about what I should do if this arises again in the future. My manager told me it was okay to ask for help setting the room how I wanted if it was close to my start time. She told me I shouldn't be afraid to talk with the other teachers when something like this happens. I took her advice, and she fired me for it. I couldn't believe that I had gotten fired for protecting my student, and for doing what I thought was the most ethical thing to do. I handled it in a shy and non-aggressive way, but I guess I still rubbed this teacher the wrong way. I did feel like I had a little "mama bear" energy in me that day.

I asked my manager how I was supposed to go about telling people and my future jobs about what had happened. Their response was for me to tell people that *it wasn't a good fit anymore*. I suppose in a way they were right. I care more about the customer's experience and also about being able to express myself if I need to, without being criticized or judged. It was the first studio I ever went to as a student, and it was the first studio I ever taught at as a teacher. This place has definitely played a huge role in my growth, but what I was witnessing was that my growth was extending outside of what this place could offer me. I didn't want to be put in a cage or tamed because it made them feel better. I had a hard time pushing my emotions to the side and playing the "only good vibes" yoga teacher motto. We are human and we feel all the things, too. Some days are good and some days aren't.

I was in the third month of my sobriety at this point, and it took everything I had to stop myself from going to buy a bottle of wine, and sit at home and mope. I stayed strong though and didn't buy that bottle. I don't even think my managers took into account that I was recovering from alcoholism. That might have played a part in my snappy attitude towards other teachers. Who knows, maybe I was a bitch to some of them and didn't even realize it because I was stressed and trying to cope with a new way of dealing with life. I'm not going to say that it's a cakewalk to quit drinking. I would maybe warn your bosses ahead of time, so they can sympathize with you. I chose to keep quiet because I didn't know any better. I was bitter for a while from this abrupt ending at High Low. I was ripped away from my students without a warning, but I soon realized that this was going to be the greatest blessing I could've ever asked for.

These moments are the ones that shape us, and encourage us to grow. I could've chosen to have a glass of wine, but this was a true test of my devotion to this path. I made it through the pain and made sure to feel everything that was happening to me. I didn't want to hide it or numb it out with a glass of wine. I need to feel what's going on inside of me, so it doesn't happen again. I need to evaluate what happened and how I can grow into a better human from it. Like I said earlier, even more dangerous than ignorance is certainty. I was sure I'd have this job for a lot longer than a year and a half. I had been building such a huge fan base over there and I was starting to make some good money. The part that hurt the most was that they did this right before the holiday season. This is the high season for yoga teachers and there weren't many options for me to start at other studios, nor was I ready to. I had to process my ego being shot to the ground. I was too nervous and I didn't even know what to say when people asked the question, "Why'd they fire you?" without showing my bitterness.

*Side Note: Sometimes your growth and your light shining brighter will intimidate others. Keep growing anyway! Don't let this stop you from shining, because the world needs your light. Take moments like this as signs that the universe is trying to open up a new door of opportunity for you to discover. Also, LET GO of the things that you cannot control. Learn from the lesson and keep progressing in life. Never stop being a student to life. There is always room for improvement. Let your inner warrior guide you, and never dim your light for anyone.

CHAPTER THIRTY

FROM THE WORST EXPERIENCE
TO THE MOST MAGICAL

When I was let go from my job, I saw the support and love from the community that I had built. I had so many of my students reach out to tell me how much they would miss me and how upset and shocked they were that I wasn't there anymore. There was an overflow of emotions to be in this position where I felt like I was ripped away from my family. The other teachers might not have liked me, but their students loved me. The outpouring of people's responses once I came out with my story was proving exactly that. I made sure to take screenshots so I could look back one day at my "love bank" from my students showing me what my life's work is doing for people.

I finally got to see the seeds that I had planted in so many individuals as they were coming out with their stories of how I touched their lives in one way or another. It was such an overwhelming feeling of not being alone that it was hard to beat myself up. Plus, I knew the real reason why they let me go. I was shining too bright for them and they didn't know how to handle me anymore. It was an easy out to a sticky situation that they preferred not to deal with, which is fine in its own sense. I know I don't need to be with anything that doesn't align with my morals and core values. That job was hard on me, energetically. I could feel the resistance and how unwelcomed I was with some of the teachers. It was my time to leave and see what I could make of myself.

With all this extra time on my hands, I had the opportunity to truly devote myself to falling in love. The night when it all felt right, and I gave in and committed, I remember I would normally be teaching my 9 p.m. class on a Friday night. I told Stuart to help me get through the pain of this void of not teaching with helping me get creative. I needed to make something with my hands, but something that I could sell to make my rent money. This was the moment I fell in love with Stuart. He has all the tools at his place to make pretty much whatever I could imagine. He helped me create these beautiful moon shelves that can be turned into an altar or used to organize your crystals. He was so patient and taught me how to use all the machines. His brain knew how to build things naturally, and it was such a bonding experience for him to walk me through the steps. Instead of doing it for me, he showed me the skills so that I could do it on my own.

These little crystal moon shelves were the beginning of our love story! Not only was it such a good release to work with wood and bond with Stuart, but I learned that I have a whole new skill that I'm actually good at. I feel like we are all meant to have multiple skills, yet for me personally, I've always put all my eggs in one basket. Needing to make an income all of a sudden was the driving force behind this for sure, but when it came down to it, I wanted to be adaptable and versatile in how I could spread my love. It was such a sweet moment with Stuart that after our first production run, I was smitten by him. I was sitting on the countertop in the kitchen with him, giving him the biggest bear hug. That's the moment I knew I wanted to be with him. I was amazed at how much he was willing to help me get through this time. He showed me his patience over the last three months, waiting for this moment. The sweetness from the blossoming of a new business, and how well we worked as a team, gave me hope that this truly is something different than all of my past relationships. I will always remember this night, when we decided it was time to break down the walls and let love in. We made the sweetest love; one where we could feel the souls combining and the truth was spoken in our eyes. He made me forget that I was ever sad, and gave me a new focus and a drive that I'm so grateful for.

Not only was he great at teaching me new skills, but he was kind, gentle, understanding, smart, and genuine with his willingness to help me. I fell in love with his brain and the way it worked. I was proud to call this soul my boyfriend. Honestly, we looked like we would be together. It was as if all the pieces were coming together when I thought my life was falling apart. It took three months to finally be able to get to this point, but it was worth the wait. It takes time to build trust. It takes time to get vulnerable. It takes time to open up, especially when you're sober. It takes time to get to know someone to see if they're the right match for you. I say take all the time you need before you take that leap and get physical. If they can't wait for you, they aren't meant for you. It makes the physical connection that much better, not only because of the anticipation, but because you know it's coming from a genuine heart (from theirs but also from yours.) It's easy to get the wires mixed up when sex is involved too soon. Well, it is for me, anyway. I knew it needed to happen this way and felt like my relationships were beginning to make a promising turn.

The first batch of seven moons sold out instantly, from my Instagram posts on my **AlliBeeYoga** page. I had so many of my students wanting to help me out, and most of these sales were from them. I had the demand to make a second round, and that also sold out within a couple of days. People were liking these moon shelves so much that I finally had to make an Etsy page--**WoodBeeUniques**. This was a cute and catchy little name and I was pumped to start seeing things unfold with this new business. I was on a high from being able to make a living with my hands and getting creative. Plus, I was putting so much love into each moon and it felt good to still be able to share my love with the world. I never knew crystal moon shelves would be such a hit, but they are. I was feeding off of everyone's excitement about them! We decided to make a couple of other size options so we could also get the lower price range people as well. We made some that could hang, and we made some that could sit on a tabletop. I was so happy to have been able to create this with my love and still be able to pay my rent on time. These moons were honestly saving my ass. It was nice to have his support with this, too. I would have been lost starting this up by myself. I spent so much time becoming independent and strong that I had forgotten that there is strength in numbers. I forgot what it was like to be a "team." It was magical to watch our special bond unfolding.

I needed this kind of love in my life at this exact moment. It was like the universe knew I was about to embark on a crazy journey. I don't know what would've happened to me without him and his genius brain. Even though Stuart may not be my *"forever man,"* I'm extremely grateful that he was able to open up my heart to the idea of love again. It was so nice to have Stuart there to help be a guiding light and lift me up out of my depression during this time.

Being fired from my job taught me how much of my identity was wrapped up in it. When I didn't have it anymore, it was like I was a clean slate and needed to start back at square one. I gained a couple extra shifts at Practice Yoga Austin after this happened. I was grateful I had Practice to still work for, but I wasn't teaching nearly as much as I had been. From being fired, I learned that I'm more than just a yoga teacher. I have so much more to share with the world than my teachings. This time was truly a blessing for me because I had the time to hunker down and end the first draft of this book. I spent hours devoting myself to perfecting the process of healing. I was finally able to hear my truth and everything started to feel right when I was able to give in and surrender to the situation. I stopped resisting what had happened to me and instead began to see all the beauty that was unfolding from it.

Now that I had WoodBeeUniques going on in my life, I was making about the same as what I was while teaching my ass off every week, yet I wasn't as exhausted. I couldn't believe how much of my time I spent driving around town, chasing my own tail and trying to hustle all the time. I would spend a full day or two with the moon production and then have the rest of the week to write or rest. I was falling in love and having a damn good time doing so. I didn't know it at the time, but this is exactly what I needed in order to stay on my deadlines and finish this book.

With my extra shifts over at Practice Yoga Austin, I was still able to share this outlet with the community. Because I wasn't over-teaching, my classes became more impactful. Plus, I had more time to focus on my retreat to Costa Rica that was supposed to happen in May. I was planning all the smaller details like the schedule and the food menu. I had time to devote and give this retreat the attention to its details in order to make it extra special. I came in contact with one of the inmates that I met while I was in Nicaraguan jail. He reached out to me on Facebook, recalling meeting me in there. His name is Marlon, and to my surprise, he was still in there. I was shocked that he still remembered me, but he said that he would never forget that experience with me getting released like that. He said he hasn't seen anything like it since. He wanted me to send him a book on how to do yoga, so I started putting that together for him. In exchange, he made a bunch of these beautiful macrame bracelets from plastic bags for my retreat guests; the same bracelets they made for me while I was in jail. Things were falling into place with all the smaller details in my life.

One day, I had the urge to be more productive with my life, and find another job. I wasn't ready to go to another studio and get more teaching gigs yet. I had my tail between my legs and it was hard for me to explain why my last studio let me go, so I avoided it. I had the intuition one day to reach out to Stretch Labs to see if they were hiring. I heard it so loud and clear that I knew this was the job to go after. I called them and asked if they were hiring and they told me to look online on a job search site to see if they were hiring. If they were, the application to apply would be there. Of course, I looked online and it was the third job on the list. I filled out the application and the next day got a phone call interview. It was easy. There was no resisting or questioning what I was doing. Everything lined up perfectly. I got hired that week at Stretch Labs and started an intensive training to become a Flexologist. I learned how to do assisted stretching for people, so they can gain better range of motion. This worked perfectly with my yoga teaching background and if anything it was a nice addition to my skill set. The two jobs could be intertwined and my knowledge about the human body would be growing even more. Knowledge is power, and I was like a sponge soaking it all in. I always enjoy adding new skills that I could use to make a living. Especially if they were going to pay for my training.

Good things are happening right now. I had to be freed from my old job and their negativity to be able to open myself up to all of these beautiful gifts. I believe the world is what you make of it, all depending on your perspective. I did my best to keep myself in a positive mindset. I tried to keep moving my body, filling my thoughts with creativity, and spreading loving kindness into everything I was doing. I was focusing on putting these vibrations out there into the world, and I noticed that all of these things were returning back to me, tenfold. I can feel myself stepping into my light when I notice my energy feeling light. I feel more calm and secure with who I am, and where I am on my journey. I feel like I have done the work of diving inwards, and am still doing this work to this day. I am now able to honor the process of growing and welcome change with open arms. It is in these moments of riding the waves of life that I feel most alive. You wouldn't be able to enjoy the good moments to the maximum if you never had any bad times in your life.

*Side Note: Use your pain on a creative endeavor to allow for the release of energy when something like this happens (paint, write, woodwork, it doesn't matter--just create.) It is important not to remain stagnant and dwell on your loss. Channel this energy somehow, and release what's holding you back. It is not until you release the past that you can unlock the future.

Chapter Thirty-One

You Had the Power All Along, My Dear

The truth is, life will always find ways to dim your light. It is in the challenges and these moments where you have a choice. That choice in how you choose to show up for yourself will determine your fate. You have your own path to walk down, and only you know what is right for yourself; no one else does. There will come a time in your life when you will want to create the space for your growth and nothing will be able to stop you from finding it. You can't swim against the resistance of everything forever. Take a step back, breathe, and find a way to go with the flow of what the universe has in store for you. That which no longer serves you will find a way to slough off of you so you can make space for the new. I found it impossible to reach my highest potential and experience everything the world has to offer when I remained in my comfort zone. It takes a leap of faith and feeling the freedom of free-falling, not knowing how you will land. It takes gaining the courage (or asking your Angels for it) to let go of everything that you knew was real and tangible to be able to reap the fruits of the unknown forest. Letting go creates rebirth. This life will always unfold in a way that is meant for growth and a higher purpose for all of us.

When we learn to ride these waves and allow ourselves to feel our emotions, we are able to slow down and hear the messages that these gifts bring us. Take the time to process these feelings instead of hiding away from them with distractions or substances. Instead of looking at life happening to you, look at life happening for you. *What is this teaching you?* Just know, when you grow and evolve into someone that is beaming, it will make some uncomfortable. It's inevitable. The goal is to keep growing anyway! No one else is walking in your shoes or has the power to change your life; only you can.

This life is constantly shifting and shaking us, forcing us to grow. I have spent my life trying to figure out how to find my light and how I can shine in the brightest fashion. It took shaking up my world to allow the light to shine through. At this point in my book, I'm finally realizing that **I've had this power all along**. This light lives within each of us, waiting to emerge to be seen and heard. It comes forward when you find a way to step into your truth, and be honest with yourself. Do the work, forgive the past, and thank those challenging moments for making you the strong badass that you've become (or are meant to be). It is in these cracks in our wounds that brings forth the light on the other side. If those moments never happened to me, who knows where I would be now. I might have never become a yoga teacher or I might not have been given the courage to speak up and finally complete the ten-year project of writing this book. I have found my peace within my pain, and I have made my pain become my power. I made the conscious choice to live a different life that can provide me the clarity, and the kind of peace that my soul was craving. I have used these wounds and this pain to become the fire in my belly that would serve as a catalyst for my growth. This life is not meant to be perfect and pleasant all the time. No change would happen and no growth would be gained if it wasn't for these experiences in the dark. Welcome these challenges with open arms, if anything. The trick is to learn from them and try a different route, until you get the result you want. Get curious with these feelings, and find a way to express yourself. Be honest with what you want out of this lifetime, and have a clear vision on how you are going to make the inspired action to follow through.

I found yoga to truly be the key that unlocked many doors for my healing. Yoga helped me process my emotions, and gave me a new addiction. It saved my life when I was in the darkest of places. Yoga gave me power and a sense of purpose. This practice taught me to honor myself and my body, along with how to follow my heart to find my light. When I practiced, I was showing up for myself. I was meeting myself where I was each day with a new perspective. My teacher, Shanti Kelly, says "Your body is a metaphor. How you do your practice is how you do your life." So when I did my practice, I cared. I cared with every cell in my body so I would care about my life. That sense of love for myself only seemed to grow when I didn't think I knew how it could. When you slow down and observe what is happening in your practice, you are able to witness what is truly happening deep within the surface of your skin. This practice also gave me a community of people that were all experiencing a similar awakening.

I was able to see and feel why I was put on this earth, and that was to spread this loving kindness out to others. I am here to share my experiences and prove the research that I've collected over the last ten years had a purpose. I'm here to guide others with movement, making it their medicine. I'm here to share my creativity with the love from my hands. My moons get to bring in a space in your house where you can worship your crystals, so you take a moment to appreciate their strengths, and feel calmed by them. I am also here to continue my own healing. You can expect workbooks and a sequel from me soon! Our work is never finished, as we continue to grow and evolve. The healing journey is a lifelong commitment. We are all students here on Earth, learning from each other. Just remember, don't ever stop growing, and have faith and not fear. You have the power within you to conquer the highest peaks and the lowest of lows.

I found getting creative and allowing myself to get in my flow state allowed me to figure out what feels right in my life. I learned to follow my heart to find my light and listen in, especially when my intuition is loud. Writing to all of you for all these years has been the biggest blessing for me. I was able to feel your eyes reading this and somehow, I knew I wasn't alone. I don't regret anything that has happened to me on my journey. I know the rawness of my experiences and the depths of the darkness were meant to help others. Yes, in the moment, I feel just as naked and vulnerable as my cover photo, but I know this will only make me stronger by sharing these experiences. I wanted to show you all that no matter where you are on your journey, there is a way to find your truth and let your light shine. It took some time for me to learn this, but I knew I was going through these painful experiences so that I could be more relatable. I seemed to have found almost every dark corner to fall into, to be able to touch more souls with being able to say, *I've been there too*.

I found that getting lost is sometimes the best way to find yourself. It's a great way to let your instincts kick in and give yourself the opportunity to practice in trusting the universe. I found walking and running helped to clear my mind and ease any tension in the body. I'm so grateful I have my wolf by my side that would encourage me to do this daily. If you don't already, I recommend getting a dog for this exact reason: They force you to stay active and get your ass outside!

I found that being alone isn't always a bad thing. Sometimes, the only thing you need is the space to be able to think for yourself so you can listen to your heart and process your emotions instead of projecting them onto other people. Especially if you're dealing with trauma or an abusive relationship, it's best to spend some time with yourself so you can process your feelings without someone else interfering with your truth.

Surrounding yourself with people who can lift you up is also clutch to shining your brightest. Be around people who inspire you and encourage your uniqueness. If you have people in your life that bring you down and make you feel inferior or like a cockroach, weed those people out so you can make space for people who can fill up your cup! Make a boundary and let go of those that cross your line. Sometimes, you can't avoid these people that drag you down, so it's important to protect your energetic space. Maybe in the shower, bless the water and ask for it to cleanse your energy. I personally like to do this method when I get home, or *after* an unpleasant situation. Or you can imagine a big, bright, white bubble surrounding you *before* you have an interaction with someone that normally takes your energy. Ask your angels for support, guidance, or protection. **Remember: Angels become more present when you ask for their presence, so don't ever be shy to do so.** We all have our own squad of angels that are here to protect us and help us on our journeys.

You have to let go so you can make space to let in what is right. It's hard sometimes to let go because we have become so attached to the pain or the drama. We only know what we know and it takes a sacrifice to finally leave the comforts of being uncomfortable. It's a choice that only you can make for yourself. Choose wisely and take your time when it comes to dating. Be so picky about who you let in on a sexual level. Especially for women, we pick up and carry the men's DNA with us for life (that is, if they cum inside of you). No need to rush what is right in your life. What is right for you will be around when you are ready; what is wrong for you will be hard to keep around, either emotionally or technically.

If you are in an abusive relationship, know that there is always a way out. Find a backup plan of a house you can stay at for a while if you live together, and make an exit strategy. Once you're out, you can begin to get clear on your own thoughts and the next steps to build yourself back up. It's a process of regaining your power and reclaiming what is rightfully yours. It can be confusing when you're stuck in it, but once you are freed from it and cut the cords of attachment, you'll be able to see the light at the end of the tunnel. No one deserves to be treated in this manner and you are worthy enough to stand up for yourself and walk away, but, once more, only you can choose this for yourself.

If you are dating, take your time. Make them wait for it! You get to see if they have the patience to put up with you, and their willingness to try to understand who you are. You also learn a lot about a person when you use this time to talk and see if your lives line up with one another. Be honest, vulnerable, and open from the beginning so you both know what you're getting into. If you have to fake who you are, why would you want to keep up with that lie for the long run? If they don't like you for the real you, then you don't need them in your life anyway. Talk about your past so they can sympathize and understand you better. If you are a booty call for someone and having fun, by all means do so, but just know that as you get older, it weighs on your conscience as you think about all the things you did, and all the nights you can't remember. So choose wisely and wear condoms!

Another pro-tip I learned the hard way: Your body is your temple. Be careful of what you feed yourself, what you choose to put in your body, and how you alter your brain. I know sometimes the feelings get too real for most of us, and most of us want to hide from the truth. This pain is an important teacher; feel these emotions instead of numbing them out with substances. Not drinking has gotten easier over time and I feel so much more comfortable in my own skin since I made the decision to quit. It's as if my body and my karmic path are thanking me, continuing to bring me abundance and blessings. Plus my intuition has gotten stronger with a clearer mind.

Listen to your body and eat right for your Dosha (Ayurveda). Pay attention to the stars and what's happening in the sky. The stars and the moon can be powerful tools when it comes to your manifesting powers and opening the portals to magnify the process. Manifesting and the magic behind it are real. Use this tool to help you on your journey. If you begin to believe and have patience, you'll be surprised how the universe will work in your favor. You must be clear with what you want, and when you are ready and ripe for it, the universe will be there to present its gifts. Have patience, devotion, and compassion when it comes to your growth. Nothing good in this life is ever easy, and it will be an ongoing journey of discovery. You have to show up with faith in yourself, if nothing else. Know that you are the ruler and the creator of what you wish to surround yourself with. Make wise choices that can progress your path and know that **you are worthy of happiness**. You are capable of finding your light and your purpose on this planet. Understand that you are perfect, just as you are, and you are made this way to learn and heal your karmic path. **Your past does not define you, and your pain does not create your identity for your future**. Your willingness and openness to grow will help you find your light and bring you a sense of inner peace. This will shape you into the soul you are meant to evolve into. If you can think it, dream it, and feel it in your heart, then you can manifest it into reality. You can make anything possible as long as you believe it's possible.

It has been my absolute pleasure to create this book of my wild journeys on my way to finding my light. The truth is, I've had this light and power all along, I just didn't realize it. I was so lost in alcohol, drugs, and boys, that I was stuck in the darkness, running into walls. Yet, that darkness is where I could practice my faith in myself and see the light shining through the cracks. It was in these moments of rock bottom that my higher self was the loudest. Sometimes it takes losing everything and falling on your face to be able to start fresh again. I followed my heart to find my light and made one hell of a story out of it. I hope you all have enjoyed this book and I wish you all the best of luck on *your* wild journey to the light. Just remember, surf those waves of life and know that you've got this!

~ XO ~

Allison Bee Levy, a.k.a. Alli Bee

Acknowledgments

I couldn't have compiled this book without the loving support of my parents, Carol and Eric. Thank you for giving me the space to explore and become my own unique individual. (Cover design created by Carol with Giraphics)

I also want to give a special thank you to my friends who have been there through thick and thin. My love goes out to Katelyn, Amanda, Emily, Dina, Nadley, Zach Kracht (He's the one who took my cover and about author photos!), my sister, and for all of the others that have crossed my path. You know who you are!

This book was completed with the help of my life coach, Alison Tugwell, and my wonderful friend and editor, Meredith Canmann. Thank you for your help and encouragement throughout this process!

Thank you to my beta readers for helping me craft the polished product, and thank you to my launch team for helping me promote this book's release.

A special thank you to Frank Cimino for helping me on my healing journey. I am so grateful that you saw the light in me when I couldn't.

Thank you Buzzy, for being a guiding light and for helping me learn all of these wild lessons in this lifetime.

Most importantly, I want to thank my pain for being a source of power and inspiration, instead of debilitating me. I also owe some credit to my exes for making a great story for me.

A special thank you to Kevin Butler for being so patient and helping me with the audible version of this book. There was so much healing that happened from being able to record this book with my voice. Thank you for capturing it beautifully.

Audible Book Recorded and Produced by Kevin Butler with Black Bird Creative.

References

Easwaran, Eknath. *The Bhagavad Gita*. Cambridge Scholars Publishing, 2010.

Harris, Elena. "Bat Spirit Animal." *Spirit Animal Info*, 1 July 2014, www.spiritanimal.info/bat-spirit-animal/.

Jones, Norah. "Premium Astrology Norah." *Premium Astrology Norah RSS*, 27 Feb. 2012, www.premiumastrologynorah.com/.

Continue the Journey with Alli Bee - Additional Perks from the Author

If you are looking for inspiration, blogs, retreats, events, meditations, or even some yoga classes with Alli Bee, check out her website www.allibeeyoga.com.

Visit www.wildjourneytothelight.com for more information about this book and the journey. On this site, you will also find wellness bundle packages and gifts to help brighten your spirits. If you are interested in the writing journey, the healing process, or the path to self-discovery or manifesting join Alli Bee for group workshops or one on one mentoring. Find "How To" workbooks and healing techniques to improve your ability to self-heal along with guided meditations.

Be sure to follow AlliBeeYoga on Instagram to stay updated with her inspirational posts, daily messages, yoga schedule, and upcoming events.

www.allibeeyoga.com
www.wildjourneytothelight.com
Instagram: AlliBeeYoga

If you enjoyed this book and want to support me in my mission to helping others find their light--please write a review and share your expereince on Amazon. Thank you!

Made in the USA
Columbia, SC
06 January 2021